❖❖

Psychoanalysis,
Language,
and
the
Body
of
the
Text

◇◇

*Martin
Gliserman*

◇

Psychoanalysis,

Language,

and

the

Body

of

the

Text

UNIVERSITY PRESS OF FLORIDA ⧽ ⧽

GAINESVILLE TALLAHASSEE TAMPA BOCA RATON PENSACOLA ORLANDO MIAMI JACKSONVILLE

01 00 99 98 97 96 6 5 4 3 2 1

Library of Congress Cataloging-in-Publication Data
Gliserman, Martin J.
Psychoanalysis, language and the body of the text / Martin Gliserman.
p.   cm.
Includes bibliographical references and index.
ISBN 0-8130-1416-6 (alk. paper)
1. English fiction—History and criticism.   2. Body, Human, in literature.   3. Language
and languages in literature.   4. English language—Style.   5. Psychoanalysis and literature.
6. Mind and body in literature.   7. Defoe, Daniel, 1661?–1731.   Robinson Crusoe.
8. Brontë, Charlotte, 1816–1885.   Jane Eyre.   9. Woolf, Virginia, 1882–1941.   To the
lighthouse.   10. Bradley, David, 1950– . Chaneysville incident.   I. Title.
PR830.B63G58   1996
823.009'36—dc20   95-11053

The University Press of Florida is the scholarly publishing agency for the State University
System of Florida, comprised of Florida A & M University, Florida Atlantic University,
Florida International University, Florida State University, University of Central Florida,
University of Florida, University of North Florida, University of South Florida, and University
of West Florida.

Excerpts from *Moments of Being*, by Virginia Woolf, copyright 1976 by Quentin Bell and
Angelica Garnett, reprinted by permission of Harcourt Brace & Company.
Excerpts from *To the Lighthouse*, by Virginia Woolf, copyright 1927 by Harcourt Brace &
Company and renewed 1954 by Leonard Woolf, reprinted by permission of publisher.
Earlier versions of chapters 4, 6, and 7 were published, respectively, in the following issues of
American Imago: vol. 47, nos. 3–4 (Fall–Winter 1990); vol. 40, no. 1 (Spring 1983); and vol. 43,
no. 2 (Summer 1986). Reprinted by permission of The Johns Hopkins University Press.

University Press of Florida
15 Northwest 15th Street
Gainesville, FL 32611

For
Mom
and
Dad

Two
impressive
menschen,
one
great
couple

◇◇

Contents

◇◇

Preface

This book is about how the human body makes its appearance in those literary texts we call novels and what message that body transmits. By demonstrating the powerful presence of the body in the novel, I hope to clarify further the intricate relationship of body and mind, in particular the role that language plays in integrating these major centers of being. I want to show how inextricably the body laces into the language of narrative. In literary texts, at least, the body evidences itself in the language that is the literary text. It does so by mentioning the body explicitly as well as by alluding to it; by offering shared symbols with personal variations; by presenting structures indicative of motion, dimension, tension, and stability; and by its protean disguises, including its seeming absence.

In investigating the presence of the body in the language of the text, I bring together the description and analysis of language which Noam Chomsky forged and the sensitivity to the presence of the body in language which Freud articulated as psychoanalysis. The general contribution of this work is to a growing field of "body studies." In bringing this synthetic analysis to literary language, literary critics, teachers of literature, and historians gain a new dimension to seeing the body of the text—something that has hitherto been described in relatively flat ways. Specifically, I am adding a major element to aid in the analysis and perception of the body in literature by examining the syntax of the text (sentences, paragraphs, and chapters) as bodily gesture, appearing in the shape of both desire and despair. I see the body as embedded in the syntax of the sentence. This aspect and those described by others together develop a quantity of redundancy that in turn precipitates a fuller sense of the body. I think I have succeeded in making the body more dimensional and thus more apparently present, at least given a willing suspension of disbelief or a willingness to participate in a thought experiment— that the body can be tangible without being corporeal.

Although the work is not clinical, I hope psychoanalysts find interest in this work insofar as psychoanalysis works in and with language, knows the body to be of importance, and places stock in consciousness (interpretation) as well as in the power of the unconscious. However, as psychoanalysts we receive virtually no formal training in language or linguistics, and thus lack a certain level of conscious understanding of language. We lack a metalanguage, so we miss some opportunities to understand our patients better. As psychoanalysts, we know that language, for all its sophistication, also carries the primitive, and in this work I develop ways to see that nonverbal primitive embedded in language.

Last, I hope to contribute something to current discussions of trauma. In looking at the body within the context of a group of novels, I discerned trauma at the center. Each novel lays out the history and ramifications of some trauma, making each into a discourse on pain and its directional paths—past, future, inward, outward, or transcendent. Insofar as pain goes beyond what is tolerable and is continued long after inflicted, it is profoundly disruptive. Trauma breaks down boundaries, radically caves in defenses and ordinary discourse. The literary artist is able to transmute trauma enough for us to glimpse it. The intricacy of connection between body and mind is evident in trauma, for there the whole being is pushed beyond capacity and transmutes, more or less radically, depending on the person and the extent, duration, and intensity of the traumata. The ensuing pain dissolves any easy conceptions one has about the boundaries of such compartments as "mind" and "body."

I did not embark on this journey with the intention of examining trauma, but that is what has shown up. This autopsy on trauma is significant insofar as world politics, both micro and macro, seem ruled or propelled by it. Trauma is our world's most general epidemic: it strikes infants, children, boys and girls, men and women, the elderly, people of all economic classes, all colors, shades, and ethnicities. If we can know more about trauma, its etiology and ramifications, we might be better off.

The foundation for this book seems to me to have been built early in life, so, as my first book, my acknowledgments go far back. My family of course were the first people to teach me about the body, its rules of process and interaction as they understood them. They did, as D. W. Winnicott would say, a good enough job, giving me ample love. Mother, father, and sister took care of me. My brother gave me lessons on the vulnerability of the body. There was relative silence on the actual subject of the body at that pre-Spockian time, and that silence filled up my curiosity.

In addition to the curiosity of desire, a darker interest also grew in me.

Along with many others of my background, I went to an after-school Hebrew school for six years. I remain grateful as an adult for learning about the history of the Jewish people in Egypt, Spain, and Germany. I am grateful for being taught the horror of people's inhumanity to others, for it stirred up strong feelings—anger, fear, and fascination—and forged strong values. The concrete details of torture allowed me to realize something about the nature of human interaction at the bodily level. The question of how human beings could do such things to other human beings has driven my life—trying to understand it and trying to move without violence to shift it.

For my intellectual foundations, I want to thank Bill Wees, who introduced me to Freud in a Colby College January Plan on Dreams and Surrealism in 1965 or so, and, also in the Colby community, Abbott and Nancy Meader for their openness about bodies in paint, pottery, and film.

I want acknowledge the impact of Susan Elmer Gliserman (1945–73), with whom I grew up intellectually (1963–73), whose concrete feminism helped me grow up humanly, and whose death at the hands of a drunk driver seemed to change every cell in my being.

I appreciate the human impact people have had on me and my work along the way at Indiana University, Rutgers University, the Center for Modern Psychoanalytic Studies in Manhattan, through *American Imago*, and at the University Press of Florida. I particularly want to thank Merritt Lawlis, David Bleich, and David Smith with whom I began formal thinking about what I had been learning. My ideas moved forward another notch in the early years of Livingston College, where ideas developed in teaching with David Leverenz, Steve Zemelman, and Peter Parisi, and more generally in talking with George Levine, Dick Wasson, Jackie DiSalvo, Ann Snitow, Barbara Masekela, Kate Ellis, and Wesley Brown. On a more personal level, I want to acknowledge a person who was what Toni Morrison might call a "friend of my mind"—Gina Sangster Hayman.

I owe special thanks to Barry Qualls for unfailing support, for helping me move forward, and for tastefully renovating Murray Hall. I am grateful for the helpful and accepting readers of my early work—Harry Slochower, Ruth Velikovsky Sharon, and Marilyn Rye—and to other readers for their encouragement, comments, and observations—Maynard Solomon, Ellen Handler Spitz, Peter Rudnytsky, and Andrew Gordon. I offer great thanks to Arnold Bernstein for teaching me how to heal and grow. I especially want to thank Walda Metcalf at the University Press of Florida for her interest in the manuscript, her moving it along expeditiously, her hospitality, and her help along the way.

I once wrote a manuscript when I was in misery; it didn't make it. This book was not written in misery. It was written with love and support from Marilyn Rye, who read, encouraged, suffered rejections, commiserated, and made suggestions. Moreover, without Marilyn I would have missed out on two great children—Jane Berlin and Nicholas Gliserman—and two wonderful canines—Maximus Dog and Agatha Dog. They all helped with this work. It is probably not a hip or postmodern thing to say, I know, but love has been enabling.

1

The
Body
in
the
Text

In this book I would like to show that the body is integral to the text of the novel and how the body reveals itself in the language of that text. My proposition is that the body is variously encoded in language and communicates to us through language. In this project of seeking the relationship between body and language, I join others in different areas of study who are questioning the categorical framings for "how we are"—body, mind, feeling, thought, emotion, language, and so on. The categories are useful, especially as names for clusters of phenomena, but they become problematic for us, their users, when we mistake the formulations for the reality or fail to see the continuities and inextricable links between and among the phenomena. Most "radically," when I talk about "the body of the text" I do not intend "the body" as metaphor; rather, I want to maintain that there is a bodily presence in the novel in the sense that DNA is preserved in amber. What do I take a novel to be? In a Buckminster Fulleresque mode of expression, a novel is a sustained imaginative experiential (interpersonal, intrapersonal, social, psychological, political, historical) linguistic artifact. Inevitably, when a person authors such an artifact, the body that is embodied in language will become embedded in the text with the personal signature of the author.

Language Is Embodied and Embedded in the Body, and the Body Is Embodied and Embedded in Language

The body is a feature of our being that is and has been a ubiquitous subject of discourse and object of technologies.[1] In this book I want to demonstrate how the body is embedded and embodied in various layers of language in a spectrum of novels. A central assumption here is that the vital, deep-structural presence of the body is a core phenomenon of language, sometimes exquisitely represented in the novel—and it is that body in the novel to which we respond; it is to be connected to that body that motivates our reading. The body is what, in part, the language of literature communicates. (The new "virtual reality" is really much less awesome than our own capacity to generate our own virtual reality—embodiment—when we read.) The assumption that language is embedded in the body is posited by Noam Chomsky: *"we may regard the language capacity virtually as we would a physical organ of the body and can investigate the principles of its organization, function and development in the individual and the species.* Personally, I feel that this is just the right way to approach the study of human language" (1980, 185, my emphasis). I want to take this notion one step farther by suggesting that language is an organ, an organ about organs, and an organ that writes itself into its communications. *And* it replicates itself where and when it can. We will be able to see how the body makes its appearance in different layers or facets of (the structure of) language. Language is the most wily way yet found of networking, creating webbings that any spider would have to admire.

Historically, the human voice (which represented or spoke on behalf of body) and language coevolved.[2] That is, whatever the precise history of the development of language, language was initially from the body and about the body—a metabody, altered, transposed, displaced, metamorphic. Language (as an organ) is intricately connected to the body at higher and lower levels via genetics, physiology, neural networks, mouth, lungs, blood, muscles, heart, tongue, and so on. Language, when exercised, is physical—it puts things into motion and draws energy; it displaces (e.g., air), consumes, organizes, creates new pockets of chaos, stirs up resonances. Language, then, is a physical/bodily experience at each level: as hard wiring, character, software, output, and input. We find fundamental and foundational, symbiotic and synergistic, relations of body and language; the body has embedded itself in language. And language that is laid out in the print of a novel does not become disembodied just because it is not emanating from a living, breathing body. The body lies inside the language, like a seed in its shell, waiting for the medium in which to germinate.

This book investigates the way the body is presented in novels. The particular language map that any given novelist constructs contains traces of the writer's body—needs, desires, fears, histories—which mirror ours or allow us to reflect on them, thus Baudelaire's "mon semblable, mon frère." The body's traces show up in various ways, some overtly and explicitly, some structurally, encoded as forms in action, syntactic gestures. A novel articulates a body as much as it tells a story. It develops a preverbal, ur-gender, non-verbal, and/or unverbalized visceral experience as much as it develops an intricate symbolic interpersonal interaction in a complex setting over space and time.

Some Mappings of the Body

The body has, of course, always been a focus of interest, from its anatomy to its representation. In recent years the interest seems to have accelerated as both discourse on the body and discourse on discourse on the body, as in Michel Foucault's *History of Sexuality* (1980, 1986), increases. Yet it also seemed to have been accelerating three decades ago when Jean Starobinski (1989 [1964]) noted with a smile that the recent enthusiasm about the body made it seem as if "Everything is related to the body, as if it had just been rediscovered after being long forgotten" (353). In the modern period, I would point to Freud as responsible for making the body open to public discourse. Freud begins with the body in his studies as a physician and moves into psychoanalysis with a similar focus. The first case presented in the *Standard Edition*, "Observations of a Severe Case of Hemi-Anaesthesia in a Hysterical Male" (1886), is, as the editors note, largely "concerned with the physical phenomena of hysteria . . . only some very slight indications of an interest in psychological factors" (24). Although Freud's theoretical interest shifts to sexuality, to transference, to superego, and so on, he remains to what is virtually his last paper ("Splitting of the Ego in the Process of Defense," 1938) concerned with the body, especially as it manifests pain, fear, confusion, and other emotions.

Our contemporary discussions about the body have been profoundly shaped by feminist criticism, which has played a large role in bringing the body into consciousness, partly from the observed imposed restrictions on the female body. An early feminist document, the first issue of *Our Bodies, Our Selves* (1971), spoke concretely and directly about reclaiming and remapping women's bodies in many contexts (such as anatomy, pleasure, abuse, and medical encounters) in which they had been misappropriated. Setting the ground for further analysis is early feminist criticism: Betty Friedan's *Feminine Mystique* (1963) analyzed popular fiction as a way to address the new constrictions of the 1950s; Kate Millett's *Sexual Politics* (1969) analyzed male attitudes toward women, seeing a tendency to negate the Other, giving her only bodily form and bodily use. A more recent work,

Dorothy Dinnerstein's *Mermaid and the Minotaur* (1976), argues that the relative absence of male caring for babies—direct, concrete bodily (physical and visceral) contacting and caretaking—generates a profound human absence for both child and father (and thus mother, too). The outcome of this bodily skewness is what Luce Irigaray speaks of as madness: "Each sex has a relation to madness. Every desire has a relation to madness. But it would seem that one desire has been taken as wisdom, moderation, truth, leaving to the other sex the weight of a madness that cannot be acknowledged or accommodated" (1993, 10). And in her *Thinking Through the Body*, Jane Gallop notes that Roland Barthe's writing in the 1970s "passed out of his scientific stance (structuralism) into something that seemed softer, more subjective, *more bodily.* The Barthes of the seventies authorized my own push out of objective, scholarly discourse into something more *embodied"* (1988, 11, my emphasis). Central to all these works, and many more, is questioning the situating and constructing of the body in a particular manner and the vast consequences to all of that. Feminist thought shifted the monologue on the body to a dialogue and thereby made a family body, and that helped evolve a new sense of family and thus "family therapy" and a new major focus on abuse to the child's body. Fundamental to the questioning feminist thought raised is the mistreatment of the body, its constrictions, restrictions, and deformations. But equally important, much feminist thought is also on reclaiming the body, along the lines of Toni Morrison's sermon on the mount: the moment in *Beloved* when Baby Sluggs, holy, says, "Here . . . in this place here, we flesh; flesh that weeps, laughs; flesh that dances on bare feet in grass. Love it. Love it hard" (1991, 108). Or again, feminist spirit also emerges in the celebration of the body, its powers and beauty, in Judy Chicago's *Dinner Party* (1979), in which a table is set with each famous female guest represented by a dinner plate, a crafted vulval image.

An excellent "statement" about the state of current body studies is the landmark three-volume work edited by Michel Feher, *Fragments for a History of the Human Body.* The collection brings together fifty contemporary essays including a 100-page bibliography of other sources focused on the body. Feher notes: "As the notion of fragment implies, the texts collected here do not pretend either to form a complete survey or to define a compact portion of the history of the body. The fact that so many problems are addressed only indicates the extent of the field to be explored" (1989, pt. 3:11). The texts examine the body as related to machines, animals, and gods; they examine how the body communicates; they examine the relation of body and society. The overall vision of Feher's collection is to show that "the history of the human body is not so much the history of its representations as of its modes of construction" (pt. 1:11). Barbara Duden's "Repertory of Body History," an extensive bibliography and index, also gives the reader a sense of the immensity of the field, from Paul Ableman's *Anatomy of Nakedness* (1982) to Harry Wolfson's "Internal Senses in Latin, Arabic, and Hebrew Philosophical Texts" (1935).

Last, I note an increased focus on trauma—the ramifications of abuse, torture, murder, and being a witness to such violence. Understanding the depth of damage generated by physical abuse has major political and legal implications. For example, the relatively recent psychiatric category of "post-traumatic stress" has concrete consequences for men in war, women in rape, and children in destructive families. Perhaps the most articulate of all more theoretical work is that of Elaine Scarry—*The Body in Pain* (1985)—which I discuss in the first chapter. An essay by Paul Fussell, "The Real War, 1939–1945" (1989), likewise brings to consciousness what he observes has been publicly repressed: the complete horror of what man does to man. The recent work on trauma has crystallized the information on and from the Jewish Holocaust, particularly now that the stories of so many individuals have been told in, for example, films of Claude Lanzmann or the videos made at the Video Archive for Holocaust Testimonies. The works of Bruno Bettelheim (1960, 1979), Dori Laub (1991), and Lawrence Langer (1991) explore the aftermath of surviving the witnessing and experiencing of relentless bodily suffering. The articulateness and concreteness of all these works lend credence and support to efforts of Amnesty International.

The psychological roots, the emplacement, of violence in the individual body (and the consequences of that emplacement) have been studied in Alice Miller's work in general and, relative to this discussion, is her psychological analysis of Hitler (Miller 1983). Eric Erikson (1963 [1950], 326–58) also wrote of Hitler and the fathers and children of that era in that culture, particularly the collective and individual "dominance and harshness" of the father. Janine Chassequet-Smirgel's work (1985) on narcissism and group psychology, although abstracted from direct focus on the body, describes how individual perversion can be perverted into a group perversion in which perversion—the destruction of others—becomes the Good; these works also call back Freud's *Group Psychology and the Analysis of the Ego* (1921) in which he describes the ways the body is released by the group while at the same time, of course, enslaved by it. An excellent portrait of how the beaten body progresses in a fascist state is George Orwell's *Nineteen Eighty Four*

(1983 [1949]) to which I will return in another chapter. Perhaps needless to say, many novels present significant trauma.

A New Mapping: Le Style est le corps

The particular area in which I want to see the body and study its vicissitudes is the language of novels. I have a notion that inasmuch as "style is the person," "style is the body." That is, through the writer's style we find the body. By style I mean a writer's habits of syntactic and semantic constructions. A writer's style is the linguistic expression of his or her body. Because the body is not generally expressed in the manifest narrative—the novel is ostensibly "about" its characters—there is a way in which it is not heard or spoken of. Nonetheless, the body is encoded in the language, expressing itself and resonating with the reader.

The psychoanalytic analysis of the body embedded in language that I have in mind would not have developed without the work of Noam Chomsky, particularly his landmark *Syntactic Structures* (1957) and *Aspects of the Theory of Syntax* (1965). Chomsky's theory cracked open language in a way that parallels the discovering of the language of genes. His work opens up a new dimensionality to language in his way of seeing a deep structure that allows the complexity of the surface structure to become more apparent. Previous ways of thinking of sentences—as simple, compound, or complex—were not adequate for describing literary (or other) sentences and could not make fine distinctions; they were not adequate in description or explanation. In Chomsky's theory two central areas are significant for the analysis I am working on: recursion and distinctive features.

What we think of as a single sentence in the surface structure—from the capitalized beginning to the period ending—may well be a series or grouping of embedded sentences. In a more technical formulation, "sentence" is a recursive element, such that at major junctions in a sentence—at nouns and verbs particularly—other sentences may, in a transformed way, be inserted. A "sentence" is a transformable element; "he runs" can be transformed for purposes of embedding: "running," "his running," "for him to run," "to run," "when he runs," "who runs." The significance of these syntactic matters (rules) for literature is that a writer develops syntactic habits, syntactic patterns, that is, a pattern of patterns, a signature. In some respects I am pursuing an avenue that Richard Ohmann (1969a [1964], 1969b [1966]) once pursued though he did not seem to pursue all of the dynamic possibilities therein. As I see it, syntax is a gesture, a motion with inherent relationships. Although "the words" of a sentence move forward, the structure of phrases and groupings that make up the sentence are more multidirectional and dynamic. The sentence forms show how the body holds and releases tension and how much tension can be tolerated.

The centrality of patternment in communications (whether genetic or linguistic or other semiotic forms) is emphasized in Gregory Bateson's *Steps to an Ecology of Mind* (1972) and Douglas Hofstadter's *Godel, Escher, Bach: An Eternal Golden Braid* (1977). Both stress the importance of patternment, of patterns and metapatterns; both stress the impact of redundancy in information. For me, the pattern matrices that Chomsky's ideas of syntax developed allow a new vision of, if not insight into, the writer's sentences. The ideas of transformational generative grammar enable one to speak with more precision about the complexity of one of Henry James's or Virginia Woolf's sentences or the way a text as a whole coheres to a particular way of seeing and imaging, ordering, giving rhythms to. Of course, I may not have seen what I did in the writer's sentences unless I had been equally interested in psychoanalysis, a discipline that asks, among other questions, what repetition signifies (both particularly, in this person's repetitions, and generally, in the species). Bringing psychoanalysis to the structuralized dream world of the Chomskian sentence, I "naturally" wondered what the forms added up to.

A second pattern-opening perspective that Chomsky's theory develops involves each item of the sentence: each semantic element (i.e., every word) can be seen as having a complex of distinctive features, a group of on-off differences (+/- animate, +/- human, +/- count, +/- abstract). Given these defining differences and similarities, words have their own habitat, implicit rules that describe how they interact with others. My thought here is that there is a descriptor [+/- body] among the distinctive features so that, for example, verbs like "look" or "eat" or "see" have embedded in their feature matrices something that defines them as related to the body, even though abstracted at times ("I want you to look at the situation this way"). Moreover, some semantic elements acquire or are authorized at times to take on the characteristics of [+body], for example, in John Cleland's *Memoirs of a Woman of Pleasure*, (1963 [1749]), a sword must be read as "sword" with such characteristics as [+hard, +penetrating, +body, +genital, +male]—the phallus. Realizing that just below the surface of the text is a vast network of information in the form of descriptive rules is akin to recognizing the transference-countertransference matrix in the psychoanalytic setting—discourse #1 (the story of this or that relationship) is also carrying with it discourse #2 (the story of the dyad). The rules of relationships structured by being in them at the most vulnerable time of one's life are as inexorable as the laws of language acquired at the same time of life.

In addition to dominant words, significant for redundancy as well as being qualitatively important, individual semantic units form semantic webs. Words have at least a double life—they generate and fulfill our narrative lust, but they also live in another (deconstructed, synchronic, slipped) universe of discourse. When we focus on the semantic webs of the body, untangling them from the narrative, we see how embedded the body is in the text and that it articulates its concerns.

Eyes, for example, are often the most dominant bodily redundancy in novels—they and their related verbal networks are the most often mentioned bodily parts. In general, they are seen as incidental to the narrative (although cinema studies has emphasized the gaze). The role the eye plays varies immensely from novel to novel, however. In David Leavitt's *Lost Language of the Cranes* the eyes are mostly described as opening, looking, and closing; they seem limited to an infantile state of eating, gazing, and sleeping. In *Jane Eyre* the eye has a complex narrative of its own concerning male destruction, female healing, and sexuality. Given the dominance of the eye in most fiction, their scarcity also marks a work like Kathy Acker's *Kathy Goes to Haiti*, in which the genitals dominate the bodily languagescape (and thus perhaps telling another story of Jane Eyre from a different angle).

Hands are also strongly represented. For Daniel Defoe in *Robinson Crusoe*, the hands are largely aggressive, performing male-related behavior (work, violence, defense, punishment), but they also perform other functions (speaking, feeding, healing, making). In Keri Hulme's *Bone People*, there is an almost complete discourse on the hand. It speaks (in sign language), touches and contacts, and violates the other. In *Emma*, by contrast, there are roughly three instances when a hand contacts someone else, and it becomes a highly charged emotional matter when it does.

The embedded body is made accessible by the kind of microanalysis that Chomsky's linguistic model allows. Having opened up this particular theater of the body by way of linguistic observation, I am interested in highlighting that body as pregendered as well as gendered, multigendered, and transgendered, and the body as wounded or terrorized. It will be clear in the analysis of particular works that the body is in some sense much larger than gender. Culture may impose whatever it wishes on the body and its gender, but desire will articulate itself, will assert, for example, its being both male and female and neither one nor the other. At the same time, we notice how vulnerable the body is and how being pushed beyond its limits alters our vision, our existential core. The wounded body may have a gender, but the pain is transgender. As useful and necessary as is current discourse on gender and race, we must also remind ourselves of the commonality of flesh and the ultimate need for us to treat each other like people.

◇◇ The introductory chapters focus on how the body manifests itself in the novel linguistically and psychoanalytically; they also examine the body in extreme situations where it is highlighted—in erotic novels and novels with themes of violence. In the final four chapters, the detailed study of the body in the four separate novels—*Robinson Crusoe, Jane Eyre, To the Lighthouse,* and *The Chaneysville Incident*—presents various strands of the genre: eighteenth-century, nineteenth-century, modern, and contemporary; male and female; white and black. The discourse of the body in most novels focuses on primal bodily pain and vulnerability. In *Robinson Crusoe* it is hunger; in *The Chaneysville Incident,* it is a frigidly cold inside; in *To the Lighthouse* the bodily center is threatened with implosion and decay; in *Jane Eyre* the center, seen within the eye, is starving and raging.

The study of the four novels is also a study of gender configurations. The bodily representations of all the writers point to similar concerns with bodily integrity, creative capacity, and violence or violation. We expect differences in the representation of the body by men and women, and they are there, but the particular similarities are unexpected (in these times of increasing separations of intellectual territories). All the texts show the tension between trauma and creativity, survival is in question for all of the central characters. Although the male and female characters in these texts play out their separate gendered roles, within the deeper forms of the fiction the bodies are reconfigured in nonconventional ways.

Last, the individual analyses point to the particular concerns of each novelist. Scrutiny of the semantic networks and layers of syntactic patterns reveals the primitive body as fraught with a desire shaped and distorted by fear, pain, and conflict. This primitive body in turn structures the psychological politics of interpersonal relations as represented in the texts, for example, the deep fear of starvation in *Robinson Crusoe* is placed in the context of the Other's cannibalism.

2

The
Embedded
Body

Writing, reading, and imagining all involve the participation of the body. The body not only does, it speaks of what has been done. The body has a mind and memory of its own and an articulation of its own in our multi-voiced language. The body speaks through our ordinary language at the very same time we are speaking of other matters. One aspect of a string of sentences may be a story with its hero or heroine moving in time and space with others. Another part of that string is its *physical* form and structure, the dynamic of its movements and tensions. These dynamics express the body; they are coded in the language, presented in a non-narrative manner, and easily passed over by the eager reader, who is not, however, unaffected by them.

The sentence is no simple matter. Chomsky's work and the work it has stirred up have forever enriched our vision of the sentence's dense complexity and its inner workings—the rules required to generate it, the intricacy of its structural and meaning-making networks. The sentence has depth, reaching back into unconscious processes, into histories. Given the sheer quantity of neuronic activity related to writing and reading an affiliated group of sentences, we know the body is in motion. How a reader moves through a sentence is partly or largely dependent on its architecture, its layout, its internal system, especially as it comes to be defined and differentiated by other sentences around it as we read further. The author presents us with the shape and energy of sentences, and as we enter that realm, we try on those shapes and forces, as we might try on someone else's gesture to see what it feels like, or as when our face or hand spontaneously gets into a position that calls to mind another person's gesture and then feeling we understand that person for a moment. The sentence is physical; it puts us in various positions.

We engage the tale, but we must also engage and negotiate the sentences. The physical qualities of the sentences are expressive: they are the body language of language. We can easily think of the Chinese ideogram as having that quality of physicalness, for example, the brush stroke is physical and expressive. That physical quality is not absent in Western sentences; it is found by looking at the syntactic form as crossed with various semantic networks. The sentence is an ideogram whose abstract (ideogrammatic) form is seen in the relationship of its parts to one another, especially the relation of embedded sentences to one another and to the matrix.

The human body pervades narrative fiction. Transformed, it appears in the text as language although it does not speak and is not read through the usual process. Certain aspects of a sentence are not "about" what the sentence is overtly "about" (although the two aspects may have related concerns). A sentence speaks many channels simultaneously. That is, a sentence or a discourse is made up of bundles of information—one set of signals focuses on the relationship, say, of one person to another, but another set of signals emanating from what looks on the surface as the very same sentence or discourse focuses on relationships as a more abstract pattern with primitive, bodily roots. The language of fictional narrative (or drama or poetry) is not a flat, one-dimensional, dedicated channel but a multidimensional one. The sentence is hologrammatic. This quality of language is akin to what Freud speaks of as the overdetermined nature of any given moment in the stream of thought and what Jacques Lacan discusses as the sliding/slipping of the signifier/signified relationship. In addition to speaking of general, concrete instances—of symbols, motives, words, or signs (*parole*)—I am speaking of the whole of language (*langue*) and suggesting that as a vehicle for conveying information, it works somewhat in the way a fiber optics communications line does: carrying thousands of messages simultaneously. In the case of language, one set of messages it generates is from the body, about the body, to the body, for the body. How can the body be seen in order to be read? By overlooking the semantic flow of syntactic forms and looking at the vertical patterns woven by the forms and the intricate networks woven by the semantic relationships out of the flow.

The body in-forms the text; the text embodies its writer; the reading reader embodies the body of the text: all this is our communion, our benign ecology of mind, which some see as essential to our psychic health as individuals and as a global culture.[1]

The embedded body, transformed by and into language and particularly in the pain it expresses, articulates what R. D. Laing might call the politics of the body. Bodily pain, interactions through which it is generated and ways in which it is remembered, has major consequences. Bodily pain is transformed into politics, ideology, and behavior, that is, war, small-scale inter-nalized or private (a person, a couple, a family), and large-scale and secret or public. The pain of the body has of course been explicitly spoken of from the thrashings in *Tom Jones* to the mercilessness in Morrison's *Beloved*, Keri Hulme's *Bone People*, Robert Stone's *Flag for Sunrise*, or Russell Banks's *Affliction*. My focus is on the relatively unspoken pain, or unspokenness of pain, of primitive deprivations or assaults or of trauma experienced by mature persons: this pain may well be "on one's body/mind" without being "on one's mind/body." Indeed, the pain is inscribed on the body: as Maxine Hong Kingston's title story in *The Woman Warrior* graphically illustrates, when Fa Mu Lan returns home and her parents literally carve their grievances on her back (1977, 41). Double pain is carved into Fa Mu Lan's back—the pain of the parents' losses and the pain of the knives expressing it. Carving the pain passes it along, and it will be passed along some more. Pain is carved into the body, and though one has ceased to feel it, it remains "on the body" and emerges in writing through axes other than the linear sentence. Virginia Woolf was sexually abused by a relative for many years; traces of that abuse show up in the very syntax and semantic networks of her sentences. How is one to see that? The sentence has body; the sentence has dynamics—flow, forward and looping, chaos, counterpoising this and that; the sentence is an architectural structure of tensions.

The intense presence of the body is revealed in the novel's language: the significant redundancies within and between syntactic and semantic networks and patterns. Syntax is a gesture from the body, a signature with a permanent structure and an encapsulated motion. That is, the form of a sentence is replete with interactions which in any given writer become habitual patterns, and these patterns articulate deep sets of relationships—deep in the sense of primitive and powerful. Thus the structurings of an opening sentence may be reflected at the higher levels of organization—paragraph, chapters, images—indicating through the redundancy a central tension or way of aligning tension

Semantic units (words, the sign) and webs of them, taken out of narrative structure, reveal the body as a voice (a sound image by way of the name) and an image (a visual image). The semantic network reveals bodily preoccupations and connections and points to the story of the body embedded in the text. A semantic analysis of *Jane Eyre* reveals a striking redundancy that could be considered statistically significant of "eye/s" and of verbs associated with seeing and looking. Redundancy of this sort is significant. The ubiquity of the eye in *Jane Eyre* and the quality of its presence—different from other of Brontë's works in which it plays a minor role and different from other texts in which the eye is significant—invites us to see it, to speculate. Why is it so present? What does it mean? Despite all the articles and essays written about *Jane Eyre*, none have observed the tale of the eye, though aspects of it (e.g., Rochester's blinding) do receive attention. Jane Eyre, of course, presents us with a similar problem of both wanting and not wanting to be seen.

The interplay of the syntactic (motion, structure, and pattern) and the semantic (name, sound and image, relational network) builds up a dimensional body, articulating memory, desire, anger, pain, and grief. The psychological significance of the body's presence—its vicissitudes, its modes of repetition, its branching into relationships with others and with the inanimate—unfolds in the relationship between these axes of language and somewhat at an angle from the sentence's surface.

◇◇ Examining the human body in a range of English and American novels, I hope to contribute to a growing, multidisciplinary study of the body, some of which I noted in chapter 1. The present interest in the body is related to a growing recognition of its vulnerability. That is, the collective treatment of the body has major political ramifications. I interpret the emerging literature on the body as speaking to concerns about certain out-of-control, runaway situations between sexes, races nations, and classes, within the self, and with the environment that threaten bodily survival. It is the sense of Dorothy Dinnerstein, for example, "that there is in fact some basic pathology shaping our species' stance toward itself and nature, a pathology whose chances of killing us off quite soon, if we cannot manage to outgrow it first, are very good indeed" (1976,4). The studies of the novel offered here demonstrate verbal transformations of primitive bodily understructures which in turn give shape to de facto political behavior, that is, the way people treat their own and others' bodies. The psychoanalytic perspective on the body I have chosen for its capacity to discern the roots of bodily conflict which are later transformed.

A recent philosophical-linguistic work by Mark Johnson—*The Body in the Mind: The Bodily Basis of Meaning, Imagination, and Reason*—reveals connections of the body and language that can help us see how vivid[1] literary works bring the body to the fore. Johnson explores "some of the more important ways in which structures of our bodily experience work their way up into abstract meanings and patterns of inference. . . . My argument begins by showing that human bodily movement, manipulation of objects, and perceptual interactions involve recurring patterns which without our experience would be chaotic and incomprehensible. I call these patterns "image schemata" . . . [they] emerge first as a structure of bodily interactions . . . [and] can be figuratively developed and extended as a structure around which meaning is organized at more abstract levels of cognition" (1987, xx). Johnson analyzes specific connections between bodily orientations and linguistic instances, such as the idea of "force," and persuasively demonstrates "that there is a meaning that comes through bodily experience and figurative processes of ordering" (17). Johnson's work on the encoding of the body in language confirms my notion that the body informs and is embedded in the texts it generates; as he observes, there "is no aspect of our understanding that is independent of the nature of the human organism" (209).

The relationship of the body and language has also been studied in a remarkable work on the radical separation of them by Elaine Scarry, *The Body in Pain: The Making and Unmaking of the World*. Scarry examines the relationship of body and language as they are destroyed in violence and embedded in culture in more benign situations. In the following passage Scarry discusses the relation of the body to culture and the way the body is severed from language (as the springboard of culture) in the context of torture:

> Every act of civilization is an act of transcending the body in a way consonant with the body's needs: in building a wall, to return to an old friend, one overcomes the body, projects oneself out beyond the body's boundaries but in a way that expresses and fulfills the body's needs for stable temperatures. Higher moments of civilization, more elaborate forms of self-extension, occur at a greater distance from the body: the telephone or the airplane is a more emphatic instance of overcoming the limitation of the human body than is the cart. Yet even as here when most exhilaratingly defiant of the body, civilization always has embedded within it a profound allegiance to the body, for it is only by paying attention that it can free attention. Torture is a condensation of the act of "overcoming" the body present in benign forms of power. Although the torturer dominates the prisoner both in physical acts and verbal acts, ultimate domination requires that the prisoner's ground become increasingly physical and the torturer's increasingly verbal, that the prisoner become a colossal body with no voice and the torturer a colossal voice (a voice composed of two voices) with no body. . . . All those ways in which the torturer dramatizes his opposition to and distance from the prisoner are ways of dramatizing his distance from the body. The most radical act of distancing resides in his disclaiming of the other's hurt. Within the strategies of power based

on denial there is, as in affirmative and civilized forms of power, a hier-
archy of achievement, successive intensifications based on increasing distance from, increasingly great transcendence of, the body: a regime's refusal to recognize the rights of the normal and healthy is its cart; its refusal
to recognize and care for those in agony is its airplane. (1985, 57)

Scarry's work is a profound analysis of a major political epidemic that takes
place not only at the level of the state, which Scarry examines, but also at the
level of the family, as, for example, Alice Miller and R. D. Laing have examined. In the successive denials Scarry outlines—denial of the body, denial of language—in the descent into human hell, her work confirms those
of others working in the psychological realm in the area of the family, for example, Gregory Bateson's formulation of the double bind in which very similar successions of denial occur, engendering madness. Similar layers of denial are articulated by various channels of language in literary texts. Scarry's
work gives voice to the unspeakable. I have concluded that literary texts likewise give voice to the unspeakable, in experiential and unconscious ways.
The voice of the body in literature is in the matrix of patterns beneath the
alluring surface of the narrator's.

The Body in the Text: Explicit, Symbolic, Syntactic

The body's image in the novel can be seen in three overlapping ways—explicitly, symbolically, and syntactically—as briefly exemplified below and
elaborated in chapter 3. That the body should be presented on different layers of the text finds confirmation in such ideas as "redundancy," "recursion,"
and "pattern" as found in information theory, cybernetics, or systems theory.
That is, if my hypothesis that the body is deeply embedded in the literary text
is accurate, then for it to be communicated, it must recur, not only on a single level but on several. As Gregory Bateson notes, " 'Meaning' may be regarded as an approximate synonym of pattern, redundancy, information, and
'restraint' [reduction of probabilities]" (130). Bateson defines redundancy as
the "patterning or predictability of particular events within a larger aggregate
of events" (1972, 406). Douglas Hofstadter has explored the issue of redundancy in music, visual art, and mathematics and in the following lines approaches it in relation to DNA and RNA: "Why encode genetic information
in DNA, when by representing it directly in proteins, you could eliminate
not just one, but *two* levels of interpretation? *The answer is: it turns out that
it is extremely useful to have the same information in several different forms*"
(1979, 616–17, my emphasis). In a similar vein, Bateson discusses the infor-

mation received by the two eyes to illustrate that the redundancy in fact creates a bonus of dimensionality: "In principle, extra 'depth' in some metaphoric sense is to be expected whenever the information for the two descriptions is differently collected or differently coded" (1979, 70). By looking at the different orders of bodily representation in the novel, we find a similar dimensional bonus—we learn to see the textual body move.

The body is explicitly present as an image in being named or less overtly present by being implied by verbs. For example, in Toni Morrison's *Beloved* a minor character, Amy, is described thus: "Arms like cane stalks and enough hair for four or five heads. Slow-moving eyes." Aspects of Amy's body are simply named by nouns—arms, hair, eyes—and described to give a sketch, an impression of a figure. The body may also become an object of self-conscious observations, as in John Barth's *End of the Road:* "It is impossible to be at ease. . . . The Doctor sits facing you, his legs slightly spread, his hands on his knees, and leans a little toward you. You would not slouch down, because to do so would thrust your knees virtually against his. Neither would you be inclined to cross your legs in either the masculine or the feminine manner: the masculine manner, with your left ankle resting on your right knee, would cause your left shoe to rub against the Doctor's left trouser leg, up by his knee; the feminine manner, with your left knee crooked over your right knee, would thrust the toe of your shoe against the same trouser leg, lower down on his shin" (1960, 6). In Barth's lines the body is explicit, on the surface; its self-consciousness and extensiveness make its psychological significance more complicated than Morrison's sketch above. The body in Barth is relatively paralyzed; Jacob Hornet can imagine other postures but is unable to take them up—they all lead to contact with the Doctor. Alternative positions lead one to "thrust," "rub," or again "thrust" some part of the body at or against the Doctor. In another line from Morrison's work, the body is called up by verbs and nouns: "Above the patter of pea sorting and the sharp odor of cooking rutabaga, Sethe explained the crystal that once hung from her ear" (58). The bodily imagining called on here involves hearing a sound, smelling an odor, seeing hands sorting peas, imagining a crystal and an ear, and listening to a voice. Only the ear is mentioned; other parts of the body are called on, invited in, implicitly. Another variant of an implicit body can be seen in a few lines from Robert Stone's *Flag for Sunrise:* "Holliwell finished his rum, thought about having another and decided on it. He poured it quickly and guiltily . . . raw rum drained the disease of his mind." The body here is not mentioned by nouns, but aspects of the body come into play—hands for pouring and raising to drink, the mouth, gullet, and gut.

The absence of the body, the failure explicitly to mention any local physical sensations, parallels the desire to absent the body to have "drained the disease of his mind." Holliwell has "drained" the rum from the bottle and from the glass; in turn it "drained" him. In and of themselves the explicit mentionings of the body only add up in the large verbal context work. For example, in Mary Gordon's *Final Payments* we find many references to the back, especially the backs of men—"The sight of his back was so beautiful that I felt a kind of despair." This explicit mention fits into a network of symbolic representations concerning the power of the male (the strength of his back), a fear of some inner badness (the father turns his back to her), and expressions of self-disgust (fecal).

The body presents itself in symbolic forms as well as being explicitly visible or conspicuous at the level of nouns and verbs. Just as Johnson invites us to see the bodily implications, the direction and thrust of certain "abstract" verbs, I want the reader to see the bodily possibilities in more concrete settings such as interior spaces, landscapes, and objects for similar reasons. The symbolic body is an image of the something other than the body, but it shares various central descriptive and interactional possibilities with the body. Johnson, for example, examines instances of verbs with the particle "out"—go out, let out. He takes the body as the prime "container" and sees other in-out orientations—"squeezing out the toothpaste"—as "the projection of IN-OUT orientation . . . a first move beyond the prototypical case of *my* bodily movement" (33–34). Thus "our IN-OUT schemata [however abstract they become, e.g., 'picking out' themes in literature] emerge first in our *bodily* experience, in our perception and movement" (34). In keeping with Johnson's IN-OUT schema of the body as container, consider the opening lines from Mary Gordon's *Final Payments*: "My father's funeral was *full of* priests. Our house had always been *full of* priests" (1). The phrase "full of" is one whose predicate is often filled, in American slang, with "malarkie," "baloney," or "shit." And the subject position of the sentence is generally a "you" or a "they." Thus a person/container is filled with negativity, filth, waste. Bringing the resonance of "full of" into Gordon's work, priests fill the syntactic position of shit: "After the priests left, the house emptied quickly" (34). As we look into the novel, we do see that the negative inside is very strongly represented by this syntax and by many symbolic interiors, for example, "the defeating stench of rotting food . . . broccoli liquefying at the bottom [of the vegetable bin]" (42). The referencing in these forms to things excremental is reinforced at the level of particles as well—"back," as in look back, give back; we find a far greater concentration of verbs with the particle "back" in Gordon's work than in any one hundred novels. Moreover, the anatomical "back" is a favorite aspect of the male body.

To see other aspects of the symbolic body we can look at examples from Cleland's *Memoirs of a Woman of Pleasure*, and Defoe's *Robinson Crusoe*. In both cases we will look at an object that penetrates something, often some-one — the body and various of its parts are capable of penetration. In Cle-land's work the body is thinly disguised: "He looked upon his weapon him-self . . . guiding it with his hand to the inviting slit . . . thrusts . . . draws it again . . . re-enters, and with ease sheath'd it now up to the hilt" (1963 [1749], 73). We must equate the weapon with a penis or the passage becomes ludi-crous, even though the sentence carries the metaphor to the bitter end and the woman receiving this weapon cries out " 'I can't bear it . . . It is too much . . . I die . . . I am going.'" In Defoe's narrative there is an incident involv-ing Crusoe, Friday, and Crusoe's gun. Crusoe shoots several animals, as he had previously shot Friday's pursuers, and Friday is amazed: "He thought there must be some wonderful Fund of Death and Destruction in that Thing . . . if I would have let him, he would have worshipp'd me and my Gun" (1972, 212). There is no intention here that the reader should be reading the weapon as anything but a weapon, an image of power. Nonetheless, the weapon has recognized linguistic relations with the phallus — established long before Freud pointed them out. When we trace the image of the gun and examine the linguistic surround in which it appears, we see that the gun is more than a gun and, though different, not so removed from the vaguely sadistic phallus we find in Cleland. In addition to penetrating and killing, however, Crusoe's gun is a container — "in" it must be a "wonderful Fund of Death and Destruction." Fundament and/or phallus, it is an object of narcissistic veneration — Crusoe worships it, for it defines the source of his power. As will be discussed further, the inside is a central locus in Defoe's work.

The syntactic appearance of the body is more elusive than explicit men-tions or symbolic representations. The syntactic image is one of "pure" rela-tionships whose possible meanings are determined only in the context of se-mantic matrices. The syntactic image is that of the preverbal; its shapes and forces are given voice later. In Edgar Allan Poe's "Fall of the House of Usher" the opening sentence demonstrates how the body may be syntactically placed: "During the whole of a dull, dark, and soundless day in the autumn of the year, when the clouds hung oppressively low in the heavens, I had been passing alone, on horseback, through a singularly dreary tract of country; and at length found myself, as the shades of evening drew on, within view of the melancholy House of Usher" (1972, 244). The structure of this sentence situates the body in the midst of time and space. That is, the "I" who "found myself"—the body "on horseback"—is literally embedded in the sentence between descriptions of time and space. In a sketchy way, it looks like this: [time/duration (during . . . whole); times (day, season); space (clouds . . . low)] [I/alone/horse] [space (through . . . tract); time (at length)] [found myself] [space (view . . . House)]. This schema of being contained within dominates the tale. Thus the narrator successively enters deeper levels of interior space. First, he "entered the Gothic archway of the hall" and is then "ushered . . . into the presence of [the] master" and notices how "gloom . . . pervaded all" (248–49). As days go on he finds a "closer and still closer intimacy admitted me more unreservedly into the recesses of his spirit" (253). Within this "spirit" Usher himself has a particular fantasy of "the interior of an immensely long and rectangular vault or tunnel, with low walls, smooth, white, and without interruption" (254). The story itself hinges on Usher's twin sister's "entombment" (259) and being "entombed" (260). As the "secret" is let out, the narrator finds the terror of it "creeping upon" him (260) and notices a "faintly luminous and distinctly visible gaseous exhalation which hung about and enshrouded the mansion" (262). And in the end, the narrator witnesses the faint "fissure" in the house "rapidly widened—there came a fierce breath of the whirlwind . . . the mighty walls rushing asunder . . . and the deep and dank tarn at my feet closed sullenly and silently over the fragments of the 'House of Usher'" (268). In the opening sentence the narrator is syntactically situated in the middle of darkness and silence; in the process of the tale, we enter a succession of interiors until the revelation of Usher occurs: "*We have put her living in the tomb!*" (266); and, in the end, the House of Usher is explicitly split, fragmented, and silently buried. Suffice it to say here that the syntactic image of the opening, locating the narrator's body in negativities—dark, dull, soundless, oppressively low, shades, melancholy—is emblematic. The burial of the body is successively passed on—the narrator is buried first, then in a cycling around, Usher and his sister are buried; she is entombed, he is in the house that becomes entombed.

Images of the Body in Psychoanalysis

The foregoing discussion has established the general idea that the body is represented in the novel through hierarchical patterns of language. The body's presence is neither anomalous—it is always embedded at some level of the novel, as it is in any cultural artifact—nor is it without meaning, though it may at times be fragmented, frozen, melted, or otherwise distorted. We can now focus on some of the ways the body has been perceived and investigated by psychoanalysis because it is a discipline that has studied representations of the body and articulated its primacy in human development and relationships. The body is the ground from which the self emerges; its treatment and handling are thus central to the development and perception of the individual. More than other disciplines, psychoanalysis has studied the vicissitudes of the body. Psychoanalysis has always had a focus on the body as it emerges through verbal language and other semiotic systems such as gestures and symptomatic acts, children's play constructions and drawings, and the visual arts.

From Freud's early interest in physiology to his late interest in the broad matter of Eros and Thanatos, his work is connected to the body. From a therapeutic perspective, Freud sought to de-repress the body by speaking of it and its repressed, systematically encoded representations. He studied the body from many angles: its development, gender, enactments, transformed representations in cultural artifacts and dreams, sensitivities, dis-ease, erotics, wounds, grief, destructive rage, and fear. Freud uncovered the wishes of the body in dreams and the pain of the self in bodily symptoms. He argued that the body would speak its pain until the pain could be spoken in language, allowing deeper pain to emerge. He read the secrets of the body in its own language; as he said in *Dora*, "He that has eyes to see and ears to hear may convince himself that no mortal can keep a secret. If his lips are silent, he chatters with his finger-tips; betrayal oozes out of him at every pore" (Freud 1953b [1905], 76–77). Freud knew that the body spoke a language about itself and that our everyday language spoke of it also, on different registers. He believed that if the muted language of the body could be spoken about, it might lead one to see a connection between the drama of the mute language and its history. Health, for Freud, consisted of making connections and staying connected by use of language.

The body continues to be a focal area of psychoanalytic exploration because, I suspect, there are very few treatment cases in which the body does not at some point figure prominently. The following brief catalog indicates some areas of psychoanalytic investigation: the body's development (Abraham 1927, Erikson 1963, Mahler 1968, Spitz 1965, Anzieu 1990); gender (Horney 1967, Dinnerstein 1976, Benjamin 1988, Mitchell 1974); identity

(Lichtenstein 1977, Erikson 1963, Searles 1979, Laing 1960); transitional needs (Winnicott 1971a); armor (Reich 1949); rage and aggression (Klein 1981, Fromm 1973); self-attacking (Spotnitz 1976, Kohut 1985); parental treatment (Winnicott 1965, Miller 1986, Dinnerstein 1976); representations in dreams, drawings, and play (Klein 1975, A. Freud 1969, Winnicott 1971a, Erikson 1963, Coles 1964); and in culture as a whole (Roheim 1952, N. Brown 1959, Bettelheim 1960, Lasch 1978, Kovel 1981, Marcuse 1962, Gay 1984, Foucault 1980, Segal 1981). Additionally, a brief trip to the *Chicago Psychoanalytic Literature Index* (1978) reveals how much focus there is on the body in psychoanalytic journals; one finds such headings as abortion, addiction, aggression, alcoholism, allergy, amputation, anality, asthma, auto-eroticism, beards, and beating children.

At the moment, I want to extract some body images from these writers to establish an array of images so that when we approach the appearance of the body in the novel, the reader will have visceral, visual, sensuous, and dimensional associations. By and large, the focal aspect of the body which psychoanalysis examines is primitive in that it is shaped early in life before verbal language has been formally implanted or is later so traumatized that it simulates, regresses to, the fragmentation of early life. The images we will look at in what follows will give a sense of the body of the infant and the consequences of its handling and the images of the body (as a consequence of its treatment) which the child and adult symbolically articulate. Thus we will look at a spectrum of mother-child relationships—"good enough," abusive, and abandoning—and a range of distressed body images that psychoanalytic and feminist readers have reconfigured from verbal, visual, and behavioral configurations created by children and adults.

A foundational idea in psychoanalysis is that the routine treatment of the infant/child—experientially located in the body—profoundly shapes the psychological makeup of the individual. Thus, as Peter Ritvo (1974) notes, "Because the child's internal bodily needs and rhythms are not from the beginning in time with the patterns of the adult environment, he is liable to developmental disturbances involving bodily functions. . . . How the bodily needs are managed by the mother is significant for later personality development and psychopathology. The child's ego will take an attitude toward the instinctual drives which is similar to that of the mother" (162). Being an infant is to be in what Bettelheim might call an "extreme situation"—the infant is exceedingly vulnerable, utterly dependent, and replete with needs vital to survival. Any pattern of caring is thus nearly "hard wired," as Heinz

Lichtenstein writes: "The mother does not convey a sense of identity to the infant but an *identity:* The child is the organ, the instrument for the fulfillment of the mother's unconscious needs. *Out of the infinite potentialities within the human infant, the specific stimulus combination emanating from the individual mother "releases" one, and only one, concrete way of being this organ, this instrument.* This "released" identity will be irreversible, and thus it will compel the child to find ways and means to realize this specific identity which the mother has imprinted upon it" (1977, 78). Although Lichtenstein does not directly speak of the body, he recognizes the child as an "organ" that gets shaped into an identity by the interactions with the mother, that is, by the way the mother treats the body. When the treatment of the child is regarded from a collective perspective, that is, when we can see certain uniform practices of child rearing in groups, it becomes clear that the culture has certain values—a group identity—which is also impressed, through the mother, on the child's body. The work of Erik Erikson often focuses on this transformation from culture, to mother, to child. For example, in studying the Sioux Indians, he notes, "Sioux child training forms a firm basis for this system of centrifugality [of aggression] by establishing a lasting center of trust, namely the nursing mother, and then by handling the matter of teething, of infantile rage, and of muscular aggression in such a way that the greatest possible degree of ferocity is provoked, channelized socially, and finally released against prey and enemy. We believe we are dealing here, not with simple causality, but with a mutual assimilation of somatic, mental and social patterns which amplify one another and make the cultural design for living economical and effective" (1963, 156). Erikson's work draws our attention to the basic redundancy of the body; thus the body's need to survive, to compete with others and with the environment is a group body need which is met in part by how the child's body is shaped to encourage it to be able to meet the needs of both the individual and the group.

The nature of this vulnerable, primitive body emerges as we consider the myriad ministrations of the mother and the concomitant bodily needs they fulfill. Dorothy Dinnerstein gives an excellent concrete description of what Winnicott would include in his sense of the "holding environment" of "good enough" mothering. The description gives us a sense of how utterly in one's care the infant's body is:

> It is in a woman's arms and bosom that the delicate-skinned infant—
> shocked at birth by sudden light, dry air, noises, drafts, separateness,
> jostling—originally nestles. In contact with her flesh it first feels the ec-

stasy of suckling, of release from the anguish of hunger and the terror of isolation. Her hands clean, soothe, and pat its sensitive bottom. Her face is the first whose expression changes reciprocally with its own. Her voice introduces it to speech: it is the first voice that responds to the voice of the child, that signals the advent of succor, whose patterns of rhythm or pitch correspond to events the child notices or body sensations it feels. She is the one who rocks or bounces it when it feels tense, who thumps it when it needs to burp. She comes when it feels anxious or bored and provides the sense of being cared for, the interesting things to look at, touch, smell, and hear, the chance to use growing powers of back-and-forth communication, without which human personality and intellect—and indeed the body itself—cannot develop. (1976, 78)

Dinnerstein's specificity develops an image of how much the body is attended to and handled. The body is stimulated, soothed, comforted, given space, fed, touched, caressed, kissed, stroked, rocked, warmed, cooled, cooed, bathed, swung, sung, bounced, cradled, and the like—if the child is lucky. The relationship of body to body, of mother (and father) to child is complexly charged as the primal needs of the child come together with the unconscious needs of the parents.

A child whose needs are adequately met will grow in relatively healthy ways, flexible enough to adapt and/or change systems. Inasmuch as the child adapts to its culture, however, with its own collective bodily needs, it carries the dis-eases particular to that culture—for example, aggressivity channeled toward a bias about skin color or anatomy. Dinnerstein's particular concern is that given the essential split of gender in our culture, men and women cannot grow in healthy ways because each is half and neither is whole. Under the best of conditions, we grow up warped, alien. Dinnerstein says that the unequal distribution of both caring for the child (a "female monopoly") and making something in the world at large (a male monopoly) is *the* problematic in our culture. The imbalances ensure that the intricate web of male-female infantilization will continue its negative dialectic and play out its violent possibilities. The body is not wholly realized; it is out of touch, the male with caring and the female with what Dinnerstein calls "enterprising." Enterprise without caring and caring without enterprise create ecological dysfunction—intrapersonal, interpersonal, and environmental. Thus, even in a relatively benign situation—a healthy infant and a good enough mother—the outcome may be damaging to both men and women. Even with good mothering, without fathering there is a missing piece, a "difference that makes a difference." Dinnerstein's point is that we enter the world with monocular vision (mother-child) rather than with binocular vision (mother-child and father-child), hence some depth is missing. The child's body is shaped by one pair of hands; there is a distinctive absence of the other Other for the child and the presence of that absence in the first Other—the mother's anger, grief, depression, frustration, exhaustion, depletion. The double absence (gone for the child, gone for the mother, and thus gone for the child in another manifestation) creates exaggerated needs; the body embeds the feelings of the body that holds it.

Dinnerstein's work argues that the asymmetry in child rearing has large-scale political ramifications. Without forgetting her perspective, I would like now to focus down from the large-scale issues to more individual ones as they emerge in the absence of maternal care. Given the amount of power embedded in the mother-child dyad when it is a good enough situation, what happens when it is not good enough, when it is deprivational or abusive? René Spitz demonstrated that the body of the deprived infant fails to develop and often dies (1965, 267–92).[2] One group of children he reports on were in a foundling home in which he says they were "adequately cared for in every bodily respect. Food, hygiene, medical care and medication, etc. were as good, even superior [to those in other facilities]. . . . But, as one single nurse had to care for eight children . . . they were emotionally starved" (278–79). The image of these infants is one without vitality; they become increasingly "passive," "vacuous." Even by age four most "cannot sit, stand, walk or talk." Spitz notes that "when the emotional deprivation continues into the second year of life, [it leads] to a spectacularly increased rate of mortality" (282). The body which is technically even humanely attended to but not loved fails to develop and thus withers away. The body initially requires fairly steady care and attention. The children Spitz describes as being "emotionally deprived" are physically deprived as well in that there is not enough of the explicit connectedness depicted by Dinnerstein—there is not enough physical information to tell the infant to live and thrive. In fact, the infants Spits describes were *not* "adequately cared for in every bodily respect." Radical absence destroys the body by preventing its unfolding. The image of the body of these children is vegetative and dying.

Alice Miller's work examines different extreme situations in which there is abuse and abusive contact—premature and overstimulating, harsh and violent, or neglectful.[3] She traces the roots of violence and self-destructive living to what she calls "poisonous pedagogy." This is a belief system documented by individual cases and historical studies of child-rearing practices.

It entails molding a child's behavior by harshly treating its body, denying the harshness, and disallowing dialogue. Miller says:

> The desire for "true nobility of soul" justifies every form of cruelty toward the fallible child, and woe to the child who sees through the hypocrisy.
>
> The pedagogical conviction that one must bring a child into line from the outset has its origin in the need to split off the disquieting parts of the inner self and project them onto an available object. The child's great plasticity, flexibility, defenselessness, and availability make it the ideal object for this projection . . . children who have grown up being assailed for qualities the parents hate in themselves can hardly wait to assign these qualities to someone else. (1983, 90–91)

Miller examines the ways that violence stays alive and is propagated, sometimes to turn against the self and sometimes against the other. She notes, as does Bateson, that the child's enforced inability to express a response is likely to send the pattern into repetition: "If there is absolutely no possibility of reacting appropriately to hurt, humiliation, and coercion, then these experiences cannot be integrated into the personality; the feelings they evoke are repressed," later to be acted out individually or collectively (7). In the absence of care, the body withers. In cases of abuse and neglect, the violation to the body creates a desire to violate another's body, to undo the wound, or to recreate the original abuse. A last possibility is that the abused child will manage to transform the pain and speak of it in some new, creative manner, eluding the censors of the internal or external worlds.

Although being attacked promotes desires to attack back, there are strong prohibitions against attacking (especially, for example, against attacking one's parents) and survival realities that prevent it; hence the attack is often displaced on to one's own body. Wilhelm Reich found conflict imprinted on the body and used the metaphor of "armor," which develops in response to pain, to control it, block it out. Reich says, "The total expression of the armored individual is that of 'holding back.' This expression has to be taken literally: *the organism expresses the fact that it is holding back.* The shoulders are pulled back, the thorax pulled up, the chin is held rigid, respiration is shallow" (1949, 364). Reich's work speaks to how the body expresses the existential position of the self—the paradox that to keep itself protected, it cuts off its lifeblood. And to express itself, the posture—the syntax of the body—communicates the same message. Other investigators have also reported the effects of bodily distress becoming internalized. Arthur Valenstein describes one patient, for example, who reports, "'This discomfort in my body, roiling about all the time, cramping and pains—everything hurts and is uncomfortable; it is as if I hold on to it as the only thing I have ever known, the familiar, and I go back to it. . . . It goes way back, as long as I can remember'" (1973, 388) Valenstein notes that on top of preverbal or pregenital distress others will form: "Thus, object experience moves progressively not only from 'who eats whom,' but also to 'who controls whom,' 'who shreds whom,' 'who dumps on whom,' 'who pierces whom,' 'who shafts whom,' and 'who screws whom'" (389). As this sort of bodily pain, this self-hate of the narcissistic disorders, becomes collective, it forms the core of what Christopher Lasch (1978) characterizes as the "culture of narcissism."

The body of the infant develops in relation to both its own inner being and its relations with others; it may be well cared for, neglected, abused, or abandoned. Those who work with children have been able to study the symbolic expressions of bodily images and of violence, felt, experienced, or feared.[4] Melanie Klein's work is focused on what the primal body imagines doing to the mother: in its frustration and rage, it wishes to tear open and eat the mother's goodness; in its grief, it wishes to repair it; and in its anxiety, it fears its own body will be eviscerated. Lacan describes Klein's contribution thus: "Through her we know the function of the imaginary primordial enclosure formed by the *imago* of the mother's body; through her we have the cartography, drawn by the children's own hands, of the mother's internal empire, the historical atlas of the intestinal divisions in which the *imagos* of the father and brothers (real or virtual), in which the voracious aggression of the subject himself, dispute their deleterious dominance over her sacred regions" (1977, 20–21). Klein impresses us with the visceral quality of the child's world as it emerges in play, fantasy, rituals, games, learning patterns (inhibitions), and everyday behavior. For Klein the preverbal universe—eating, weaning, toilet training, parental sexuality—often leads to violent, primitive bodily fantasies acted out in daily behavior, especially when the preverbal universe has been overstimulating, frightening, or deprivational. For example, Klein writes of one patient (Ruth, aged four and a half) who experienced, among other things, severe anxiety attacks, especially at bedtime. Klein sees the attacks as a repetition of a complex configuration beginning when the child was two and the mother was pregnant; she explains: "Saying good-night before she went to sleep meant saying goodbye forever. For, as a result of her desires to rob and kill her [pregnant] mother, she was afraid of being abandoned by her forever or of never seeing her alive again, or of finding, in the place of the kind and tender mother who was saying good-night to her, the 'bad' mother who would attack her in the night" (1975 [1932], 29).[5]

In another case, a young girl wants to learn but has inhibited the desire and stopped learning. Klein says, "Arithmetic and writing symbolized violent sadistic attacks upon her mother's body . . . these activities were equated with tearing, cutting up or burning her mother's body" (57).

On less primitive planes, others have explored the symbolic representation of the child's body. On the "simple" level of the genitals, for example, Erik Erikson has noted that the spatial configurations constructed by girls and boys seem often to represent the genital dimension of the body. The play configurations created by girls tended to be circular; the focus of concern with these structures had to do with intrusions, openness, and shutting out. The configurations of boys tended to be vertical, with concerns of standing up and falling over (1963, 97–108). Representations of greater complexity — portraying the psychological conflicts engendered by interpersonal forces — have been examined by such people as Robert Coles and D. W. Winnicott.

Coles's work (1964) has often demonstrated how the body of the child as represented in drawings is a function of an intricate web of relationships. He is less concerned with primitive conflicts of the body than with the representation of here-and-now existential conflicts as they are translated into images of the body, which in turn provide an understanding of how the body is psychologically treated. The study of Ruby, for example, documents how a young black girl sees herself — images her body — as she grows up in a white society and particularly as she enters a school that is becoming desegregated in a highly oppositional atmosphere. Some of the features Coles notes in Ruby's early drawings are that black and brown were rarely used, and if used covered over with other colors; white people were "larger and more lifelike"; black people's bodies were "less intact" so that an eye or an ear might be missing and the arms were "shorter, even absent or truncated." Interestingly, one ear of a black person might be missing, but the one shown would be bigger than a white person's — the better to hear — and, complementary to the big ear, the black person often "appeared with no mouth" (46–47). For Coles, the body drawings are the child speaking her existential perspective on being a black child; the drawings are the intrapsychic mapping of multilayered conflict. The distortions of the body's representations signify external malevolence and internal adaptations. Thus to speak may be dangerous so there is no need for a mouth, but listening is important to survival hence the need for a large ear.

In D.W. Winnicott's consultations with children, he asks the child to play a squiggle game — he draws a line, a squiggle, and the child completes it, and then they reverse the order (1971b). In this process Winnicott sees in the gestures of the body as well as the body's representation in drawings and play, metonymic messages, encapsulated history, interpersonal relationships. The drawing is a middle point between reality and dream. Winnicott used the drawing game as a way to allow the child to reenter and thence to leave the conflict through the symbolic process and through talk. For example, an eight-year-old girl who had begun stealing things at school had a consultation. As Winnicott saw it, the problem revolved around maternal deprivation: the child's mother became pregnant and subsequently ill, and the child was relatively neglected. Through a series of squiggle drawings and talk, the child "caught the feeling of becoming deprived and of feeling hopeless. Having recaptured this experience in full consciousness . . . Ruth . . . lost the compulsion to steal" (229–30). Whatever was missing inside became clear. In other consultations the body or its representation emerges as a mute speaker of embedded conflict. Thus in working with a young boy, Alfred, Winnicott noted two bodily statements — one is that Alfred "made a little push with his breath," and the second is that he stammered. In the course of talking and drawing, both gestures are connected to "making an effort" and in fact trying too hard and thereby fouling things up. It turns out that the bodily message repeats the experience of Alfred's father — he tries too hard and then goes into a hospital for several months as a result (110–12).

Feminist consciousness has contributed another perspective on the formation of deformation of the body, particularly the female body. Thus an early publication, *Our Bodies, Our Selves,* was dedicated to demystifying the body, establishing its sexuality, and disentangling a woman's body from the male-dominated medical business. Betty Friedan's *Feminine Mystique* articulated the matter of women's bodies and their treatment thus: "In the second half of the twentieth century in America, woman's world was confined to her own body and beauty, the charming of man, the bearing of babies, and the physical care and serving of husband, children and home" (1963, 31). By and large, women were seen and treated solely as bodies, and as such they were mistreated. Friedan's observations came in part from the study of popular literature, and the feminist study of literature in general has had a sharp focus on the body — how it is treated by men, how such treatment is perpetuated, how one overcomes it. Thus Elaine Showalter notes that in its early years "feminist criticism concentrated on exposing the misogyny of literary practice . . . emphasizing the connections between the literary and the social mistreatment of women, in pornography, say or rape" (1985, 5). Later studies have turned to women writers and their own representation of the body. For example, the works of Sandra Gilbert and Susan Gubar (1979) on nineteenth- and twentieth-century women writers often examine concerns with the body, for example, food and eating, sexuality, maternity, and childbirth.

In all these various works of psychoanalysis, social psychology, and feminist analysis the body figures prominently. The body that is mistreated—overstimulated, hurt, neglected, existentially denied—carries secret pains. At times the body withers under the pain, the deprivation or constriction of language, as works of Spitz, Bettelheim, Miller, Harold Searles, and others have demonstrated. In less oppressive circumstances, the secret pain is embedded but may slowly unfold when images, constructions, play activities, and gestures lead to language. Thus we see the body represented in play, drawing, posture, gesture, symptom, dream, and art. However condensed or displaced, the body carries with it a tale it is dying to tell.

◇◇ The body writes itself into the culture and is richly embedded in language. Thus civilization is at risk when a radical split is created between language and body (inversely demonstrating their connectedness).

The works of many writers consciously call our attention to the centrality of the body—Laurence Sterne, Toni Morrison, John Barth, Kathy Acker, Ernest Hemingway, D. H. Lawrence, Margaret Atwood.

The Body Emerges: Explicit, Symbolic, and Syntactic

This chapter further maps out the three basic ways the body emerges from the language of the novel as outlined in the previous chapter and explores in a preliminary way some of the psychoanalytic themes of that body. First, aspects of the body are presented on the surface of the novel by being explicitly named. Second, the body is presented in a symbolic manner through spatial descriptions and images such as objects, interior spaces, and environmental shapes. Last, the body is present in the shape, force, and motion of syntax. These categories are heuristic, allowing one to see each of three kinds of images: directly named, described symbolically, and inscribed by syntactic patterns. In fact, they overlap and often occur simultaneously. As will be clear in the four analyses of novels, the power of the body in the text lies in its redundancy, that is, it appears in all these guises, and we make meaning from their interplay. In the overlapping, in the juxtaposition of these image types, each informs the others.

My specific interest in these presentational modes is on the primitive body—not only skin, bones, organs, blood, semen, and the like but also more complex motion and interaction. The body experiences ranges of sensation, feeling, movement, force, tension, relaxation, displacement, coming both from within and outside the body. One is born with a body with its own setup; it meets a body that will in some measure adapt to that setup and will in some measure get that baby's body to adapt to the environmental setup. The body that emerges from such processes and in the literary text is generic as well as gendered—it has a preverbal history, a repertoire of gestures, a

range of transformations; it carries universal griefs and desires; it is fragmented, conflicted, and broken as well as integrated and healing. The body
of the text "speaks" about its primitive tensions as they occur within or at the
surface of the body, and especially as they were originally cultivated in the
relationship of the child and its environment, animate and inanimate. The
body speaks of its needs, desires, fears, and anxieties as they have been generated within or manipulated by relations with others. Thus we find tensions
in such polarities as pleasure and pain, anxiety and relief/release, symbiosis
and separation, good and bad insides, creation and destruction, secure and
anxious, passive and active.

As in other domains, the issue for the literary analyst is to explore why the
writer has made certain choices—why, for example, does "knee" show up so
often in *Tom Jones* and so rarely in other novels? Why do "hands" and "faces"
(in people and clocks) dominate in *The Sound and the Fury*? Why "back"
and "breasts" in Mary Gordon's *Final Payments*? Why "egg" in Doris Lessing's *Memoirs of a Survivor*, Margaret Atwood's *Surfacing*, or Louise Er-
drich's *Love Medicine*? We move toward understanding that a particular
bodily feature is a dominant redundancy or an outstanding singularity by examining the semantic contexts in which the feature appears and attempting
to understand the associational network. Let me use an example I will elaborate on in chapter 7: in David Bradley's *Chaneysville Incident*, the belly is
a major bodily focus. As we examine the passages in which the belly is present, a subset of concerns becomes evident and the following matrix is built
up: (1) the belly is cold or warm (or trying to be warm); (2) attempts are made
to warm the belly with coffee, hot toddies, or a hand; (3) coffee is associated
with females (mother, lover) and toddies with males (father, great-grandfather, father substitute), and the hand is associated with a central love relationship (male-female). In the course of the novel we learn the primitive
roots of the cold belly, its individual genesis, and the multigenerational embedding there of death, rage, and fierce struggle. As the belly is genuinely
warmed, it transforms from a locus of cold death (bowel) to a locus of warm
love and birth (womb). A psychoanalytic perspective allows us further to explore the formation of a bodily symptom (the cold belly) by examining such
matters as separation, splitting, and transgenerational rage.

The Body Named

Most linguistically obvious, the body, its parts, are directly named—hair,
hands, feet, eyes, and so on. The body that primarily appears in the novel is
the public and perceptual body, the body as visible on a more or less clothed

person, the body as it might become conscious to us in day-to-day life. For example, take a sentence randomly selected from Keri Hulme's *Bone People* (winner of the 1985 Booker Prize). "He shows her over the house first, the child beside her, holding her hand again, and making surreptitious comments with his fingers" (1986, 79). The physical contact and bodily communication initiated by the child cause discomfort for the woman — the child's tactile comments are "lost on" her; she is "using most of her attention" for something else. The child is related to the man with whom the woman is having a relationship (nonsexual), which the child was the medium of originating. The child is originally found by the man; he was washed up on the beach after a shipwreck. The child is mute and communicates through many channels — with gesture, writing, and behavior. The woman fights off the relationships with man and child; contact is uncomfortable for her. The issue of allowing the body to be touched is central to Hulme's novel; we find a spectrum ranging from the woman's avoiding touch (and promoting being out of touch, via alcohol), to a violent laying on of hands (by the father on the son) which completely shatters everyone. Thus the sentence in which the boy's contact and communication is described is part of a large matrix of other such descriptions. A central thread of that matrix is the story of the relationship of the hand to the body of the other — who can or does touch whom, and how, why, where, when, and with what consequences? There are many psychoanalytic issues involved — symbiosis, separation, withdrawal, trauma — and these evolve into issues of politics. The body in Hulme's novel is explicitly present; indeed, its redundancy and narrative intensity demand attention.

In most novels the body is not the surface subject or focus; rather human relationships and their development are the center of attention. Nonetheless, the body can play a central, self-conscious role in novels. For example, the body is in the forefront of Sterne's *Tristram Shandy*. Sterne's concern with health is mentioned in his preface, and throughout the novel the vulnerability of the body is a focal issue: for example, Tristram's very conception, his birth and circumcision, his breathing difficulty; Toby's wound and Slawkenbergius's tale. Hemingway's *Sun Also Rises* hinges on a bodily fact — the war wound of Jake Barnes. At whatever level of awareness, the explicit body is virtually always present. Its presence, in turn, informs its other manifestations, seen later in this chapter.

Although the body is openly presented in most novels, it is most visible and naked in novels that focus on sexuality, violence, and drugs. Novels in which these themes dominate provide us with examples of the most overt and extreme representations of the exterior and interior body depicted in intense pleasure, intense anger/pain, and intense interiorizing, withdrawing. The intensities are all in some sense narcotic; and to some extent each type shares all the intensities (pleasure, pain, and disappearance). They also have in common the subversion of language and no doubt some originating motivation. In the contexts of these intense bodily situations, the body is vulnerable, regressed, infantilized, not in control. Sexuality, violence, and drugs are nonsublimated activities, directly tapping into the body and circumventing language. Each has a transcendent possibility—erotic love, strength to build, visionary flight—but literature generally focuses on the dark side of each. Sexuality, violence, and drugs expose the body and its primitive modes of interaction. In one respect they are linked by their symbiotic/narcissistic aim—a drivenness to merge, to dissolve the self with the other (in sexual fluid), or dissolve the other into the blood of violence, or dissolve the self by taking something biomagical into the body. There is, then, some connection to the mother. The vicissitudes of this trio of forces in relation to one another and to their aim (mother) are as many as there are people. One configuration, however, seems generative: a sense that violence (violation, deprivation) initiates most of the forms of degenerative symbiosis or separation. The body, to use a phrase of A. R. Ammons's, is a "form of a motion" which is directed by the violence it suffers and the care it is offered. Those who are violated might exact displaced justice by hostile or ungenuine sexuality (using money to replace relationship), violence, or both; one might forget about pain and revenge with drugs, though the user often becomes absorbed by getting what is needed in order to forget about pain, thus finding him or herself wrapped around again, self-screwed—and thus having to remember the pain. The body does not forget its pain, and when it is not spoken of, it is enacted, reenacted, and remembered for generations, multiplying but not being fruitful. Violence creates violence, speeding up entropy by killing off language, bending it beyond itself.

Having briefly discussed the explicit presentation of the body, I would like to explore a thematically varied group of explicit representations, focused on sexuality, violence, drugs, and eating.

Eros

When the private body reaches a critical mass in a text, the body becomes the subject of it. In works such as Cleland's *Memoirs of a Woman of Pleasure* or Anaïs Nin's erotic short stories, *Delta of Venus*, the body is overtly "presented," in the ethnographic sense of sexual display. The objective of the text is largely to stimulate genital excitement for the reader. The work arouses us as we unconsciously loosen the map-territory boundaries: we respond with sexual arousal sparked by the redundant presentation of breasts, thighs, hands, penises, vaginas, and the like in dynamic interaction with one another. We image and sensuate those organs and their interplay. In imagination, we are seeing, touching and being touched. We reembody the text.[1] When analyzing these texts, as distinguished from experiencing them, we find the intensity of the genital focus suspect, indicative of more primitive desires and conflicts, for example, merging with or controlling the other, splitting the object. (Cf. Freud's "Special Type of Choice of Object Made by Men" [1910] and "On the Universal Tendency to Debasement in the Sphere of Love" [1912] and Karen Horney's "Distrust between the Sexes" [1967 (1931)].)

In Cleland's work ([1749] 1963) the body is the subject—paragraph after paragraph presents bodies or leads up to an exposure of them. A brief example does not adequately demonstrate the erotic power of the text because that power depends on a substantial amount of verbal foreplay and the reader's decision to read. The heroine, in something of the situation of the reader, has been watching a sexual scene; her response is as follows: "I stole my hand up my petticoats, and with fingers all on fire, seized, and yet more inflamed that center of all my senses; my heart palpitated, as if it would force its way through my bosom; I breathed with pain; I twisted my thighs, squeezed, and compressed the lips of that virgin slit" (65). The reader is here implicated as a voyeur, as one likely to be sexually excited by what he or she sees, and not unlikely to go into action—masturbation. The reader is willing to pay someone to provide a sexually exciting image which in this passage is of someone paying someone else to provide an image that is sexually stimulating.

In addition to exposing the body and its sexual desires, Cleland's work raises issues of the language used to describe the body. Here is a passage concerning Fanny Hill and her true love: "My beauteous youth was so glewed to me in all the folds and twists that we could make our bodies meet in; when, no longer able to rein in the fierceness of refreshed desires, he gives his steed the head and gently insinuating his thighs between mine, stopping my mouth with kisses of humid fire. . . . I began to enter into true unallayed pleasure of pleasures, when the warm gush darts through all the ravish'd inwards; what floods of bliss! what melting transports! what agonies of delight!" (89–90). We could find more explicit passages in contemporary sources—letters to the editor in "men's" magazines depicting sexual escapades, or novels like *The Story of O* or *Nine and a Half Weeks*. Nonetheless, we note how much of the body comes into play in two passages from Cleland—hand, finger, thigh, vagina, heart, lungs, bosom, mouth, penis, sexual juices—and how much movement the body makes—breathed, squeezed, glued, compressed, insinuated, kissed. We can see as well how boundaries break down as Fanny in the first passage identifies with the lovers she watches or in the second is "melting" into her lover. As important as the explicit aspect of Cleland's sexual descriptions is the symbolic aspect. That is, Cleland often relies on linguistic slippage; in an overtly erotic work, the body is often described in other terms. The body becomes a field of battle, a horse, a landscape, a space. For example, the heroine describes her virgin genital as a "theatre" that "did not yet afford room enough for action." The phallus is often described as a "machine," a "weapon." The female body is often a natural form—"unripe budding breasts," "virgin flower . . . yet uncrop'd"—or a "luxurious landscape." *There is nothing novel about such descriptions and that is precisely what is important about them.* That is, the association, for example, between the body and the landscape or animal or weapon is part of the linguistic fabric; it is based on analogues of shape and motion such as being interior and intruding. The erotic writer highlights these associations. Thus in a novel like *Robinson Crusoe* in which the erotic body is almost entirely absent, we can discern its presence through the landscapes, building structures, and the like. In some sense the erotic writer offers a Rosetta stone that can be employed to see the bodily dimensions of other texts.

In Cleland's work the body is amply represented, with the strongest focus on its sensual and erotic aspects; thus the major surface action and repetition is erotic play and orgasm. But as D.M. Thomas's *White Hotel* more consciously suggests, the sexuality is a cover to forget, abolish, and deny pain. Thus the opening of Cleland's novel involves a sequence of losses—of parents, guide, virginity, love, and values. Fanny is orphaned at fifteen and then abandoned by her guide in London. She feels "most bitterly the severity of this separation" (35). She is then recruited for prostitution—overstimulated and nearly raped. She meets and falls in love with Charles, to whom she gives her virginity, but loses him to other forces. She speaks of her relationship with him as symbiotic—"I . . . breathed . . . existed but in him" (107). And on losing him she becomes depressed and suicidal; she has "no view . . . of anything but the depth of misery, horror and the sharpest affliction" (107).

The sexual body of this text is, by and large, an exploitative one, turning the body to sexual labor and turning abuse seemingly on its head. Fanny Hill, that is, goes from her first procurer, who deceives her and is after "a good market for my maidenhead" (42), to Mrs. Cole, a later procurer, with whom she conspires to deceive someone else: "all my looks and gestures ever breathing nothing but that innocence which men so ardently require in us, for no other end then to feast themselves with the pleasure of destroying it, and which they are so grievously, with all their skill, subject to mistakes in" (217). Men can be fooled, and sexuality has a payoff, in money, that allows the heroine to obtain those comforts which mitigate the pains of her initial losses. Thus while the explicit body of this novel is the mature sexual one, the desire beneath sexuality is symbiosis, union with the mother. This desire emerges in the last explicitly described lovemaking scene of the novel, taking place between the heroine and her long lost love, Charles; it is described as "a transfusion of heart and spirit . . . making one body and soul with him. I was he, and he, me" (293). A comparison that Fanny makes in which vagina and penis are juxtaposed to mouth and breast clinches the sense of her deeper desire. The vagina is "that part [which] thirstily draws and drains," and the penis is "the nipple of Love," thus, "with much such an instinctive eagerness and attachment as . . . kind nature engages infants at the breast by the pleasure they find in the motion of their little mouths and cheeks, to extract the milky stream prepar'd for their nourishment" (294). Making love with Charles, presenting sexuality for the last time in the novel, the adult sexual act, so dominant in the novel in a more distanced, narcissistic way, transforms here to a more primal symbiosis; paradise lost is paradise regained.

The explicit erotic body is the subject of erotic writing, but it appears as well in texts with other, more whole, subjects. In these cases sexuality is often paradigmatic of more existential and primitive aspects of a character's relationships, as we can see in works by D. H. Lawrence (*Sons and Lovers*), James Joyce (*Ulysses*), Henry Miller (*Sexus* series), Mary Gordon (*Final Payments*), Rita Mae Brown (*Rubyfruit Jungle*), Margaret Atwood (*The Handmaid's Tale*), and others. As feminist critics have noted, the erotic body in action is a body politic, defining power. The naked body, the desiring body of eros, reflects in its interactions the nature of other dimensions of male-female and homosexual relations. The various feelings aroused by the intensity of sexuality are carried over from nonsexual interactions. Thus Paul Morel's relationship with Miriam in their naked sexual scene indeed lays bare his relationship with her—fraught with fear, holding back, disgust, apprehension, sacrifice—and through her, his relationship to his mother.

Nekros

In novels in which violence is a central theme, the body as agent and recipient is also explicit and thematically dominant. As in sexual narratives, the thematic *insistence* on violence indicates the working out of a psychic repetition. Psychotic rage might express a desire to merge or a fear of the same, a desire to control, a compulsion to undo what had been done to one. Whatever the motivation, the ramifications are similar; there is a severing of a connection between bodies and between body and language which distorts and injures both parties.

Sexuality, as it moves toward the perverse, is often connected to power, hence violence is often associated with it. When the body is open to pleasure, it is vulnerable. Taking pleasure seems often to shade into taking pleasure in vulnerability itself—sadism or masochism—perhaps to express in displaced form to the Other (mother) an infant pain, the same as alleviated by alcohol or drugs. Elizabeth McNeil's *Nine and a Half Weeks* is a contemporary example of sexuality entwined with escalating violence. From the first sentence, power is asserted and granted: "The first time we were together he held my hands pinned down above my head. I liked it. I liked him. . . . The fourth time, when I was aroused enough to be fairly oblivious, he used the . . . scarf to tie my wrists together. That morning, he had sent thirteen roses to my office" (1978, 1–2). Soon he uses handcuffs. He is meticulously caring in a baroque, macabre way—he feeds her while she is handcuffed at his feet; he bathes and massages her. The violence and the sexuality intensify until the heroine breaks down—she finds herself unable to stop crying, enters a hospital, and goes for psychological treatment. The quality of abuse, the exaggerated difference of pain and pleasure, infantilize and burn her out. She says, "I wonder whether my body will ever again register above lukewarm" (152). A psychoanalyst would reply, no, the body won't register above lukewarm if the memory of which the nine-and-a-half-week love affair was a repetition is not worked through. Such was the case in an instance discussed by Alice Miller of a prostitute who gradually uncovers the roots of her continued self-violation and phony power. Miller notes, "The more horrible her present life became, the more cruelly she was deceived by her procurers, the more brutally she was beaten, the less able she was to give up hoping that her love would change this man or that the next one would be her longed-for rescuer" (1986, 76). In *Nine and a Half Weeks* the lover is both torturer and rescuer. He is akin, to some extent, to parents described by Miller who, so as not to "spoil" the child, make him or her perform beyond capacity, thereby causing long periods of infant crying, screaming, and pain, but finally rescue the child to change, warm, hold, and feed him or her. The radical difference between pain and relief from pain—and the deeper the pain the more exaggerated the pleasure—is an infant experience, repeated by villains who were victimized as well as fresh victims.

The body is exceedingly vulnerable, and in texts of violence we are asked to imagine and thus experience to some extent the power one body takes over another. In part, we recognize violence by the verbs—wince, hunch, clench, huddle, smack, whack, slam, shoot, stick, attack, hit, beat, lacerate, burn—all of which describe the interaction of body with body, the powerful and the powerless. When the body is broken, the mind snaps, language barely exists. In Robert Stone's *Dog Soldiers* the antihero, Converse, is a first-time smuggler of heroin from Vietnam to California. Two "agents," Danskin and Smitty, catch up with him and use force to get him to tell them where the drugs are:

> Smitty turned on one of the ring burners and they watched it until it glowed bright orange. They were holding him from behind.
>
> "Please," Converse said.
>
> Smitty shoved the end of a towel in his mouth; Danskin was caressing the back of his neck.
>
> They're going to do it, Converse thought. He strained backward and he was so frightened that they had a difficult time holding him. Somehow he burned his hand. And burned it. And burned it.
>
> He screamed . . . in the fetal position with the fried hand trust between his thighs. (1973, 158)

As with erotic writing, the full impact of the passage is more keenly felt in a larger context. In this case the context is all that has preceded—Converse's involvement and anxiety, and more immediately the chase Smitty and Danskin have been making. We get closer and closer to the encounter above; the buildup is again parallel to a sexual one. Converse does, of course, "talk"—they "get it out of" him. The abuse, the burning, infantilizes him, rapes him. He tells what he knows, as Orwell's Winston Smith tells his torturer what he wants to hear. As the body is broken, language has no use—it must be given away—one is without thought, without power. As Bettelheim has observed, if the process of degrading goes on long enough, it easily becomes internalized and death follows soon thereafter.

The person who is violent is likely to be repeating violence from early abuse at the parental level; such a person may also find sanction for violence on more encompassing levels of the social environment. Danskin, for example, recounts how he ended up in a mental hospital for nine years after taking displaced revenge on a school peer, Bruce, for what to most egos would be a relatively minor humiliation. Danskin is thrown out of a movie theater for not paying, and he becomes narcissistically enraged; he waits for

Bruce with a tire iron and he attacks: "The first one is right across the face and he's down . . . not a sound. I just stood over him and bam! Bam, that's for your girlfriend. Bam, that's for your scholarship to Cornell . . . [until Bruce] is just a lot of mucus on the asphalt . . . three hundred cops are there, and I'm still pounding crud into the street . . . a meat market" (249) . There is an air of bravado in Danskin's depiction of his murdering Bruce; it is cold, stylized macho. His rage is now controlled, empowered, and exploited by the state; he makes money from his pain in a way analogous to the sexual way Fanny Hill makes money from hers (abandoned and deprived). His personal rage becomes a political tool, doing someone else's violence. The writer of violence assaults, terrorizes, and/or tortures the reader and induces strong negative feelings—increasing discomfort, anger, hatred, self-attack, depression, desire to act out. The violence awakens us to the pain of living in the world, to the mass of unnecessary abuse at any given moment, and to our own capacity for hating the Other, longing for revenge, bitter with envy. The violence to the body in the novel addresses us as both victim and victimizer.

The body is made primitive when attacked by the death machines of the sadocrats: Orwell's O'Brien; Robert Stone's Lieutenant Campos (in *Flag for Sunrise*) and his Danskin and Smitty above; the Nazis in D. M. Thomas's version of the Babi Yar massacre in *The White Hotel*. The punishment of the body scars the mind, fragments the ego; boundaries collapse. The body of the victim no longer lives as a user of language; the victim may only be empowered to commit suicide, as does Okonkwo in Chinua Achebe's *Things Fall Apart* or Richard in James Baldwin's *Go Tell It on the Mountain*.

The witness of violence is also scarred. An example is Virginia Woolf's Septimus Smith in *Mrs. Dalloway*. He is home from World War I, where he witnessed, among others, the death of his leader and friend. He slowly becomes "crazy"—he is infected with the craziness of the mass murder of war.[2] His internalized madness eventually leads him to jump out a window to his death so as to avoid the doctor who denies his pain. The death he witnessed unhinged his human connections; he psychically returns to earlier connections: "And the leaves being connected by millions of fibers with his own body, there on the seat, fanned it up and down; when the branch stretched he, too, made that statement" (1925, 32). In another situation, Jill Percy, in *Dog Soldiers*, witnesses a relatively small terrorist massacre: "Converse and Ian could tell what she had seen. Her steps were slow and deliberate and she appeared confused. If one stayed in the country [Vietnam] long enough one saw a great many people moving about in that manner" (34). The effects of violence in any single case are rarely limited to the immediate victim—survivors, witnesses, become mutants, going insane or on drugs, and often end up in the violence that shatters.

We hear the voice of the victim from survivors of wars, large-scale or domestic: Margaret Atwood's *Surfacing* and *Handmaid's Tale*; Doris Lessing's *Memoirs of a Survivor*; Robert Pirsig's *Zen and the Art of Motorcycle Maintenance*; Tim O'Brien's *Going After Cacciato*; William Wharton's *Birdy*; Elie Wiesel's *Wall*; Joseph Conrad's *Heart of Darkness*; Samuel Richardson's *Clarissa*. Wherever the violence emanates from, the body of the victim, being disembodied from within, is fragmented, dissociated, expropriated. Elaine Scarry observes that except for torture (and war), "Every act of civilization is an act of transcending the body in a way consonant with the body's needs." But in torture, "ultimate domination requires that the prisoner's ground become increasingly physical and the torturer's increasingly verbal, that the prisoner become a colossal body with no voice and the torturer a colossal voice . . . with no body, that eventually the prisoner experience himself exclusively in terms of sentience and the torturer exclusively in terms of self extension" (1985, 57). Confronting this radical severing of language and body, it is clear how much we presume their attachment.

Narke

Drugs, for the addicted, are taken into the body to take the body toward a straightforward if primitive pleasure and away from psychic pain. Drugs numb the mind, trick it into death by pleasure. For some writers, however, drugs are seen or "used" in the novel to unlock the mind into its nightmarish (William Burroughs) and/or visionary (Carlos Castaneda) potential. In either case, the body "returns" to earlier, fragmented or blissful states. The addict, for example, getting a fix seems related to how an infant might feel at being so relieved to have been fed that the ordinary pleasure is intensified; not only is hunger being satisfied but anxiety is allayed. In Stone's *Flag for Sunrise*, Pablo Tabor takes amphetamine for the intense "rush" it gives him. We track him for pages at a time when he is looking for a place to buy drugs, waiting for a moment to take them, and so on. Here is a typical moment when he finds a place to buy: " 'Benzedrin,' said the druggist. It was the most beautiful Spanish word Pablo had ever heard." He walks elsewhere and buys a Coke; he walks on and inspects the drugs: "Benzedrino all right, little yellow tablets, three hundred migs. Hot shit, Tabor thought; he swallowed two of them. . . . On his empty stomach, he began to get the rush fairly early on and it felt the like real thing. 'Thank you, Jesus,' Tabor said. *His being began to come together.* . . . Tabor experienced his true rush. He was moved almost

to tears" (1981, 96–97). He is willing, compelled, like others of Stone's heroes and heroines, to go through hell and torture to have that inner orgasm,
that moment of pleasure with its euphoric sense of empowerment. For Pablo
the addiction is not simply to the drug but to the dialectic of pain and
pleasure, the repetition of being saved from what seems like death. In this
totalized addiction, the body becomes an automaton and detaches itself
from the here and now—from others, language, culture, and thus conscience. The broader political ramifications that Stone points to, using drugs
as a metaphor, is that any such total addiction—for example, to money or
power—brings the same dominance of the body and absence of conscience
on a large scale.

Alcohol and drugs, each in its own way, are often associated with violence,
intrapsychic and interpersonal. For one thing, taking these substances into
the body allows one to "forget" one's relations to others. Thus the person becomes as primitive as a child but with the power of an adult. For example,
in Lawrence's *Sons and Lovers*, Mr. Morel's drinking relieves the brutality
to his body of the miner's labor and his family's disappointments, and at
times it allows the release of his physical anger—he strikes his child and his
wife. In *The Great Gatsby* the Buchanans' drinking is also associated with
the release of violence: Tom Buchanan, drunk, hits Myrtle across the face
and breaks her nose; Daisy Buchanan, driving drunk, accidentally runs Myrtle down. Drugs, in the novel, are not associated with violence in the same
way as alcohol is, but they are often found in the vicinity of violence and
connected to money and power. The violence around drugs is primarily over
"controlling" them and the money they generate. Many crimes are perpe-
trated while the perpetrator is on drugs, but that is not the purpose for which
most want to take drugs, and the greatest direct violence takes place at the
higher levels of the organization that buys-sells-distributes. Converse's
father-in-law tells him that he should not try to sell the heroin he obtained
in and shipped from Vietnam because of the agents, his competitors, who
are fiercely organized and territorial: "'They'll shoot you full of STP and put
a blowtorch to your balls'" (209). At the individual level, drugs are generally
a way to forget and to avoid the madness engendered by violence, such as
Septimus Smith experienced. Thus Marge, Converse's wife, snorting heroin
for the first time, feels greatly relieved from her various anxieties. She says,
"'I see how it works. You have it or you don't. You have it—everything's o.k.
You don't, everything's shit'" (171).

The turn to drugs for Converse stems from violence he directly experiences as a correspondent in Vietnam. He is taken into a battle zone:

> Converse had watched with astonishment as the world of things trans-
> formed itself into a single overwhelming act of murder. In a manner of
> speaking, he had discovered himself. Himself was a soft shell-less thing
> encased in a hundred and sixty pounds of pink sweating meat. It was real
> enough. It tried to burrow into the earth. It wept.
>
> After his exercise in reality, Converse had fallen in with Charmian and
> the dope people; he became one of the Constantly Stoned. Charmian was
> utterly without affect, cool and full of plans. She had taken leave of life in
> a way which he found irresistible. (24)

We learn that Converse witnessed and survived a fragmentation bomb attack—"bits of steel began to cut them up. . . . Around him the screams, the
bombs, the whistling splinters swelled their sickening volume until they
blotted out sanity and light" (185). Drugs here are linked with death—witnessing it, wanting to go in some other direction from it and away from "life"
and "reality" when these turn out to be murderous fragments. Drugs allow
one to leave the present body with its encumbrance of language and to return to an earlier, preverbal state. If most cultural activity allows one to transcend the body, drugs allow one to descend into it.

Eating

In novels with dominant themes of sexuality, violence, and drugs, the body
becomes intensely primitive. The body expresses its primitive, regressive
qualities with other, less intense processes such as eating. Eating brings with
it the mouth, teeth, lips, digestive and eliminative organs; it brings as well an
object, the breast—that which was and would be eaten. A book is waiting to
be written on eating in the novel, beginning with *Robinson Crusoe*. Although eating is not what literary critics focus on as a major theme in Defoe's work, most of Crusoe's twenty-eight years on the island focus on eating:
he plants, cultivates, protects, harvests, processes, stores, cooks. Moreover, he
is often concerned with being eaten—by the sea, animals, and cannibals.
Another early English novel, Henry Fielding's *Tom Jones*, asks us to consider
the novel itself as a "public ordinary," hence to be consumed by the reader;
eating and drinking are a very regular part of all relationships—sexual, com-
radely, hospitable, and familial. In Jane Austen's *Emma* we find Mr. Woodhouse: "His own stomach could bear nothing rich, and he could never believe other people to be different from himself. What was unwholesome to
him, he regarded as unfit for any body; and he had, therefore, earnestly tried

to dissuade them from having any wedding cake at all . . . and . . . earnestly tried to prevent any body's eating it" (1957, 12). The undifferentiating, infantile father offers people digestible "gruel" as if to say there must be no perceptible aggression (chewing, grinding) or adult pleasure (cake, wedding).

Deprivation and self-deprivation of food is a theme we find in works from *Jane Eyre* to Margaret Atwood's *Handmaid's Tale,* and it has been explored in feminist/psychological readings. Male representations of the conflict are found in Defoe's work, in George Gissing's *Odd Women,* and very strikingly in Orwell's *Nineteen Eighty Four.* Orwell's work is laden with matters of eating, the good breast and the bad. We find, for example, the following description of Victory Gin: "It gave off a sickly, oily smell — Winston poured out nearly a teacupful, nerved himself for a shock, and gulped it down like a dose of medicine. Instantly his face turned scarlet and the water ran out of his eyes. The stuff was like nitric acid, and moreover, in swallowing it one had the sensation of being hit on the back of the head with a rubber club. The next moment, however, the burning in his belly died down" (1983 [1949], 8). Virtually everywhere we go in the novel with Winston, we encounter a punishing and deprivational environment. Whatever one needs to take into oneself has a awful smell, a terrible appearance, or a miserable taste. The entire alimentary process is abused. Counter to this aspect of the text is Winston's relationship with Julia, the good breast: "He could feel her breasts, ripe yet firm, through her overalls. Her body seemed to be pouring some of its youth and vigor into his" (113). She gives him real chocolate and real coffee. When this goodness is discovered by the Party, it must be ripped out of his body. As O'Brien says, "'We shall squeeze you empty, and then . . . fill you with ourselves'" (211). The thread of eating is continued as Winston is threatened with rats; O'Brien tells him, "'They will leap onto your face and bore straight into it. Sometimes they attack the eyes first. Sometimes they burrow through the cheeks and devour the tongue'" (235). Winston betrays Julia at this very moment so as to preserve his physical being, and he thereby gives up the good breast. In the last scenes of the novel Winston gazes, like an infant, at Big Brother's face, drinks the noxious gin, and exclaims to the face, to himself, "O cruel, needless misunderstanding, O stubborn, self-willed exile from the loving breast!" (245). The bad breast is the good breast. Although the book is focused on an adult level, the issue of eating and how it is described brings one into a more primitive atmosphere. The language slides from the public body and the private body into the primitive body, the infant's body, hungry and distressed, wanting something and feeling bad at having something bad yet feeling good for having something at all.

The Body Symbolic: Spaces

Freud's *Interpretation of Dreams* began a conscious cultural convention that regards various shapes and forms in dreams and cultural works as transformed bodily manifestations, popularly called Freudian symbols. We can clarify the relationship between spatial configurations and the body by observing, through a linguistic eye, that in descriptions of spaces, objects, movements, and interactions, we find distinctive features that cross-reference with those of the body and its processes. This is the same slippage that occurs in Cleland's erotica, describing the phallus as a "steed" or a "sword" or the body as a landscape. The unconscious (or the "right brain") uses this same slippage and re-presents the body in new guises. So we find the body in domestic interiors, landscapes, seascapes, cultural artifacts, and natural objects. Even "the mind" is described in such ways that it mirrors the spaces and movements of the body—for example, things are said to go into and out of it, or it is filled or empty, or it is blocked from getting something in or out.

There are times, as well, when the explicit appearance of the body is ambiguous; it is presented as a public form, but one senses a deeper, more private, possibility. That aspect of the body which is mentioned doubles as that aspect which is not mentioned. For example, in Gissing's *Odd Women* the heroine, Rhoda Nunn, is introduced if not set up in the chapter called "An Independent Woman." The description of her appearance demonstrates the doubleness I want to point out. At first, her face "seemed masculine . . . eyes shrewdly observant and lips impregnable." However, as one studied and waited, "when the lips parted to show their warmth, their fullness . . . one became aware of a suggestiveness . . . an unfamiliar sexual time, remote . . . from the voluptuous, but hinting of a possibility of subtle feminine forces that might be released by circumstance" (1977, 20–21). Rhoda's features are initially seen as masculine and not erotic (penetrating, phallic, "shrewdly observant"), but they could shift to being feminine and sexual if some "circumstance" were right: perhaps the proverbial "right man" who knew what to do or how to do it? The lips are described as "impregnable," which shifts them into the realm of the genital. In addition, the lips seem also to suggest breasts—"an unfamiliar [i.e., repressed, unconscious] sexual time, remote . . . from the voluptuous . . . subtle feminine forces might be released." The desire of the observer shapes Rhoda into a complex sexual body—masculine and feminine, sexual and maternal. Often when we enter the realm of the body there is a loss of boundaries, linguistic markers slip from organ to organ, and psychological states slide into a dreamlike permeability.

The process of slippage from external spaces to bodily ones can be clarified by looking at a variety of interiors, all of which focus on a similar thematic—they are related to bodily interiors, particularly the bowel and its contents. In *Robinson Crusoe* (1972), when Crusoe first brings his goods into his newly built cave, it "was a confus'd Heap of Goods . . . lay in no Order . . . I had no room to turn my self . . . [but after he works on it, he] had every thing so ready at . . . Hand, that it was a great pleasure to see all my Goods in such Order, and especially to find my Stock of Necessaries so great" (67–69). The space is initially messy and blocked up, and later orderly and full; initially there is depression and anxiety, later there is ease, comfort, security. A similar "Heap of Goods" comes up in a different way in David Bradley's *Chaneysville Incident*. The hero describes his mother's habit: she tends to pile things up in rooms such that no space "went . . . unfilled . . . until one day there wasn't any space . . . and the original shape of anything that had been there was lost under the piles" (1981, 128). Here the piles smother things and blur boundaries. In contrast to Crusoe's cave, the interior of John Grimes's house (Baldwin 1952) as we might gather from his name as much as anything else, is impossible to clean: "John hated sweeping the carpet, for dust rose, closing his nose and sticking to his sweaty skin, and he felt that should he sweep it forever, the clouds of dust would not diminish, the rug would not be clean . . . for each dustpan he so laboriously filled at the doorsill demons added to the rug twenty more; he saw in the expanse behind him the dust that he had raised settling into the carpet; and he gritted his teeth, already on the edge because of the dust that filled his mouth" (26–27). This space rises up to penetrate and engulf the inhabitant in its dirty negativity; it is a bad interior which "filled his mouth." In this murky area one senses a bowel but a bad breast as well. A similar feeling occurs in Mary Gordon's *Final Payments*. The heroine, Isabel Moore, tells us her father's attitude toward their house: "He seemed to take a pride in the curious degradation of our surroundings, as if the mess, the pileup, was an index to the richness of our interior lives" (1978, 35). She opens the refrigerator one day after her father's funeral and finds the "defeating smell of rotting food . . . broccoli liquefying at the bottom" (42). Gordon makes a conscious analysis of "interior" for the father who equates the house with "interior lives" by which he would refer to an intellectual life, but the interior of the house reflects more of the Moores. The fullness of the house satisfies, as it does Crusoe; the good breast is within, can't be taken away. But since it doesn't work that way, in fact, the interior, hoarded breast is likely to liquefy and rot. The inside of her refrigerator brings to mind an interior in Orwell's *Nineteen Eighty Four*—the Parsons's flat: "dingy . . . battered . . . a litter of dirty dishes . . . the usual boiled-cabbage smell, common to the whole building, but . . . shot through by a sharper reek of sweat . . . kitchen sink was full nearly to the brim with filthy greenish water which smelt worse than ever" (21). In Orwell we get a sense of collective smell in all space, sometimes intensifying, as in the Parsons's flat, but as omnipresent as Big Brother, as if one were living in and eating from a vast bowel.

In all these configurations, the interiors are related to the bowel and its functions; they have a concern with matters of order and disorder, piles, blockage, dirt, and smells. The semantic networks associated with the bowel in our culture are, in the unconscious, ascribed to analogous forms. Not surprisingly, in many of the interiors, there is an overlay of orality—food, eating, smelling food, rotting food—suggesting a bad breast in these interiors, confirming Melanie Klein's sense that the interior houses all manner of bodily functions, organs, and persons.

There is a moment in Woolf's *To the Lighthouse* when the operations of the mind are described in a similar fashion—as an interior, as a bowel—but the moment depicts a release rather than a buildup. Lily Briscoe, who finds socializing difficult and has no desire for anyone to see her work, has some amiable conversation with Mr. Bankes, to whom she shows her painting; Woolf describes a climactic moment thus: "Suddenly, as if the movement of his hand had released it, the load of her accumulated impressions of him tilted up, and down poured in a ponderous avalanche all she felt about him. There was one sensation. Then up rose in a fume the essence of his being. That was another" (1927, 39). She concludes by noting to herself, "you [Mr. Bankes] are the finest human being that I know" (39). In this passage, an unstated space, the locus of impressions, and actions relative to it and its content, are analogues of a bowel movement: "load . . . accumulated . . . down poured . . . up rose . . . fume." What are we to make of this? Her impressions of Bankes are associated with defecation, yet she thinks of him as "the finest human being." Perhaps Freud's sense of the feces as gift is apropos here. Just earlier in the scene she decided to allow Bankes to see her picture—to open herself to him. Mr. Bankes is described as "old enough to be her father . . . very scrupulous and clean" (31). She feels relieved with Mr. Bankes and released by the relief. Lily's difficulty with painting is also described in this section of the novel, and it adds a new twist to the movement of something from one space to another. She explains the psychic difficulty of her work which "made this passage from conception to work as dreadful as any down a dark passage for a child." The processes of birth, bowel, creating, feeling, thinking, writing all have visceral connections to one another in Woolf's work.

External spaces as well as interior ones also map out bodily spaces, for similar reasons—distinctive features link landscape and body. Crusoe discovers a place on his island where he "found Mellons upon the Ground in great Abundance . . . Grapes were just now in their Prime, very ripe and rich . . . delicious Vale . . . a secret Kind of Pleasure" (99–100). The place is a "Garden"; he is "Enamour'd" and "king and Lord of all." The island is the body of the fecund mother, as omnipotent in the infant's mind as the infant himself. In Lawrence's *Sons and Lovers* (1973 [1913]), the movement of Paul and Clara into the realm of sexuality is described as movement into a muddy landscape (308–11). It is a trip "down to the river," a "declivity" which they chose to "climb down" even though it is "risky" and "messy." They "descended" down the "decline," and she was "coming perilously down." He is "disgusted" at what is there as they walk along "the river's lip." The movement is down to the "risky," "messy" genital-anal area of the body. It is exciting: "They were hot and flushed." But there is some stigma, something "dirty" about pleasure for Paul. When they return to "the ordinary level" he says to her, "now I'll clean your boots and make thee fit for respectable folk." As a last example, consider Charles Dickens's use of citiscape in *Bleak House* (1956 [1853])—he intends to give us some sense of "the law" and how it works: both the environment and the processes of the law are excremental. There is "mud" ("as if the waters had but newly retired from the face of the earth"), "smoke," "a soft black drizzle, with flakes of soot in it as big as full-grown snow-flakes," "mire," "fog everywhere," and "gas looming through the fog." "The raw afternoon is rawest, and the dense fog is densest, and the muddy streets are muddiest, near the leaden-headed old obstruction, appropriate ornament for the threshold of a leaden-headed old corporation: Temple Bar . . . at the very heart of the fog, sits the Lord High Chancellor." In this body politic, the law seems to be a kind of cancerous blockage, giving rise to an image of the city as a spewing bowel and its ruler as hemorrhoidal. Thus whether we are in an interior or exterior space, the descriptions mirror the body and its primal processes. The descriptions slip from register to register because the associational networks of the selectional features of words we have all built up allow them to do so.

The Body Syntactic: Images of a Different Sort

The body and its psychological ramifications also manifest themselves in the syntax, micro and macro, surface and deep, of the novel. Syntactic patterns create images, which I will call syntactic images. These are distinctly different from what we generally refer to as "images" in literature: the syntactic image is virtually present, a gestalt waiting for the reader to experience it or recognize it. Images, as usually referred to, are imagined "in the mind" of the reader upon reading a sequence of words. The images are not literally present, as they are in a painting, but are potential, in some way visualized—with greater or lesser awareness and intensity. The image formed by syntax, however, is graphic and "there" on the page. Syntax is, to me, Western calligraphy—a group of markings organized in dynamic relationship to one another. Thus we find all manner of configurations which reveal the body of the person whose tracings they are.

Syntax is on one level the manifest sequence of words, phrases, clauses, embeddings, or chapters. This surface syntax creates for the reader its own spatial and active images. These images, like those formed by semantic webs, can be seen as transformations of bodily configurations and interactions. The gestures of movements and shape of the sentence "say" on another line than the "words"—this is the coding of the encoding, the methax of syntax. We cannot entirely separate syntax from semantics, but we can magnify the web to see how syntax cogenerates meaning, how it influences our reading, how it shapes nuances. Syntax has a dynamic aspect—we move forward with it; we anticipate, assume, expect in one phrase, and shift with the next. Syntax has, as well, a static side, a particular gestalt, the pattern of the dynamic. In some texts, perhaps those we find most rewarding and enduring, the syntax of a sentence makes a shape and establishes a pattern that repeats on different registers of the text.

An exceptional example of a syntactic image is one that will be elaborated on in the chapter on Woolf's *To the Lighthouse* but which I will note here briefly—the opening lines, the first paragraph of the novel: "'Yes, of course, if it's fine tomorrow,' said Mrs. Ramsay. 'But you'll have to be up with the lark,' she added." Her tripartite remark—(yes [if] but)—moves from positive (yes) to potential negative (if) to a qualification of the positive (but). The psychological impact of the structure is clearer when an alternative is posited—suppose Mrs. Ramsay left the verbal situation as "yes . . . if." That would give one a very different sense. Mrs. Ramsay's return ("But") to the possibility and ramifications of going negates the negation ("if"). The syntactic image of the sentence is not oppositional in the same way as it would be as a "yes-if" structure. Instead, the image is of a positive enfolding and disguising a negative. There is a static image which we are left with upon completing the opening and a dynamic motion which we experience as we are completing it. The mother embraces the negative, wraps it up, and protects her child from it. As

we work with the novel and its writer, it will also become clear that the image is one of a female protecting her center from that of the intrusive male.

The image of Woolf's sentence is of a center and a frame; the center
threatens the frame and the frame enfolds the threat. The distinctiveness of
this image is sharper when seen in the context of a different syntactic image.
Looking at the opening of Hemingway's *For Whom the Bell Tolls* (1940), we
find an image of horizontals and verticals, created by two central clauses:
"He lay flat on the brown, pine-needled floor of the forest, his chin on his
folded arms, and high above the wind blew in the tops of the pine trees." The
sentence's major clauses are demarcated by "and"; they form two horizontal
planes—the floor of the forest and the wind in the treetops. There are as well
vertical planes: the forest is a collection of vertical trees; the pine-needled
floor is the product of pine needles fallen from above; and the narrator's and
thus the reader's scan moves from "flat" and "floor" to "overhead" and "top."
The human body, which is present in the sentence, is inert—it "lay flat"—
and presented as a sculptural image rather than one in the process of forming. That is, the phrase "his chin on his folded arms" would, in the deep
structure (in transformational grammar) read: [he folded the arms [he had
arms]] [he put the chin [he had a chin] on the arms]. The phrase in the novel
inverts the actual process (he would have folded the arms and then put his
chin there) and deletes the active subject and verb so as to suggest the
formedness of the posture. The images suggest a psychoanalytic reading: a
relatively small body (baby), passive, horizontal (unerect), earthbound
(breast, death) person in the midst of a large (parental), vertical (erect), active ("wind blew") universe. Although the body is named in the sentence, it
is through the patterns of organization of the sentence that the deeper body
emerges. In an abstract way the opening might look thus: [[flat/folded/down:
inert] [up/top: active]]. Whether or not one approves of the reading, it is
clear that the syntactic image is different from Woolf's.

In the opening sentence of *The Ambassadors* (1960) James forms a more
complex calligraphic movement, one that moves feelings with precise
strokes of syntactic positionings: "Stether's first question, when he reached
the hotel, was about his friend; yet on learning that Waymarsh was apparently not to arrive till evening he was not wholly disconcerted." There are
two major clauses between which there is a pivot, "yet." Each clause has a
three-part phrasing in which the central phrase breaks up, postpones, the
completing of the first. And the two clauses together create yet another pattern of interaction—anxiety to relief, perhaps.

The opening clause conveys to this reader a degree of importance. The first character we meet (Strether) in the first sentence of the novel asks a "first question." I want to know immediately what the question was, and I sense it is important because it was the "first." The middle phrase ("when he reached the hotel"), although not answering or revealing the question, delimits the possibilities—the question is likely to be about persons, time, and space and is likely to be quite general and "impersonal." The answer may nonetheless be significant to the recipient. In any case, by being frustrated, the drama of "the first question" continues to build in the embedded clause. The verb phrase of the frame sentence ("was about his friend") reveals the focus of the question but not its content or import to the asker of the question. Indeed, this reader is more curious than ever. The other vector in this piece of the sentence is one of distance and proximity—hotel and friend. Hotels are relatively impersonal and usually afar; friends are emotionally close.

The answer to the question and thus the nature of it are revealed in the second major clause ("yet on learning"). And most important, we learn of Strether's response to the answer to his "first question" in the last phrase— he was "not wholly disconcerted." Reading the response, we return to the expectations set up in the opening clauses. The emotional energy of the sentence shifts with "yet"—it has an impact not unlike the "if" in Woolf. "Yet" indicates in general that some element in an earlier clause is not quite what one might have expected. The importance ("first question"), the action ("reached"), the distance ("hotel"), the possible warmth and closeness ("friend")—all these, whatever odd emotional lot they comprise, is about to be qualified and not as gently as "But you'll have to be up with the lark."

Strether's question concerned the time of arrival, at the same location, of his friend Waymarsh. The phrase in the middle of the second clause ("Waymarsh was apparently not to arrive till evening") indicates that Waymarsh would be later than agreed, anticipated, or expected. Strether's response to the answer to the "first question" is what the "yet" is at the head of. He "was not wholly disconcerted." The phrase is complex and best understood in light of a group of differences:

1.0 . . . he was disconcerted. This is what we might have expected as a response to the "first question" before we encountered "yet." Maybe, one thinks, he should be disconcerted, disappointed.

1.1 . . . he was wholly disconcerted. This might indicate a very high ego investment, a fragile ego, an inflexible person.

1.2 . . . he was not disconcerted. He would feel "cool," if not cold. But perhaps he is simply prepared for this and had alternative plans.

1.3 . . . he was delighted and relieved. This would feel callous and cyni-
cal; one might wonder what the nature of the "friend" is.

1.4 . . . he was partly relieved. This feels possible, mundane, not very exciting, a bit exhausted—a different "character" than Strether turns out
to be.

The specific phrasing that James does use allows for several feelings at once:
there is a feeling of a loss (disconcerted) but not a complete feeling of loss;
indeed in the hiatus is a pleasure that can only be understated. Meeting with
the friend is temporarily postponed, and Strether will not suffer whatever ag-
itations he will on the arrival of the friend. Intimacy, that is, is put off.
Strether can withdraw into the impersonal world of the hotel (there is no
subject just yet in the surface structure for "the staff"—no one to whom he
asks the question and no one from whom he learns the answer). The emotional move is from anxiety to a dropping of tension; if he is "not wholly disconcerted" that Waymarsh is not there, he might have been partly disconcerted if he had been there, and now Strether need not have that feeling.
The sentence, then, creates a bodily, emotional pattern—tension to relief,
arrival and delay, high to low, intimacy to withdrawal.

In addition to the physical and emotional movement of the sentence, I
sense that the doubleness of the two major clauses describes, or is an inscription of, the eyes which like the clauses have a three-part aspect—
cornea, iris, pupil. This hunch finds substantiation in the first paragraphs of
the novel; toward the very end of the second paragraph the narrator remarks
about Strether that he "was burdened . . . with the oddity of a double consciousness" (18). The eyes are a kind of double consciousness. And the eyes
appear implicitly in several phrases—"there was little fear that in the sequel
they shouldn't see enough of each other"; "delightful . . . to find himself
looking . . . into his comrade's face"; Waymarsh had been "invited . . . to a
tryst at the inn and had even invoked his aid for a 'look round' at the beau-
ties of Liverpool"; "he both wanted extremely to see him and enjoyed extremely the duration of delay." Last, to round out this hypothesis, the eyes
are explicitly mentioned in the closing sentences of the novel when Miss
Gostrey says to Strether, " 'It isn't so much your *being* 'right'—it's your horrible sharp eye for what makes you so" (365). The psychological complexity
of the eye in James's work is far beyond this brief exposition; suffice it to say
that the eye is central to his tale, as James himself notes in his preface: "He
now at all events *sees*; so that the business of my tale . . . is just my demon-
stration of this process of vision" (2).

The opening of Jane Austen's *Emma* displays a different psychological setting than those above, where Hemingway's character is nested in nature; James's is afar but urban, in a hotel; Woolf's is on vacation in a home nesting her child, protecting him from the "beak of brass, barren and bare"; and Austen's is nested in possessions. In Austen, the focus is solely on the character—there is virtually no relationship, just narcissism. There is a thematic tension between having and being, between child and adult. The linguistic structure helps us see how dominated the sentence is by Emma and how pampered the body of Emma is: "Emma Woodhouse, handsome, clever and rich, with a comfortable home and happy disposition seemed to unite some of the best blessings of existence; and had lived nearly twenty one years in the world with very little to distress or vex her." When we look at the linguistic deep structure of this sentence, we see, among other matters, that the surface structure deletes a highly redundant feature, the subject noun, Emma Woodhouse. One set of rules posited by transformational grammar allows for the deletion or substitution of redundant items within and between sentences. Raising the deletions of this sentence enhances one's perceptions of its focus of the sentence. The deep structure could be loosely mapped thus:

> *Emma Woodhouse* [Emma Woodhouse is handsome] [Emma Woodhouse is clever] [Emma Woodhouse is rich] [Emma Woodhouse has a home [the home is comfortable]] [Emma Woodhouse has a disposition [the disposition is happy]]
> *seemed* TO DO SOMETHING [she united some of the best blessings of existence] AND Emma Woodhouse lived in the world nearly twenty one years [[NEGATIVE] [SOMETHING distresses Emma Woodhouse] [SOMETHING vexes Emma Woodhouse]]

The deletions help us see how focused the sentence is on Emma Woodhouse. Although written in the third person, the narcissism emerges from the eightfold deep-structure repetition of "Emma Woodhouse." The overall sentence is framed with "Emma Woodhouse" ("her" in the surface structure) and almost completely filled with her.

The surface format balances attributes, gifts of a sort, with absences, gaps, which further our understanding of the narcissism. Emma Woodhouse has been more gratified than frustrated. Physically, mentally, and economically, Emma Woodhouse is well endowed; but interpersonally and characterologically, she is less well developed—hence the importance of "seemed"—she does not unite those blessings, but seemed to. There is a gap in her experience which is a deletion in the sentence that we cannot recover particularly, we are told in the surface sentence only that there was "very little to distress or to vex her." If you look back at the deep-structure representation above, it will be noted that in transformational-generative grammar the "negative" is seen as a transformation rather than a constituent—that, as in psychoanalysis, the negative is an interloper. Thus, SOMETHING distresses and SOMETHING vexes Emma Woodhouse. What? Vex suggests external forces irritating to one, while distress suggests internal anxiety or stress. I also associate distress with an infant or child who is sensitive to shifts and discomforts, hungers and digestive difficulties. This oral matter is germane — Austen raises and splits the matter between Emma's father and Emma. The father delights in nothing more than his "small basin of thin gruel" (16). "His own stomach could bear nothing rich, and he could never believe other people to be different from himself" (12). So the father is orally an infant—easily distressed. Emma seems more sophisticated than her father, but in her own way—although more advanced than her father—she runs parallel with him on her level. Mr. Knightly observes that "Emma has been meaning to read more ever since she was twelve . . . I have done expecting any course of steady reading" (26). Emma does not deal with language at a level more complex than a kind of "small basin of thin gruel." In any case, the last phrase in the surface structure initially points to a somewhat unchallenged person.

But the nearly buried negative constituent ("very little") gives me pause — negatives are suspect. And this negative is disguised, diminutive, and perhaps degrading but nonetheless present. The diminutive negative minimizes any negative psychological or interpersonal possibilities and implies overgratification. We find "very little" close to "nothing" on a spectrum between "nothing" and "everything." We discover in the following paragraphs reasons to believe that "very little" has in fact disturbed her—her father is a "most affectionate, indulgent" sort (1); and Knightley says that she "will never submit to anything requiring industry and patience," that is, work. So she will not place herself in a position of stress.

At the same time, the negative ("very little") remains suspect and invites exploring for denial—that is, something does distress her, perhaps something large, and it may be that this something is of greater consequence than Knightley's feeling that she lacks discipline, is infantile. What might it be? We learn in the second paragraph that "her mother had died too long ago for her to have more than an indistinct remembrance of her caresses, and her place had been supplied by an excellent woman as governess, who had fallen little short of a mother in affection" (1). The governess, Miss Taylor, whose getting married in some ways initiates the action of the novel, has been with the family for fifteen years, so the mother died when Emma was between four and five. The opening diminishes the loss—there was "very little to distress" her, the mother died "too long ago" to be remembered, and she was replaced by an "excellent woman as governess"—and here we find another "little" belittling—the governess had "fallen little short of a mother in affection." But what of other realms? Well, the "mildness of her temper had hardly allowed her to impose any restraint." She keeps the woman/girl a child. She does not vex her.

The mother is more missed than recognized; there is no grief, there is a denial of Emma's pain (by both the narrator and Knightley), and overindulgence (by the father and the governess) which implicitly acknowledge pain in the absence, a blurring of boundaries between governess and pupil (they "had been living together as friend and friend very mutually attached"), a concomitant egocentric and self-indulgent quality (Emma does "just what she likes" and has "too much her own way"). More important, Emma's central activity in the novel in trying to arrange a life and match for Harriet Smith and badly botching things up, almost ensuring that Harriet Smith has very little life, seems to be an indirect revenge on the mother for abandoning her (as is the governess at the outset of the novel). Emma's social acting out in its sadistic intent and her lack of discipline speak to Emma's anger, desire, and pain. The last clause in the opening sentence is both "true" in a superficial way and a little misleading. We are apt to become, like Knightley, too critical of Emma and too smug—exactly those qualities he would disapprove of. At the end of the novel even Emma seems to agree with others' interpretations when she says to Knightley, " 'I had the assistance of all your endeavors to counteract the indulgence of other people. I doubt whether my own sense would have corrected me without it' " (363). She is right that we need feedback to correct ourselves. She also indicates a need for a kind of discipline she did not get—people were afraid for her, overcompensated for the loss of the mother, and thus kept her a child.

The major syntactic move in the sentence is the deletion of one noun feature in a string full of attributes; the sense of the sentence is of overabundance coupled with a feeling that there is a gap. The gap—loss (oedipally disappearing or dying)—is actually full. That is, the gap has been experienced—the whole/hole is filled with grief—though the sentence underplays and denies that experience; the gap is the unconscious. In the course of the novel, the gap can be reenacted, consciously experienced, damaging the other, feeling guilt and grief, and repairing the damage. And having done so, one can move from the "affectionate, indulgent" and infantile father, to the more adult and lustful Knightley, who reveals to her, "'I . . . have been in love with you ever since you were thirteen at least'" (363). The body of this opening passage is locked into a series of dazzling mirrors; the body is in a rare state (reminiscent of the sleeping princesses of fairy tales), pampered, indulged, beautiful, comfortable and in a state of rest, absent of tension.

The shape of *Emma* is different again from earlier sentences; it balances good things with bad ones and puts both inside the frame of "Emma Woodhouse." Thus, [[Emma Woodhouse [handsome, clever, rich, comfortable, happy, best blessings, twenty one years] [[neg] vex, distress Emma Woodhouse]]]. The good/bad of the interior of the sentence calls to mind Klein's notion of the good and bad breast. Emma is touted and idealized and then somewhat poked at, attacked for not suffering (though suffer she might have). The inside is asymmetrical, not in balance, as it is suggested Emma is not quite balanced, existentially. This playing of one side against another is closer to James's opening than to the others in that it does not so much suggest gender as a more primitive relationship to the body.

"Syntax" has a broader focus than the sentence — entire collections of sentences have a syntax as well. As we will see in Woolf's *To the Lighthouse*, the syntax of the sentence is to be found in many other structural and descriptive aspects of the work. In Orwell's *Nineteen Eighty Four* we can observe a marcosyntactic pattern of a frame with a center. That is, in both the opening and the closing paragraphs of the novel we find a significant repetition, and the "content" of this repetition is alluded to and has some relation to the very center of the novel. First, in Orwell's second sentence Winston Smith has "his chin nuzzled into his *breast* in an effort to escape the vile wind." In the last paragraph of the novel Winston acknowledges "the loving *breast*" of Big Brother. The novel is framed with references to the breast, thus focusing on that organ and suggesting to me various psychological and semantic relationships. And indeed, the novel has a strong focus on food and drink, for example, Winston's recollection of the last time he saw his mother when he had stolen some much prized chocolate from his sibling. Descriptions of terrible food and drink are frequent. The novel shifts from its initial position of Winston's inward escape and self-nurturance ("chin nuzzled into his breast") to his finding Julia, who offers him a good breast ("her breasts . . . pouring some . . . youth and vigor into his [body]" [113]). After he finds the good breast, it is taken away ("'You will be hollow,'" O'Brien tells him [211]). It is replaced by the bad-good breast of Big Brother, "B.B.," the double-breasted God. In Orwell's work, the semantic references to the breast in privileged places—opening and closing paragraphs—alert the reader to an essential psychological matter.

Coda

The body is inscribed and embedded in the text in various image types—explicit, symbolic, and syntactic. This chapter has mapped out these types to establish how strongly the body figures in the novel. In other critical works the novel has been studied with a focus on social interactions, identity, rhetorical patterns of narrative, and the like. Here we examine the body embedded in the text. The body is explicitly mentioned and described, but there are additional traces of it in the slippage of selectional rules, the associational cross-references of the distinctive features of phonology and semantics in the explicitly named body, in spatial configurations, and in the movement and structure of syntax.

The body is a central figure in the novel. It appears in image and symbol, overtly and implicitly, in name, space, and syntax. And it shifts from one manifestation to another. The body is transfigured into language, where it is spelled out in different material. The drama of the body configured by language is often one of disintegration and reintegration in dynamic tension. It is a drama of fragmenting, severing, and loss, over against cohesion, union, and re-creation. The drama is one that Freud talked about as Thanatos and Eros; it is one Klein speaks of as being between rage and destruction, and guilt and reparation. Hannah Segal, along these lines, posits that "all creation is really a recreation of a once loved and once whole, but now lost and ruined object. . . . It is when the world within us is destroyed, when it is dead and loveless, when our loved ones are in fragments, and we ourselves in helpless despair—it is then that we must recreate our world anew, reassemble the pieces, infuse life into dead fragments, recreate life" (1981, 190). In repairing the object, one repairs the self, and vice versa. The object can also provide what is necessary to begin the movement to integration.

Disintegration occurs and reoccurs in the face of abuse, deprivation, and loss. Conversely, reintegration crystallizes around moments when one's body and spirit are being taken care of. So, for example, in one of Crusoe's closest encounters with death, he takes care of himself with various medical preparations and by reading the Bible, whose words begin to comfort him—he takes things in, and their goodness heals him from within. In Jane Eyre's tale, moments when comfort are administered to and by her are focal to the novel's major repetition. Briefly, she is taken care of by (1) her uncle when her parents die; (2) Mr. Lloyd, the druggist, after the red room scene; (3) Miss

Temple after Brocklehurst publicly (mis-)informs everyone at Lowood that she is a liar; and (4) her cousins, unbeknownst to all, after Jane flees Rochester. In turn, Jane administers comfort to her dying friend Helen and to Rochester on many occasions: (1) when they first meet by chance on the road and he falls when his horse slips; (2) on the night his bedroom is set on fire; (3) in a prefiguring event, when she takes care of Mr. Mason's wound; and (4) at the end of the novel, when Rochester is blind and lame. The theme recurs in Bradley's *Chaneysville Incident*; the hero moves into an integrative frame with the care of the woman who loves him when she is able to warm him. In one of Woolf's works, *Mrs. Dalloway*, we find that some disintegrative moments cannot be survived and surmounted—Septimus Smith kills himself. But in *To the Lighthouse*, in Lily's completed painting and vision, we see a working through of a process of grief and destruction. In all, unlike all the king's horses and all the king's men, language is able to reintegrate Humpty Dumpty if into a different order, that of syntax. The fragments of primary process, the manifest dream Freud describes as "broken . . . jammed together . . . like pack-ice," the syntactic deep structure—these are brought to the secondary process, the well-constructed surface. The autistic gives voice; the fragmented reintegrates in the communal domain of language. In a psychoanalytic setting, speaking is thought of as a transformation of action. In the novel, we can see that the transformation of action is an action itself—the transfiguring of the body and its movement.

4

◇◇

Robinson
Crusoe
and
the
Vicissitudes
of
Greed:
Cannibalism
and
Capitalism

In this chapter I begin the first of four readings examining particular fictional works for the representation of the body. In these readings I will look for central patterns and redundancies in the larger framework of an entire work, enhancing the clarity of the concise and fragmented examples offered in earlier chapters. In the context of a whole novel, the presence of the body becomes impressive in its insistence on all levels—semantic, symbolic, and syntactic. And again, as the body of one text is juxtaposed to those in other texts, one sees more of the stylistic variations and possibilities. Each text is unique. In the particular text of this chapter, Defoe's *Robinson Crusoe*, we will find a strong bodily focus on eating. This focus is cognizable in the explicit words of the novel, the nouns and verbs that speak it forth, but also in the symbolic and syntactic spaces. We find a vast semantic network concerned with food and eating-related language; we find a curious pattern of symbolic circles in the novel, circles inside of which goods are hoarded or eaten; and we find sentence forms that wrap around, not unlike the symbolic spaces. The sheer enumeration of bodily parts and representations makes it clear that the bodily need is present. Equally interesting are the ramifications of this vast presence, the transformation of the psychological into the political—i.e., the politics generated by the psychological pull and the role money comes to play in it. In *Robinson Crusoe* cannibalism and capitalism meet.

Food and the Sign of the Circle

The bodily locus of Defoe's work is alimentary. The hero's primary occupation and recurrent preoccupation in the text is with eating and being eaten, having and not having food or becoming food. Eating is a central and primitive matter, which is transcribed into higher-level relations; that is, the original monad, dyad, trio (narcissism/symbiosis, mother/child, oedipus) eventuate in a policy toward others. The schema that develop between child and mother, the routines of need, fulfillment, overstimulation, and frustration continue in analogous form in intricate adult relationships and are encoded in one's patterns of language as well.

The centrality of eating in the novel is confirmed by linguistic analysis: a major redundancy is a semantic cluster focused on eating and food. The array of eating-related verbs and nouns extends from the food itself to the processes of growing it or getting it, preparing it, preserving it, eating it, and storing it. Although I find the quantity and linkages of this network interesting in and of themselves, what I want to stress is the schema of containing represented by them, for example, we find a schema of there being something out there which I can decide to relocate to in here. Beginning with the high frequency of "eat," the network includes words describing eating, foodstuff, drinks, cooking modes, cultivation processes, and storage. Following is a sample from some of these categories: eaten, ate, feed, fed, feeding, food, nourish, victual, consume, consuming, ravenous, voracious, gnaw, chew, swallow, feast, feasted, starve, starved, hunger, hungry, dainties, diet, drink, nauseous, vomit, man-eaters, cannibals, cook, broil, boil, bake, roast, oven, banquet, dinner, breakfast; rice, meat, fish, bread, grapes, raisins, melons, fruits, butter, lemons, limes, limejuice, milk, cheese, cake, brisket, turnip, grain, barley, corn, cornbread, husk, hops, yeast, seed, wheat, tobacco, rum, liquor, beer, chocolate, cocoa, coffee, cordial, oatmeal; crop, sow, cultivate, plant, grow; dish/dishes, forks, pan, pot/pots, basket/baskets. Such a list, of course, makes best sense in the contexts of others which I am not supplying here, but one can imagine how much thinner the larder is in *Jane Eyre* or *Nineteen Eighty Four*, or how different the eating from that in *Tom Jones*. In any case, the semantic web is impressive in its range and depth.

In addition to the semantic articulation, the bodily concern for food is written into the text with an emphatic image of a circle. The circle is inscribed in the landscape of the novel—literally drawn in the symbolic and syntactic imagery. Crusoe makes more than a dozen circular forms on the island—as home, sanctuary, corral, enclosure—all of which focus on food: growing it, domesticating it, storing it, processing it, defending it.[1] The circle as a container defines a variety of bodily shapes relating in various ways to the symbiotic/parasitic, bodily child-mother relationship, that is, mouth, breast, belly, and womb.

Defoe's insistent and complex focus on food, eating, and money prefigures later analyses by Darwin, Marx, Freud, and Lévi-Strauss: Defoe offers a range of cultures, evolutionary steps, which address the problem of eating, a fundamental fact of life. The novel is a document of social and psychological evolution and conflict. Crusoe, a loner, a traveler-observer, presents various forms and aspects of social organizations—cannibal, hunter-gatherer, agricultural herder, commercial maritime, territorial/colonial capital, and more. He demonstrates a variety of systems for making money, that is, having things to eat, and he is implicitly leading us to the most current system. The best system is one that gets the most energy out of the least material with the least expenditure of energy. Money maximally condenses energy—it is the eighteenth century's brand of information. In the evolutionary terms of the novel, capitalism (especially slavery) is more efficient than cannibalism.

Crusoe's desire is very clear: he wants to get and have enough to eat. On the island, food is *the* commodity; on the mainland, commodities are mediated by money. Money is a transform of food. Money can be increased by having labor that gets less than is realized. As it turns out, those whom Crusoe fears will eat him are the very ones (types) whom he wanted to enslave (to grow crops for him) but was prevented from doing so—by the "Hand of God"—and was marooned on the island. His fear (of being eaten) is his desire (to eat). Enslavement, however, is economically more efficient than cannibalism. That is, were we to think as Marvin Harris (1977), we might say that where Crusoe's cannibal consumes a large quantity of protein at one sitting, the capitalist derives a much larger quantity of gain by preserving the object to labor. A cost-benefit analysis from Crusoe's perspective turns up in favor of slavery over cannibalism—free work is much more enduringly satisfying than a free meal. In psychological terms, the same survival lesson is true at a primitive level: better to nurture the breast enough to nurture oneself on a long-term basis than to bite it and starve, be abandoned or attacked.

Whatever way one turns in the novel, one encounters a situation that works its way to the focus on food. Crusoe reveals to us how much bodily effort goes into feeding the body, ensuring that it has a constant source and a secure surplus. The semantic concern with food and eating is reflected in the syntactic pattern of circles and encirclements. In the opening sentence, for example, Crusoe places himself syntactically outside and his father and mother inside, inverting his original position within his mother. He becomes their parent. He engulfs them. Moreover, in the symbolic spaces in the novel, Crusoe's body is painstakingly built and modified over many years: he gives birth to himself, feeds himself, defends himself, and multiplies.

The Syntax of the Circle and Cycle of Consumption: Alimentary Perpetual Motion

Robinson Crusoe revolves around conflicts of consuming—physiological, psychological, and economic—as indeed all of Defoe's novels do (see Watt 1965, Novak 1976, Berne 1956, Pearlman 1975, Gliserman 1973). The conflicts are embedded in the primitive domain of the novel, are openly presented in the surface imagery and semantic networks, and are symbolically represented in formal, syntactic ways. The novel's emphasis on consumption and its attendant conflicts is part of what has kept the text important; it is only in recent decades that our culture has begun to analyze the ramifications of consuming.[2] Defoe was among the first to examine the problem imaginatively, in a new form, and to touch on its fearful, dark prospects. We might recall that Defoe lived in the thick of the problem—as any of his biographers will attest, he was a businessman who got himself into various economic and political difficulties and debts that haunted him to his death.[3] The novel articulates, perhaps for the first time in England, the cradle of modern capitalism, a connection between a primitive desire to consume and a social, religious, economic, technological way to realize that desire without seeming to be a cannibal. The novel unconsciously posits a relationship between cannibalism and capitalism. At the same time, of course, it denies that relationship. The novel asserts an antithesis between cannibalism and capitalism without perceiving that all items on a spectrum have something in common—in this case, consuming.

This study explores the conflicts of consumption in *Robinson Crusoe*, being guided by its layers of patternment and analyzing the psychological significance of those patterns. By "layers of patternment" I mean that a given image is informationally redundant (Bateson 1972, 128–52; Johnson 1987, 126): the image appears repeatedly not only in various semantic guises but also in structural arrangements (syntax). The specific pattern in this novel is one of enclosure or encirclement: SOMETHING IS ENCLOSING SOMETHING ELSE, OR SOMETHING IS INSIDE SOMETHING

ELSE. The circle as container is the dominant geometric redundancy. We can see the complex relationship of the circle to bodily configurations and actions (e.g., consuming/consumption) in the various positional interactions it suggests: get into, get out of, put in, get out, keep out, hold in, keep in, hold on, let go, let out, let in, open up. The circle defines a space within and a realm without; it defines a boundary between and various interactive possibilities.

These positional possibilities of the circle are related to the kind of linguistic analysis Johnson suggests in his discussion of spatial configurations depicted in language which mirror bodily interactions. By examining various "image schema" of the language—for example, container, path, balance, scale—he demonstrates the slide from concrete bodily experience to abstract propositional logic: "I am suggesting that such inferential patterns [of classical logic] . . . arise from our bodily experience of containment [in the particular case just developed]. Their use in abstract reasoning is a matter of metaphorical projection" (1987, 40).

In Defoe's work the body is inscribed/described as a container with its own subset of containers (head, bowel, belly, womb, phallus); in turn, the body is located within a larger space with its own subset of containers (house, room, cave). For example, Crusoe retrospectively tells us that his "head" was "empty" of thoughts of God and he was "obstinately deaf" to his father's advice. Defoe depicts the "head" as a container that has been impervious to others (father) and is consequently empty (Father). Given the preoccupation in the text with circles and enclosures, the description of the head as a container is informationally redundant. That is, it repeats an articulation of a basic set of bodily concerns articulated on other registers—for example, being full or empty, being permeable or impermeable, being entered or blocking out. These various modalities speak to the primitive bodily relations we develop with others—in the womb, being birthed, being fed, and the like— in which we are contained and container, exchanging stuff between and within. In many respects the novel is about the boundaries. E. Pearlman says, for example, that "Crusoe's sense of his psychological boundaries is inadequate; his identity needs to be buttressed. The wall that he builds is an integument that reinforces the boundaries of the self—it is a metaphorical psychic skin" (1976, 52). In addition, we see a desire to break down others' boundaries and a constant fear that one's own will be broken down by others. The circle is the body of this text, and the motions (get in, take in, hold on) define the primitive interactions of the body.

A psychological reading of the main configuration with all its attendant interactive states is necessarily complex and indeterminate. That is, the circle as container is the shape of many bodily forms and orifices—mouth, bowel, womb, breast, head—and these can be positioned in relation to all the moves mentioned above; for example, an idea can get into the mind or be prevented from doing so, or one can get supplies out of a ship and place them into a fortified circle. The matrix of possibilities is larger than any non-machine study can account for. Here, then, we will follow out the major redundancies, the darkest lines in the matrix. At the core of the text are several intense, primitive (preverbal) conflicts. I see the conflicts as so disabling that mature (genital), sustained relations with others becomes impossible and are replaced by a fetish—money.

The fantasy of the novel might be called "spiraling alimentary perpetual motion." The fantasy is to have an object which one can consume and by consuming not only have it but also replicate it. That is, one takes within for sustenance, surplus, storage, and conception; what is consumed is excreted/birthed and recycled. Money is a condensation of the fantasy—breast, phallus, bowel, and womb. The genesis of the conflicts of the novel are in the realm of eating, where we find both greed and dread of being devoured. In psychoanalytic terms, the conflict represents a primitive splitting of the object (breast/mother) into a good (nurturing) breast and a bad (withdrawing, persecuting) breast (Klein 1980, 6–10, 324–26). The split emotional valence can be seen, for example, in the dread of being encircled by cannibals as opposed to the bliss of being surrounded by money. The elements surrounded by the good circle—breast, baby, feces, phallus—are the very elements that the projected bad breast seeks to destroy and that the persecutory anxiety is focused on. The pattern of encirclement inscribed in the text in syntax, semantics, and images leads us to the schizoid-paranoid core of the fiction, the primary process of the text surrounded by its cohesive narrative logic. It is the madness into which Defoe descended that we must also face if we want to feel the dimensional power of the text.

I map out the splitting—good and bad—as encountered in both the inner and outer ranges of the novel. That is, the novel is an intrapsychic representation as well as an interpersonal representation. We read Crusoe and the cannibals as both an inner and an interrelational conflict. We can also see the interrelational aspect of the novel—the manifest text and all its subtleties—as an expression of a group wish, a sign of the times. As Virginia Woolf observed, *Robinson Crusoe* "resembles one of the anonymous productions of the race itself rather than the effect of a single mind" (1925, 34). In the space between the intrapsychic and the interpersonal, we witness the genesis of ideology. There is a moment in the text when desire is projected, externalized, and disowned, followed by a moment when the desire out there is attacked—this is the conception of ideology and its first action. I particularly trace the vicissitudes of greed to suggest how psychological constructs (e.g., fantasy), grounded in bodily experience, become ideological (socially enacted) ones.

In watching both inner and outer ranges we witness a collision in which primary process, in the guise of necessity, breaks into secondary process and appears socially and morally acceptable. In *Robinson Crusoe*, specifically, we see the transformation of primitive cannibalistic desires into a socially acceptable mode of consumption—of labor, via imperialism (slavery and property invasion) and capitalism. The transformation occurs through an act of violence, aggression directed at others, ostensibly to prevent their aggression. The catalyst of the transformation is the father. On a visionary threat of death, the I of the text is forced to open himself and take in the father. As the first transference object, the father reflects and displaces the splitting of the mother. Being a phallic object, however, he facilitates the son's identification and a new way of channeling aggression. That is, the aggression directed at the mother and feared in retaliation remains within, as self-attack or paranoia. The aggression the father demonstrates allows its release by way of death-dealing technology. The paternal split—an invasive, attacking phallus and a nurturing-engendering phallus—displaces the maternal split, allowing the attacking phallus to expunge the bad, persecuting breast (the cannibals) and the nurturing phallus to supplant or converge with the good breast of the mother. Crusoe's symbiotic fear is as great with the father as the mother. As he disembodied the mother through a displacement to money, he disembodies the father by way of the word, the text—in which form he can be taken in.

The First Circle—The Opening Sentence

The centrality of consuming and containing is inscribed in the structural and dynamic images to which the form, the syntax, of the opening sentence/paragraph of the novel gives shape. That is, the sentence has the shapes, movements, and repetitions that together with the semantic webs articulate the psychological concerns of the novel:

> *I* was *born* in the Year 1632, in the City of York, of a *good Family*, though
> not of that Country, my *Father* being a Foreigner of Bremen, who settled

first at Hull: He got a *good Estate* by Merchandise, and leaving off his Trade, lived afterward at York, from whence he had married my *Mother*, whose Relations were *named Robinson*, a *very good Family* in that Country, and from whom *I was called Robinson Kreutznaer;* but by the *usual Corruption of words* in England, we are now *called,* nay we *call* our selves, and *write our Name Crusoe,* and so my companions always *call'd me.* (my emphasis)

The sentence begins with "I" and ends with "me." Located within the first "I" and the last "me" are mother (Robinson) and father (Kreutznaer, now Crusoe), thus:

[I/born [father/Crusoe, mother/Robinson] called/me]

The "I/me" encircles, swallows up, mother and father. The retrospective narrator inscribes his introjects within a structural image, made of text. He is, in the narrative, named them and in some sense is them. The I has taken in a mapping (Laing 1970), a paternal course (anagram of Crusoe): be of "good Family" and go from place (Bremen) to place (Hull) to place (York); acquire "good Estate"; and marry someone (a female who stays in the same place) from a "very good Family." The I also embeds a value system—"good" versus "corruption."

The structural image of containing the parents within the self suggests a wish, which, in other portions of the text, is denied, split off, projected, and killed off. In its projected, persecutory form, the wish returns as a constant threat in the novel—of being "swallowed" or "devoured." Eating is a central preoccupation; Crusoe worries about getting food, having enough of it, losing it, or becoming it for some "wild beast" or "naked savage." *Robinson Crusoe* is one of the stories in our culture about the "raw and the cooked," hence it is about laws and differences and boundaries, as is clear from the dynamic form of the sentence. The dynamic aspect of the sentence in motion yields its own image: of piling up and/or elongating. It is a temporal flow of details: a paternal course, a truncated family history, a birth and naming, ending with a rhetorical flourish of repetition. The structural image is of consuming; the dynamic image is of piling up (details of time, place, and rhetorical phrase).

The list, the pile-up, is habitual in the text and Defoe's writing in general. There are those formal listings that are typeset into the text: the list of "Evil" and "Good," of "Comforts [and] Miseries" on the island (66); the list of seasonal changes (106); the list of all those killed when Crusoe overthrows the mutiny (237). And we find innumerable less formal listings: Crusoe constantly offers us his inventories: of how much canvas, ammunition, raisins, rum, seed, and other goods he has and of where all these items are distributed and stored. He offers us a breakdown of his day, an inventory of his time blocks—"I was very seldom idle . . . regularly divided my Time," he tells us (114). He details all his algorithmic systems and processes, step by step. For example, we learn how to cut, shape, and set in place poles for fortification. As J. Donald Crowley observes, "Defoe obviously delights in cataloguing . . . he relishes enumerating the stages of . . . mechanical procedures" (xiv–xv). The delight Crowley senses points both to the bodily pleasures of fullness and holding on/in, as well as the related pleasure in the fullness of an engorged/elongated genital as they are transposed into full, elongated sentences (for other examples, from psychoanalytic practice, see Reich 1973, 291).

Primarily, the listings are an insistence on orderliness, on pattern and law, often arising in the face of psychologically distressing situations. For example, in seeing the remains of a cannibal feast, he tells us, "I saw three Skulls, five Hands, and the bones of three or four Legs and Feet" (207). The defensive enumerating points to a desire/fear of chaos or "fecal homogenization" in the terms of Chassequet-Smirgel (1984). She notes that the intention of perversion is "to reduce the universe to faeces, or rather to annihilate the universe of differences (the genital universe) and put in its place the anal universe in which all particles are equal and interchangeable." The essential differences are those between the sexes and the generations. She explains the motivation for the denial of difference: "The abolition of differences prevents psychic suffering at all levels: feelings of inadequacy, castration, loss, absence and death no longer exist" (4–6). The onus of perversion in Defoe's text is laid on the cannibals: "The Place was cover'd with humane Bones, the Ground dy'd with their Blood, great Pieces of Flesh left here and there, half eaten, mangl'd and scorch'd" (207). The cannibals grind the world down into feces. So, too, at a slower pace, does Crusoe in his desire for money, although it is denied by the surface appearance of attention to difference and boundaries. The bodily pleasure of incorporating the other is displaced into an unnoticed textual inscription and is denied by the narrative action in which the listings speak of separateness.

The desire to consume, "stated" by the structural image ([I[parents]me]), is a logical precedent for a desire to reduce matter to feces, to pile up what is consumed, to be fused with it and have it always with one, which is articulated by the dynamic image. The dynamic of the sentence content seems to deny a desire to de-differentiate; it asserts a temporal flow and difference.

That is, the "I" who is "born of" recognizes the difference of generations and of the sexes in "Father" and "Mother." The assertion of difference stands against the incorporation described by the structural image as well as against the matter of "Corruption."

On the neutral skeleton of facts in the first paragraph are hung two words associated with value—"good" and "Corruption." As much as anything else, the novel presents a conflict between these two forces, as well as the corruption of the good (paradise lost) and the good of corruption (paradise regained through money). No sooner is corruption mentioned in the sentence than the sentence itself becomes corrupt by the working definition of the novel set out in the Preface—a "just History of Fact." The opening has a rhetorical flourish that seems almost antithetical to the spirit of the facts, that is, efficiency. The flourish here is this: "I was *called* . . . we are now *called*, nay we *call* ourselves, and *write* our *Name Crusoe*, and so my Companions always *call'd* me." The repetition has a biblical ring, for example, "And every oblation of thy meat offering shalt thou season with salt; neither shalt thou suffer the salt of the covenant of thy God to be lacking from thy meat offering: with all thine offerings thou shalt offer salt" (Lev., 2:13). The question is why Defoe uses this rhetorical repetition here. Why the concern with his name? And why, from a man who claims (repetitiously) not to be idle and to use his time wisely, does he "spend" over a third of the opening sentence on the matter of names? The focus on names suggests a concern with filiation—genesis and influence—and hinges on a self-reference examined below.

Crusoe's insistence on his name succeeds in calling attention to itself— "naming" is important. In fact, Chassequet-Smirgel notes that Genesis "is entirely based on principles of distinction, separation and differentiation . . . and this comes to the same thing . . . of naming." Further, "the original meaning of 'nomos', the law, is 'that which is divided up into parts.' Thus we find the principle of separation is the foundation of law" (8–9). Changing a name, then, reconstructs relationships and revises boundaries. The opening insistence on names is related to a self-reference concerning changing names and thus of the "Corruption of words." I refer to the fact that Daniel Defoe was born as Daniel Foe and that he changed his name. That change was a kind of corruption; it was an attempt to *create an image*, an illusory identity, and, most important, a way *to deny filiation*. James Sutherland says that "he altered his name to the more impressive, and certainly more aristocratic, Daniel Defoe" (1938, 2). In her discussion of grandiosity and narcissism, Annie Reich notes that "compensatory narcissistic self-inflation is among the most conspicuous forms of pathologic self-esteem regulation" and it often "arises from a striving to overcome threats to one's bodily intactness" (1973: 293–94)—a fear we see over and over again in Defoe's narrative.

Dressing up his name, Defoe creates a fake, a fiction, a pseudo-aristocrat. In the novel the matter is reversed, projected: the name is changed not by a person but by linguistic entropy. The name is ground into the more common sounds of English, and thus the "foreigner," the father, is assimilated. I raise this issue in part to indicate an important consistency of mental operations in the text. Specifically, the name transform—actively changing one's name to passively having one's name changed—is similar to the transforms witnessed in the text; for example, the desire to act (consume) is inverted into a passive fear of being consumed, or the active desire to intrude becomes a fear of being passively intruded upon (such passivity has been noted by Castle [1979] in relation to *Roxana*). The issue of Defoe's change of name is thematically related to Crusoe's act of leaving home and going "against the Will, nay the Commands of [his] Father" in that both acts separate son from father, thus from his law. They deny paternity and claim a kind of self-birth or a self-generated universe.

It is not only Robinson Crusoe whose birth is announced in the opening sentence, it is the birth of a new form, the English novel. This work required a certain perversion of past forms, including biblical narrative and spiritual autobiography, pointing to an ambivalence toward paternity—a desire both to recognize and to corrupt the law, Harold Bloom's (1973) "anxiety of influence." One strand of influence is certainly from the Bible, as indicated both by the rhetorical flourish of the sentence's last third and by the whole tale's relation to the narrative of Jonah. The Bible, of course, is a text with which Defoe was intimately familiar. He transcribed a large portion of it as a child ("I myself, then but a boy, worked like a horse, till I wrote out the whole Pentateuch") and was steeped in religion as a young adult (Sutherland 1938, 15). Another formal influence is the seventeenth-century spiritual autobiography, as several critics have noted (Starr 1965, Hunter 1966). Surely there is some fear and guilt involved in the "Corruption" of sacred texts and traditional forms?

In addition to these influences, Defoe's work also has some roots in Milton. Sutherland reminds us that Milton lived only a few hundred yards away from Defoe and died when Defoe was about fourteen. Sutherland says that "Milton he knew well and frequently quoted" (5, 16). In the preface to the novel, the "editor" says that the "writer" wrote in part "to justify and honor the Wisdom of Providence in all Variety of our Circumstances." This seems a less elegant and forceful formulation of Milton's "great argument" to assert "eternal providence, / And justify the ways of God to man." Milton invokes the muse—"I thence / Invoke thy aid to my adventurous song, / That with not middle flight intends to soar . . . while it pursues Things unattempted yet in prose or rhyme." Defoe, rather than invoking is selling: "The Wonders of this Man's Life exceed all that (he thinks) is to be found extant; the Life of one Man being scarce capable of greater Variety." But like Milton in some respects is Crusoe's drive, for he seeks to avoid "the Middle of the two Extremes," "the middle Station" of life for which his father argues. And in some more "humble" respect, Defoe also "pursues Things unattempted yet." Moreover, despite the difference of level, *Robinson Crusoe* is a reading of *Paradise Lost*, or is about one "paradise lost"; it is a more concrete and pragmatic rendition, the spiritual vision of the poem becomes the economic vision of the novel.

The allusions to the Bible, spiritual autobiography, and Milton all affirm paternity by their very presence. But "by the usual Corruption of Words in England," there is also a denial of paternity. The lofty purpose of the word or the mundane or poetic meditation is brought down to adventurism and economic gain. The ambivalence toward, the exploitation of, traditional forms (and names) speaks to the clash of value systems in which Defoe found himself enmeshed.

Although I have digressed from the immediacy of the opening sentence, we have remained focused on the issues of its beginnings. The surface of the opening sentence is a genesis—the announcement of birth, the order of events preceding the birth, the heritage, and a naming. This level of the sentence speaks to a desire for differentiation, for law. But we find a counterthrust toward de-differentiation and self-generation in the introjecting syntactic image, the obsessive textual listings, the masturbatory elongation of the sentence, and the projected "corruption." We can now examine these conflictual desires in the broader area of textual forms within the narrative.

Nurturing, Protective, and Defensive Encirclements

The dominant desire expressed directly in the novel is for money. The wish is not fully granted until the end of Crusoe's stay on the island, but many of its transformed manifestations are written in the text. Crusoe does not initially express this wish; rather, he tells us he has "rambling Thoughts," an "Inclination" for "going to Sea," and "Thoughts . . . bent upon seeing the World." These desires point to Crusoe's wish to take things in (see) and to separate from his family. As he informs us, his father "design'd [him] for the Law," and he has no desire to be enclosed and sedentary (he would end up an early version of Bartelby the Scrivener).

The dominant desire is directly expressed when Crusoe pauses in the narrative to look back and judge his past: he calls his wish "the wild and indigested notion of raising my Fortune" (16). The desire for "fortune" is a permutation of a desire for the mother/breast. That is, money purchases goods and services. In addition, money replicates and transforms itself; for example, on his first trip he takes £40 worth of "Toys and Trifles" and he returns with £600 worth of "Gold Dust." Capitalism is Crusoe's brand of alchemy, transforming the worthless (feces) into gold. "Raising [his] Fortune" is thus growing his own breast—not at all strange in a novel filled with fantasies of self-generation and self-sustenance. Seeing money as representing, among other things, the breast, we can appreciate Crusoe's response when he finds money on the broken-up ship: he "smil'd" to himself and says " 'O Drug! . . . what are thou good for,'" and then, knowing full well what good it is, takes it back to the island with him. Crusoe's reference to money as a "Drug" names the addiction that has ruled his life. He sees this himself in his analysis that his "greed" (the desire to get slaves to work his land, in this specific instance) brought him low, left him stranded on the island. It is a drug he will take from the ship because he hopes to use it again, as indeed he does. Being on the island forces Crusoe to withdraw from his addiction, to dry out, but the desire takes on new forms as he awaits his return. In any case, the references to "see" the world, to an "indigested notion," and to a "Drug" suggest a primitive desire to take things in, and money concretely represents such things.

On the island, however, there is no exchange for money. Crusoe's desire moves down the chain of signifiers to concerns closer to his primitive ones; he becomes preoccupied with food. An aerial view of Crusoe's island, after he has been there for some time, would reveal a number of circular structures—his dwelling, bower, and numerous enclosures for crops and cattle. He encircles land for food; he draws the body—breasts, bowel, and womb—into the landscape: for example, one "Hedge made a *Circle* of about twenty Yards in Diameter" (105). These benign enclosures essentially protect food, mark a boundary, hold and store good things, and keep out bad things. They differentiate what is "mine" from the rest. The analogical body expresses Crusoe's desires for supplies, security, and storage space for surplus. The circle, when Crusoe is within it, points to a desire for fusion and completeness, for no separation from the mother and all she has within (see, for example, Winnicott 1965, 153–57).

Crusoe's attitude toward the breast ranges from feelings of hungry lust, which shades into fearful greed, to ambivalence, anxiety bordering on paranoia, and manic feelings of omnipotence. These attitudes emerge when Crusoe interacts with the symbolic breasts—major sources of supplies—such as the stranded ship from which he gathers his survival supplies and by the island itself with its central fecundity (Gliserman 1973, Erikson 1982). The ship is decidedly identified as a female form from whom Crusoe has "hope of furnishing [him]self with Necessaries"—"her Stern lay lifted upon the Bank, and her Head low almost to the Water; by this Means all her Quarter was free, and all that was in that Part was dry" (49). He says, "I was resolv'd to set all other Things apart, 'till I *got every Thing out* of the Ship that I could get" (54, my emphasis), and later, "I was *not satisfy'd* still; for while the Ship sat upright in that Posture, I thought I ought to *get every Thing out of her that I could*" (55, my emphasis). The ship is the world/womb from which Crusoe is now separated; out of his anxiety, he maximizes his chance to take out its insides. The desire, though realistic in the setting, has an intensive and compulsive edge to it—to "get every Thing out" of one circle and into another, his own.

In Crusoe's approach to the island, we see less direct and immediate greed and find instead feelings of possessiveness—long-term greed—and omnipotence:

> I *found* different *Fruits*, and particularly I *found Mellons* upon the Ground in great *Abundance*, and *Grapes* upon the Trees . . . just now in their *Prime*, very *ripe and rich* . . . it looked like a planted *Garden* . . . *delicious Vale*, surveying it with a *secret Kind of Pleasure* . . . to think that this was *all my own, that I was King and Lord of all* this Country indefeasibly, and had *Right of Possession*. (99–100, my emphasis)

This edenic spot, "in the Center of the Island," Crusoe becomes "enamour'd" of and builds a "Bower, and surrounded it at a Distance with a strong Fence" (101). The breastlike quality of the land is fairly apparent from the iconography—fruits, melons, great abundance, grapes, rich and ripe, delicious vale. Though Crusoe is drawn to the female aspects of the land, he is also wary of them. So, for example, he says of the "ripe and rich" grapes, "I was warn'd by my Experience to eat sparingly of them . . . the eating of Grapes kill'd several of our English Men" (99). Nonetheless, he gathers the grapes and dries them for raisins, in which form he can store them and eat his fill. His ambivalence toward the sexual "vale" of the island is put thus: "to enclose my self . . . in the Center of the Island, was to anticipate my

Bondage" (101). There is danger as well as pleasure in the center; it is better for Crusoe to be on the edge. He does not want to be inside of anything unless it is strictly under his control. He thus enjoys "surveying" the "vale" or visiting it but does not want to live within it. This is the "Garden," and he will enjoy it as such—like a mistress. The real, "secret" pleasure is that what he has "found" he now has "Right of possession" to. Unlike the ship, this "delicious" breast of the land is a renewable resource, and Crusoe gives us a manic rhapsody on his ownership: "all my own . . . King . . . Lord . . . all . . . indefeasibly . . . Right of Possession."

The circle inscribes the breast but also an ambiguous belly—womb/bowel4—a protective shell and container of fetus (Crusoe), breast/feces (stockades of supplies), and phallus (Crusoe sleeps with "two Pistols" at his head and a "gun" alongside him). Crusoe, that is, sleeps within a circle from the beginning of his stay on the island. He creates his own womb: he "barricado'd" himself "round" (53); he "piled all the empty Chests and Casks up in a Circle round the Tent" (55). His major dwelling is built with a semicircular pale abutting a hillside—"a half *circle* before the hollow place . . . Twenty Yards in its Diameter" (59). Crusoe digs a cave into the hollow place, making the dwelling quite bodylike. He forms a womb-bowel—"I lay with all my Wealth about me very secure" (57).

If the lush bower is the body of the other—mistress, wife, mother, God's breast—his dwelling is his own androgynous body. It is phallic in front; breast and womb within; and complete with urethral and anal outlets. The dwelling is the place in which the spiritually reborn Crusoe is conceived, from which he is born, in which he is nurtured. It is the womb in which the seed from the ship will gestate. The semicircle defining the front of the dwelling is a phallic fort: "In this half Circle I pitch'd two Rows of *Strong stakes*, driving them into the Ground till they *stood very firm* like Piles . . . about five Foot and a half, and sharpen'd on the Top" (59). This masculine front defends a place of fetal sleep, of nurturance, and of containing things. It is a womb but also a bowel. Thus Crusoe is concerned with "putting all [his] Things in Order" (75). He is not pleased at "a confus'd Heap of Goods, which as they lay in no Order, so they took up all my Place" (67). The bowel/bladder of the body/dwelling requires its outlets as well: "violent Rains forc'd me to a New Work, viz, to cut a Hole thro' my new Fortification like a sink to let Water go out, which would else have drown'd my Cave" (81). Another passageway out creates a problem: "I work'd side-ways to the Right hand into the Rock, and then turning to the Right again, work'd quite out and made a Door to come out, on the Out side of my Pale" (67). Given the vast amount of work Crusoe spent building the first wall and the anxieties that prompted him to do so, this back entrance seems a counterwish to his supreme desire for a secure enclosure. He is not without misgivings: "I was not perfectly easy at *lying so open*; for as I had manag'd my self before, *I was in a perfect enclosure*, whereas now I thought *I lay expos'd and open for any thing to come in upon me*" (103, my emphasis). Although nothing ever does "come in upon" him through this door, the conflict (desire to hold in, need to let out, desire and fear to let in) is manifested in other images specifically connected to the father/Father, examined below.

Sadistic, Engulfing, and Castrating Encirclements

The deadly circle threatens the hero with engulfment and/or castration, with transforming him to food and feces. It is the bad breast, a combination of projected desire and fear of the external object. Melanie Klein observes that the child "reacts to his intolerable fear of instinctual dangers by shifting the full impact of the instinctual dangers on to his object, thus transforming internal dangers to external ones. Against these external dangers his immature ego then seeks to defend itself by destroying his object" (1975, 127–28). This is part of the process that unfolds in the fantasy of the novel—the desire to devour is given to one register of the text, the anxiety and defense are played out by another. The conflict is a central repetition and is without resolution. The conflict reaches greatest intensity in Crusoe's encounters with the cannibals but is seen repeatedly in other forms—engulfment is an ever present danger in the novel. Although feared, there is also a desire to be swallowed, refetalized, and thence reborn. This desire is in fact "realized." The fear is articulated throughout the narrative, as exemplified in the following moments.

In his maiden voyage, a storm arises, and he "expected every wave would have *swallowed*" the ship. He reflects on his "wicked leaving my Father's House," but soon after the storm subsides, he "*drowned* all . . . Repentance" with drink (8–9, my emphasis). A second storm is so intense the ship is abandoned; Crusoe is warned to stay away from the sea—"see what a *taste* Heaven has given" of what might happen. Thus to be threatened with being "swallowed" is to be given a "taste" of divine punishment, but one can in turn "drown" such thoughts. The father of Crusoe's friend who gives Crusoe these warnings also makes an important allusion: "perhaps this is all befallen us on your Account, like Jonah in the Ship of Tarshish" (15). Jonah is seeking to avoid doing the Lord's bidding and he runs away, just as Crusoe seeks to avoid his father's bidding. On one level of fantasy, the punishment is desired: to be swallowed would liken Crusoe to Jonah, would put him in direct contact with God. Punishment is recognition. The threat of engulfment (in the paternal womb) holds the promise of rebirth. But for the hero in the moment, the threats of engulfment hold no promise; the womb is a tomb.

The most dramatic threat of being swallowed occurs when Crusoe leaves for the slave-trading venture and ends up landing on the island. The ship he is in is abandoned; the crew "were all *swallow'd* up in a Moment" (44–46). The waves suck him under; one, he says, "*buried* me at once 20 or 30 Foot deep *in its own Body*." When he lands, he says he is saved "out of the very Grave." Other threats occur as well. After he has landed and settled in his dwelling, an earthquake strikes and he panics "for Fear of being *buried* alive." Note, too, "the Motion of the Earth made my Stomach sick" and "Fill'd me with Horror" (80)—the womb of the dwelling becomes a tomb, and the self is likewise "Fill'd with Horror." On one of his expeditions on the island, he "descended into a very large Valley; but so *surrounded* with Hills, and those Hills cover'd with Wood, that I could not see which was my way by any direction." He remains lost for three or four days. In addition to being threatened by the inanimate world, Crusoe is never far from a "danger of being devoured by Savages" or "devour'd by savage Beasts" or a fear of "perishing with Hunger." Crusoe is in fact threatened with being devoured by lions, wolves, and cannibals; the sea and the land overwhelm and bury him, temporarily bringing him close to death.

Beyond all else, however, the circle which the cannibals make epitomizes the complex fear of becoming engulfed as it represents all levels of sadism: "I observed a Place where there had been a fire made, and a *Circle* dug in the Earth, like a Cockpit, where it is suppos'd the Savage Wretches had sat down to their inhumane feastings upon the Bodies of their fellow Creatures" (166–67). There is a variety of sadistic elements in the cannibals' feasts—in their "devouring and eating one another up" there is oral sadism. In the mess they make of everything, there is anal sadism—thus the shore is "spread with Skulls, Hands, Feet and other Bones of humane Bodies." Or elsewhere, "The place was cover'd with humane Bones, the Ground dy'd with their Blood, great Pieces of Flesh left here and there, half eaten, mangl'd and scorch'd" (207). Finally, the "horrid Spectacle" (165), the "cruel bloody Entertainment" (168), and the "bloody Doings" (169) have a primal scene quality to them and suggest a sadistic reading of sexuality as dangerous and injurious. The desires—to consume, to ground down, to castrate—are all contained in the bad circle of the cannibals. Because they embody these desires, they must be killed off.

Intrusions, Interiority, and Displacements

The primitive core desires and fears have been mapped out, and it remains to examine how those primitive feelings are transposed—displaced and "resolved"—in the narrative. Several interrelated moments in the novel bring to a head the inner conflicts which are manifested externally and resolved interpersonally. These are the moments: Crusoe's conversion, when Crusoe takes the father into the circle of himself—a matter of filiation; Crusoe's responses to the cannibals, expressing his fear of being taken into the deadly circle—a matter of persecution; Crusoe's post-island freedom, constituted by the wealth that surrounds him—a matter of the fetish. The relationship of these moments is thus: in the narrative, as in part a spiritual autobiography, Crusoe experiences a spiritual rebirth, a new relationship with the Father. With this new relationship, he gains power over himself. He is enabled, though faltering at times, to destroy the representation of desire, the cannibals. Having done so, he becomes the master over others and is freed from the restraints of the island. Leaving the island, Crusoe is soon returned to his fetish—money—and it is a moment of such intense emotion that he is overwhelmed. The freedom money offers allows Crusoe to pursue the very desires he had convinced himself (and the reader) he had been punished for. He gives in to the very impulses his father urged him to restrain, thus bringing his conversion and filiation into question.

Crusoe describes the spiritual rebirth through his reflections about his relationship to God and his self-evaluations. The rebirth is also inscribed in a symbolic, visceral manner—we can see conception, labor, and birth. Thus the moment of conversion, of spiritual rebirth, occurs exactly nine months after Crusoe has landed on the island. He is conceived on the island-mother, born out of a self-fashioned womb, and nurtured at the paternal breast. The rebirth realigns the father-son relationship; the son opens and submits himself and is rewarded for so doing.

Crusoe conceives his original badness as stemming from his blocking out the father from the circle of his mind, breaking the law, to pursue wealth without labor. This is the magic of perversion that Chassequet-Smirgel emphasizes in stating that the pervert operates on the pleasure principle, "seeking satisfaction by the shortest route, the quickest, without detours or postponement" (1984, 192). The only things in the circle of Crusoe's mind were his own thoughts and desires. He says early on that he "continued obstinately deaf" to his father's proposals; he says he is "empty" of thoughts of God, and his "head . . . fill'd . . . with rambling thoughts" and "aspiring thoughts." The conversion process begins when Crusoe takes ill, nine months after being left on the island in the fashion of the turtle eggs he finds such a delicacy. The spiritual rebirth involves experiencing "violent pain" in his "head" and opening the mind to the Father. On the primitive fantasy level, the process involves getting rid of the bad introjects in his "head" which manifest themselves as a "violent Head-ach" (86). The inner pain—an "Ague again so violent, that I lay a-Bed all Day, and neither eat or drank . . . weak . . . lightheaded"—precipitates a "terrible Dream," the catalyst of conversion.

In the dream a "Man" emerges from a "great black Cloud" and has "a long Spear" and says that since Crusoe has not seen the light and repented, he will be killed; he "lifted up the Spear" and Crusoe awakens. The nightmare sets Crusoe to examining the "real" nightmare—his failure to be open to God. The primitive quality of the superego representative is made clear by the "spear" he carries, identifying him iconographically with the cannibals. "The miseries of Death came to place itself before me," he says (90). The threats—of castration, penetration, death—set Crusoe to "reflecting," seeing patterns of behavior and making relationships, like an infant emerging from narcissism. Crusoe deduces God: someone else must exist. Thoughts of God's relationship to man and the world "seldom enter'd into my head," he says. But the "terror" and "Horrors" of death made an "Impression that remain'd upon my Mind"—the vision in effect does penetrate. His inner being is in turmoil; there are "Vapours in [his] Head" and the "violence" of the sickness "extorted some Words" from him and "Tears burst out" (90).

In this state Crusoe moves into the most interior space of the novel: he goes inside his dwelling, and there he goes into a chest in which he finds a "Cure, for both Soul and Body." He finds a Bible and begins to "look into" it for the first time and to "read it" (93–94). He goes deep within his analogical body and takes deep within himself nurturant words and "magical" potions. The potions he takes—rum and tobacco—"flew up in my Head violently." He goes into a deep sleep, perhaps sleeping through an entire day, and awakens feeling better. As he reads the Bible, he meditates on the phrase, "I will deliver thee." He learns to see the metaphor as the "Deliverance from the Load of Guilt" (97) which he feels. Crusoe then gives birth to himself—and he gives birth to a negative self ("Load of Guilt"), hence he feels a "great deal of Comfort within." He enters a symbiotic relationship with God, with a "Constant reading the Scripture" and looking to God. It is shortly after his peak experience—"a Kind of Extasy of Joy" (96)—that he discovers the breast of the island, the "planted Garden" examined earlier. He tells us that he "Admir'd the Hand of God's Providence, which had thus spread my Table in the Wilderness" (130). Crusoe accepts God as the good breast. The payoff is an immense and immediate relief, and the long-term payoff is wealth—a load of gold for a load of guilt.

The advent of the cannibals shifts the aggressive trends of the novel and manifests its politics. The drive for the good breast—whether for "raising [his] fortune" or his crops—moves to a drive to defend the good breast against the forces that Crusoe feels are a threat to his good breast. It is no longer Crusoe who seeks to consume, it is the alien other. Crusoe's initial responses to the threat of the cannibals are desires to withdraw, feelings of paranoia, obsessive-compulsive thoughts and actions (endless fortification, vigilance), and sadistic fantasies of attacking and destroying. Having seen "the Print of a Man's naked Foot," which occurs dead center in the narrative, he says he is "confus'd and out of my self." He runs home "looking behind . . . at every two or three Steps, mistaking every Bush and Tree" (154). He fears the cannibals will "devour" him or destroy his crops—he would "perish at last for meer Want" (155). He regrets the back door he made and sets out to build another layer of fortification around his dwelling. He makes his wall "above ten Foot thick," plants muskets all around, and "set in near twenty thousand" small trees, which in five years make a "perfectly impassable" shield in front of his second wall. For much of the time Crusoe feels "surrounded with Danger, and in Expectation every Night of being murther'd and devour'd" (163). When he finds the "Shore spread with Skulls, Hands, Feet, and other Bones" his "Stomach grew sick . . . and . . . [he] vomited with uncommon Violence" (165). He now "kept close within [his] own Circle." He grows obsessed with a fantasy: "Night and Day, I could think of nothing but how I might destroy some of these Monsters in their cruel bloody Entertainment, and if possible save the Victim" (168). He tells us, "my Mind was fill'd with Thoughts of Revenge" (169). At the same time, he thinks increasingly of "escape."

He has a dream, then, of taking an escapee from the cannibals—"he became my Servant," says Crusoe, and this man helps him escape. Crusoe watches relentlessly, and nothing seems to "wear off the Edge of . . . Desire" (200). And so it comes to pass in reality: Friday escapes his captors and Crusoe rescues him. Friday is "so frightened with the Fire and the Noise of my Piece" that he is paralyzed (203). He thinks there is a "wonderful Fund of Death and Destruction" in it (211). Friday is utterly submissive to this fecal phallus, and he puts Crusoe's foot upon his head to signify his position.

Friday is easily the most beautiful—and femininely sensuous—being in the novel: "comely handsome Fellow, perfectly well made," "a very good Countenance," "manly," but with "Sweetness and Softness," "long and black" hair, "a great Vivacity and sparkling Sharpness in his Eyes." He is also a man of strength and prowess—"he runs to his Enemy, and at one blow cut off his Head as cleverly, no Executioner in Germany, could have done it sooner or better." In spite of his power, Friday makes "all the Signs to me of Subjection, Servitude, and Submission" (206). Crusoe teaches him to say "Master." Friday becomes "my Man" and Crusoe is "making him carry" one thing after another, or he "caus'd" him to do various tasks. "His very affections were ty'd to me, like those of a Child to a Father" (209), Crusoe says. Crusoe is eager to wean this child "to bring [him] off from his horrid way of feeding . . . from the Relish of a Cannibal's Stomach" (211). Friday promises "he would never eat Man's Flesh any more" (213). As a companion, a person to look at, Friday is female; as a worker/slave he is a man, but at the same time he is an infant who is to be weaned and disciplined—a caricature of Crusoe. Friday is the son Crusoe refused to be.

Soon after saving Friday, Crusoe rescues a ship under mutiny and thereby finds a way to leave the island and rejoin the world at large. Once there, he discovers his early investments have flourished. Finding out the extent of his wealth, he experiences the most powerful emotions in the text outside of his preconversion illness. As Crusoe is informed of his money, he "could hardly refrain from Weeping" (282); he says he experiences "Flutterings of my very heart" (284). When he is in the circle of his money, or as he says, "when I found all my Wealth about me," he takes ill—"I turned pale and grew sick." He is so overwhelmed by the "sudden Surprise of Joy" that a physician "order'd me to be let Blood." If he had "not been eas'd by a Vent given in that Manner," he feels he would have died (285). Crusoe's response looks like an overdose of drugs. It is as if he has taken so much in that he must let something out, or as if the blood he has shed and desired to shed must be given back in some symbolic way. The giving "vent" fits in with the alimentary schema we have seen elsewhere in the novel—he makes a vent in his dwelling; the fear of death and thoughts of God force some tears and words from him; and conversely, when he is "fill'd with Horror" by the sea, the earthquake, or the sight of cannibal remains, he vomits.

He returns to England to settle down, but that behavior lasts for only half of a sentence in which he tells us he married, had three children, and then his wife died (305). With his wife's death, he decides to go "as a private Trader to the *East Indies*." Thus he repeats his desires to indulge in adventure capitalism; he gives in to the impulse his father warned him against, leaving behind his three motherless children under the age of six, just as, in reverse, he and his brothers had earlier left their parents. It is as if the middle section of the novel—the island—never took place as Crusoe picks up where he left off.

Reflections and Coda

For Robinson Crusoe something seems to be either missing or too present. In Defoe's elaborate fantasy narrative, Crusoe spends his life seeking what has gone and avoiding what is present, creating distance between himself and others. He is paradoxically as fearful as he is desirous of the other. He must get what he wants and leave what he wants. In the process of searching, he repeatedly leaves others, beginning with his family of origin and ending with his family of creation. In the desire to leave the circle of the family, as expressed in the frame of the novel, there is a repetition, perhaps an overcompensation, a reversal—it is always the child who is left. In the novel a passive state is turned into an active one.

The sharpest example of this reversal is seen in the family situation in the opening and closing of the novel. Crusoe's initiating action in the novel is to leave his parents; he follows in the footsteps of his two older siblings. In the last pages of the novel Crusoe tells us that after returning from his various adventures he was "settled" in England for seven years, during which time he married and had three children. "But," he tells us, "my Wife dying," a nephew "drew me in" and "my Inclination to go Abroad . . . prevailed" (305). On the surface, he is active in both instances, but there is a shift between his initial and final family position—first as a child and later as a parent. Moreover, from the perspective of the child role, a reversal occurs: in the final situation three children are left by their mother's death and father's abandonment, whereas in the opening situation the three children take the initiative of leaving.

The fantasy of the novel in which children leave their parents is partly propelled by the feelings of being in the passive (and narratively voiceless) position of Crusoe's offspring, left by their parents. In Defoe's other novels, what generally propels is being orphaned, and *that* is biographically more resonant. The pervasive feeling of being abandoned found in Defoe's work may relate to the early death of his mother, when he was somewhere between eight and eleven (Moore 1958, 10, 28; Backscheider 1989, 12). And it could come from experiences relative to the Plague and the Great Fire. Some time after his mother's death, Defoe became ill and went to Bath to drink the waters; shortly after that he was sent to a dissenting boarding school (Moore 1958, 28). When Defoe's father died in 1706, Defoe was deeply in debt and his father's bequest would hardly meet it (Backscheider 1989, 198–99). Paula Backscheider notes that feelings of abandonment were frequent: Defoe "complained of the ingratitutde of those whose cause he championed, the 'betrayal' of friends," and the like (199). We see this theme as well throughout Defoe's letters to Harley (Healey 1955). My point is that for Defoe being left is a repetition, a reenactment with variations on a painful experience.

Although a shift in fantasy from passive to active can mitigate the grief and rage of loss, if these pains are shadows of more primitive ones they require more intricate psychic maneuvers. The novel's fantasy solution to the primitive bind of wanting the object and fearing both its loss and its power is money. Money splits desire from fear by separating the body of the [m]other from her desire/will, thus granting one possession and control of goods (the body) without in turn being subject to her will or control.[5]

The analysis of feminists and cultural historians of the male-qua-capitalist paradigm suggests that Defoe's solution is historically and psychologically prototypical (see Dinnerstein 1976, 53; Chodorow 1978, 73–78; Gilligan 1982, 5–23; Barker 1984, 62–63; Bateson 1972, 483). As a culturally transformational text, Robinson Crusoe sets up a new male hero, one that develops at the edge of the industrial period of capitalism and colonial expansion. As a historical manual of Darwinian survival, Robinson Crusoe depicts a hero who is indeed successful, a "Master" in the eyes of some. The long-term survival benefits of such mastery are questionable, however, as feminists observe and as environmental economists favoring a shift to a sustainable-world view argue.[6] Indeed, Defoe himself recognizes at some level of consciousness that such mastery may well go out of control (Bateson 1972, 315–37, 478–93). He depicts just such a situation in his last novel, Roxana, in which the heroine's child is murdered to protect the false identity and wealth of her mother. The psychological character of Crusoe does allow him to generate a vast quantity of wealth, but the driven nature of his feat prevents him from having any long-term, reciprocal human relationships and consequently starves him of that for which the wealth is a substitute.[7] Defoe's first novel is like the comic chapter in a larger work on the destructiveness of creating "wealth" in which Roxana is the last and tragic chapter.

Splitting the object by taking the good contents of the body and leaving the problematic desire of the other creates more rifts. The desire to be full and the fear of symbiotic relatedness generate Crusoe's often remarkable en-

ergy and inventiveness as well as his equally remarkable negative aggression—his murderousness[8]—both of which are clearly reflected in the language of the text. For example, among significant verbs with highest fre-
quencies we find on the one hand "make" and "made" and on the other
hand "killed" and "kill" (which are embedded in a complex semantic network focused on weapons and ammunition) (Spackman et al. 1987). The
novel depicts a related split of aggressivity in the two narratives of possession
and generation it maps out. One narrative line involves work and genuine
sublimation, Crusoe's generative labor on the island; the other involves using the labor of others and exploiting the bourgeois desires and addictions
(sugar and tobacco) of others for immense profit without personal labor.
There is a recognition in the text on one level that as an adult one must work
to be fed, and there is a wish on another level for a more passive role, to be
fed without work, to trust the fullness of the breast and know the fullness of
the belly—minimal friction (work, anxiety), maximal bliss. But the situation
of comfort seems to engender its own discomfort, hence the need to de-
animate desire into commodity and metacommodity, money.

◇◇ We have examined a pattern of encirclements, a pattern of embodiment
and disembodiment. The circles are drawn by the language of the text and
can be read in the manner of reading children's drawings (Coles 1964, Winnicott 1971b). The circles are containers and take on the characteristics of
the body—breasts, mouth, bowel, phallus, womb. The interaction of the circles, within and between them, points to a set of primitive wishes and conflicts. There is a desire to have what is inside the circle of the other, to eviscerate the breast—"get every Thing out of her that I could" (55). There is a
desire to have that circle within the self, to introject the mother, to make her
de-form and merge. There is a desire to be encircled by the good circle, a
circle of impenetrable phalli, a circle of gold, a self-created breast. The alimentary process I have called alimentary perpetual motion is gratified in the
narrative but remains present in the novel. In some respects the novel is a
comic romance of a man and his money/mommy: Crusoe is just beginning
to turn his £40 into a fortune when he is stranded for years, but lo and behold, when he returns, there "she" is, ever faithful, reproducing, mother
money, and they live happily ever after.

The complex of desires gives rise to intensive fears of being eviscerated,
engulfed, buried, devoured. The fear reflects Klein's "paranoid position"—
Crusoe will be punished for having, desiring, or taking too much, for failing
to observe the rules and boundaries. Several psychic maneuvers occur in the

face of this fear. One is to attack himself as the bad child. Crusoe occasionally attacks himself before his vision-dream of the man with the spear but begins in earnest after that—what he calls his "reflections" are often self-attacks, pointing to his failures, for example, "I did not now take due Ways to compose my Mind, by crying to God in my Distress, and resting upon his Providence" (159). Another maneuver in the face of fear is to attack some external manifestation of the desire—to project—and this is the main event in the novel, the pivot on which the hero revolves from poor and cut off to wealthy and connected, from shackled to free to shackle. Finally, the last maneuver is to manifest one's own desire in a modified way. In Crusoe's case, money is the way to obtain the primitive desires in a socially appropriate way.

Being surrounded by money, having successfully "raised his fortune," and finding "all [his] new discover'd Estate safe about [him]," Crusoe moves to Klein's "depressive position," that is, concern over the object that has been destroyed in fantasy. In a displaced way, Crusoe makes reparation to his parents and children. At the same time, the reparation is an aspect of the tendency noted at the outset of the chapter, to turn passive into active. That is, Crusoe's giving back is also a wish to have been given to in some psychological first place. Just as the leaving the parents in the opening looks to be a reversal, so does the reparation in the end (so it is as much to himself as to them).

A brief narrative of Crusoe and his money will clarify the possibilities. The wealth Crusoe ends with began with £40, which, he tells us, "I had mustered together by the Assistance of some of my Relations whom I corresponded with, and who, I believe got my Father, or at least my Mother, to contribute so much as that" (17). Although Crusoe never contacts his parents again, the parental imagoes in the fantasy are "requited" (285). His wealth develops: he makes £260 clear on his first trip and takes £60 with him on his next trip, leaving £200 "lodg'd with my Friend's Widow, who was very just to me" (18). His friend's widow is the wife of the captain through whose interest Crusoe made his first successful trading voyage, and it is she with whom he entrusts his money and consults throughout his life. She is the displaced mother: "I was very happy *from my Beginning*, and now to the End, in the unspotted Integrity of this good Gentlewoman" (303). On the displaced paternal side is the "Portuguese Captain" who rescues Crusoe in his escape from slavery, buys the stock he has (the stolen ship, its goods, and Xury, the slave), sets him up as a tobacco planter, and gives him an account of all the money owed him while he was marooned on the island, thus bestowing on him great wealth. When Crusoe's estate is cleared, he tells us, "The first thing I did, was to recompense *my original Benefactor,* my good old Captain, who had been first charitable to me in my Distress, *kind to me in my Beginning,* and honest to me at the End" (285). He speaks of the widow and the captain as the originary couple—as good to him in or from "my Beginning." He rewards them both with money, and the descriptions of both of them abound with feelings associated with the primitive needs articulated elsewhere—he speaks of the Captain's "humanity" and "charity" and the widow's being "just" (18); he "trusted her so entirely . . . perfectly easy as to the Security of my Effects" (303); she is his "faithful steward" (278, 286), and he feels "Gratitude to her former Care and Faithfulness" (278). Having taken the original £40 from his parents and turned it into a fortune, he can now return it, "reward . . . an hundred fold."

The novel ends happily enough with Crusoe embarking on "farther Adventures." He has filled the empty spaces of his body—mouth, belly, bowel, womb, breast, and phallus—emptied the bad things within—rage and guilt—located the body within a safe, secure circle, and extricated himself from dangerous, engulfing spaces. Nonetheless, a darkness emerges in the novel from the conflicts of "unconfin'd" desire: the cannibals replace Crusoe the greedy, the mutineers replace Crusoe the rebel. Someone else has done the greedy eating, someone else has gone against paternal law, someone else must suffer the consequences. These displacements call to mind Winston Smith's moment of conversion in *Nineteen Eighty Four*—the rats are about to be let out of the cage to eviscerate him, and he screams, "Do it to Julia! . . . Not me! Julia!" Thus he betrays himself and his love, Julia. The betrayal in *Robinson Crusoe* is not conscious or articulated. That strand of the novel we call "Robinson Crusoe" is resolved, but within *Robinson Crusoe* itself the conflicts remain, displaced, in the body of the text.

The
Eyes
of
Jane
Eyre

In Defoe's novel the presence of the body—the mouth or gut—is implicit; it can be imagined and acknowledged through a cluster of redundant verbs, to be swallowed, devoured, or starved. In Charlotte Brontë's *Jane Eyre* there is no secret, it seems: the eye is the dominant bodily focus, written even into her name. The eye is named and often repeated; the scope of its semantic network is impressively extensive. In Brontë's novel the focus on the eyes and seeing has the intensity that the alimentary system and food did for Defoe. Thus whereas the tensions in Defoe were found between eating and being eaten, being fed or starving, those in Brontë are focused on seeing and not seeing; being seen and not being seen; showing and hiding, keeping secret, disguising, masquerading.

In Defoe the bodily focus has a primitive quality which the process of the novel attempts to forge into a more mature quality. The eyes in Brontë's work have this doubleness as well. On the primitive side, the eyes as the lovers gaze at each other become a primitive, symbiotic child/mouth and mother/breast; but the eyes, for Jane, are also cognitive-linguistic organs that read and "read" and learn. The eyes are Jane's evolutionary advantage.

Virtually every character's eyes are mentioned and described: cousin John has "a dim and bleared eye"; Jane sees her own eyes at one point as "glittering eyes of fear"; Aunt Reed has a "severe eye"; Adele has "large hazel eyes"; St. John's are "ever-watchful blue eyes . . . so keen . . . so cold"; Miss Temple's are "beaming dark eyes"; and the eyes of Mr. Rochester have more in them than all the rest combined—she speaks of "his great dark eyes; for he had great dark eyes, and very fine eyes, too." The eyes are very active, and the network of visual language involves many verbals: one might see, look, see by someone's look, look up, look around, observe, notice, glance, gaze, watch, survey, reveal, exhibit, open, show, behold, glimpse, examine, study, read, search, penetrate, dive into, recognize, scrutinize, see with spiritual eye, imagine. And, naturally, given a focus on the visible, various polarities show up: invisible, conceal, blind, veil, disguise, masquerade, charade, secret, mysteries. Indeed, the syntactic center, the dark pupil, of the novel is the place of greatest, most embedded secrecy. The visible is so visible it makes one wonder, What has been seen by the I/eye of the text, what is the reader invited to see?

The eye is highly visible. It and its associated network are mentioned on virtually every page, and there are at moments dense clusters of visual interactions. Brontë's insistence on the visual aspect of her work points to an intensity that moves toward the disturbing. Two embedded "seeings" strike me: the primal scene and an adolescent *stade du miroir*.[1] One disturbing reflection is one's own—the novel focuses on a very intense period of life from age nine or ten to nineteen or twenty—adolescence, sexual maturity—when the body is changing, when the body is central, when pleasure and power are desired and feared. The novel "takes place" during the time of central changes—menarche, courtship, disappointment, marriage, and childbirth. This changing body is seen by the self in a mirror, a "looking-glass," and its changes seem repulsive, unsettling, and rejected as much as they are admired and stared at. The earlier visual experience is the sexuality of others. As the cannibal feasts in Defoe are primal scenes, so are what Jane describes in the novel. She calls intense moments "spectacles" and "scenes." And, in fact, the most emotionally charged moments experienced by the body take place in a bedroom: the red room, Helen's sickroom, the fire in Rochester's bedroom, the upstairs chamber in which Mr. Mason bleeds, the dying aunt's bedroom, Jane's bedroom before the wedding. Although both Defoe and Brontë unconsciously inscribe a primal scene, the emotional nature of these scenes differs radically for the two writers. For Defoe in *Robinson Crusoe* the primal scene is bloody, violent, and destructive, with a focus on being consumed and a desire to smash the mirror of the self represented by the Other. For Brontë in *Jane Eyre* it is exciting as well as terrifying. The terror is of being ripped in half rather than of being eaten, though that is present as well. The terror is not only of sexuality but of its consequence—childbirth. Yet by recreating the other—in biological form—one's bodily power (to survive and multiply), as mirrored in the infant, is visible to all. It is through the mirror of the language of the other that one seems to recognize or find oneself, and thence to mirror the many others who have mirrored one's self.

In addition to the semantic web, the importance of the eyes is inscribed in the text syntactically by a wide variety of doubles, pairings, and mirroring of various elements of the novel:

1 the narrator has lived the life and is now reseeing it—a double take;
2 Jane is intensely involved with two families each with two sisters and a brother (one John, the other St. John);
3 we are given the following doubled description of Rochester's eyes—
" . . . his great dark eyes, for he had great dark eyes, and very fine eyes, too" (162);
4 we are able to recognize the lovers, and they each other, by their mirrored language—she sees herself in a mirror as a fairy; when he sees her for the first time, he "unaccountably thought of fairy tales."

In 1846, when Brontë began to write *Jane Eyre*, she had good reason to have a focus on the eye, besides her own nearsightedness. She went to Manchester to accompany her father, who was to have a cataract removed. During the weeks that she waited for him to recover, she wrote a large portion of the novel (Fraser 1988, 161–67). This experiential factor is akin to the day residue of the novel.

◇◇ The structural etching of the eyes in the novel is different from the way Defoe drew circles in the landscape. It emerges in microforms of sentences and paragraphs as well as the semantic webs and plays such as "I" and "eye." The opening paragraphs reveal other aspects of the structural embedding of doubleness:

There was *no possibility* of taking a walk *that day*. We had been wandering, indeed, in the *leafless shrubbery an hour in the morning;* but *since dinner* (Mrs. Reed, when there was no company, dined *early*) the *cold winter wind* had brought with it *clouds so sombre,* and a *rain so penetrating,* that further outdoor exercise was *now out of the question.*

I was glad of it; I never liked long walks, especially on *chilly* afternoons; *dreadful* to me was the coming home in the *raw* twilight, with *nipped fingers and toes,* and a *heart saddened* by the *chidings* of Bessie, the nurse, and *humbled* by the consciousness of my *physical inferiority* to Eliza, John, and Georgiana Reed. (my emphasis)

The opening paragraph is framed with strong negations—"no possibility" and "out of the question." Inside these negations is an embedded explanation of the prohibiting factors. The explanation includes a temporal frame of situational change: "that day" was endurable "in the morning" but "since dinner," which ("dinner") was "early," and which ("since dinner") is "now," it has not been. The constraints create a spatial-environmental antagonism: winter, leafless shrubbery, cold winter wind, clouds so somber, rain so penetrating. Somewhat anomalous is the parenthetical presence of Mrs. Reed — (Woolf's parenthetical mother in *To the Lighthouse*, announcing the death of Mrs. Ramsay, is clearly not the first bracketed mother). Why is Mrs. Reed there, and what can we tell of her? She is the person who seems to control the time one is to eat, is hence the mother. She is in a double surround of negativities—overriding prohibitions, antagonistic environment. She is at the center of it—perhaps the reason for it? Schematically:

> A. [(1) no possibility [(2) leafless [(3) Mrs. Reed] (2) cold, somber, penetrating] (1) out of the question]. Or,
> B. [no [deprived [Mrs. Reed] assault] no].

Mrs. Reed does turn out to be the bad mother (or the first shadow of her), and her place in the midst of the negatives suits her character perfectly. The negatives emanate from her, she is the fountain of bad things (a perfect counter to Mrs. Ramsay as the "fountain and spray of life"). The paragraph has three layers—pupil, iris, cornea?

The second paragraph has a structure of antagonism and articulates as well a structural relation with the first paragraph, which develops more conflict. Its own structure is a balanced frame that presents two conflicting sides: on one side is the "I" of the narrator ("I was glad of it; I never liked"); on the closing side we find those whom "I" plays opposite: Bessie, Eliza, John, Georgiana. We learn, in the center of the paragraph, not only about environmental but emotional antagonism. Schematically: [I/I [chilly, dreadful, raw, nipped—saddened, chidings, humbled, physical inferiority, self-conscious] them: Bessie, Eliza, John, Georgiana]. Or, "[I [physical/emotional negativity] them]." The relation of the first and second paragraphs presents us with another structure—irony, a linguistic possibility akin to bifocal vision. We might gather from the opening paragraph that a complaint is being offered, a fight against constraints, but we would be mistaken. In the opening of the second paragraph, the "I" is delighted to be indoors and implicitly away from "them." In the first paragraph the "I" is merged into a vague "we" who has no control either over the elements or over dinner (or the proprietress). Thus that the second paragraph begins and reiterates "I" feels daringly assertive, and the verbs/adverbs are equally strong in taking a position—"glad of it," "never liked" it. The remainder of the sentence, in part, offers reasons for these feelings and is structured in that respect in a manner similar to the first. In the course of exploring the reasons, the "I" loses some of its assertiveness and capitulates to the problem in the process of describing it.

Jane Eyre is glad she cannot go out because she will not have to associate with those who are antagonistic. Moreover, although she will be isolated, as we learn in the third paragraph—"dispensed from joining the group," "at a distance" and "exclude[d]"—she will experience this as being insulated from aversiveness (them)—"shrined in double retirement" and soon to be reading, the reader's double, the narrator's double, the writer's mirror. What seems at first constraining and prohibiting turns out to be to Jane's advantage and pleasure. Moreover, one reason the opening sentence speaks of time as "that day" is because "that day" is the one that has been marked as being the day Jane's liberation from the Reeds began: it is a paradigmatic condensation of the Reeds' abuse—Jane is first harassed and then assaulted with a book, blamed for the commotion, locked into the red room, frightened by her thoughts and a hallucination, is refused succor, and passes out. But the intensity of it all makes it clear that Jane needs to be separated from the family and is sent to school. That the dreary turns out for the best is a paradigm of the narrative and an oft-repeated rhythm.

In the opening paragraphs, a structure of doubles strikes me. The frame of the opening paragraph (no possibility . . . out of the question); the tension of the second paragraph (I/I . . . Bessie, Eliza, John, and Georgiana); the tension of the third (the children "clustered round their mamma" while Jane is "excluded" and "at a distance"); the "double retirement" Jane finds; and the kind of double attitude one finds between paragraphs one and two—the submissive and the triumphant, the oppressed and the jubilant. Perhaps most striking about the relation of the two paragraphs is that in the middle of them we find a double I, two eyes. Although all these doubles are different from one another, they are akin, too—they call to mind the function of the two eyes, whose doubleness, as Bateson reminds us, yields more information than a simple sum of two. In *Jane Eyre* [ey(r)e] the eye is the most redundant organ in the text—indeed, it is the most revealed organ of all the texts examined here—what does it see, what are in its depths, what does it want us to see?

Eyre's Eyes

In paintings we are often conscious of eyes—their gaze or mirroring surfaces.[2] We see a symbolic event in which seeing is represented. We watch symbolic others watching, interwatching, metawatching. In some sense we are being seen and taught how to see, how we might see or could be seen. In Charlotte Brontë's *Jane Eyre* the eyes dominate the novel's surface bodyscape. The range and depth of the references to eyes, allusions, and linguistic slippage span the primitive, nonverbal symbiotic gaze and the sophisticated, verbal, mature information exchanges (reading). The eye is the medium of mother love and sexual love—calming, exciting, and terrifying "spectacle"—and of language and I. The eye feeds one, enters one, impregnates one, opens to one. The eye may also be blind or blinded, shaded, veiled or disguised. There are dark secrets.

The "eye" comes to be the "I", das Ego. All the ways the "eye" is said to "see" add up to an "I." "I" is what "eye" sees (and doesn't see) and "sees" (and doesn't "see"). The eye has a range that extends from seeing before it had language to seeing/reading language. I sense that Brontë grew up being disallowed a voice—commanded to silence—and thus to whom words were important, hence the eyes play a major role in intellectual development (reading) and emotional communications (without voice, i.e., via the eyes)—expression and interpretation.[3]

The eyes and their various functions or operations and range of connections (semantic networks) are found at least once on every page and frequently appear in complex clusters. In the opening pages we find such words and phrases as "consciousness of" "observation," "view," "shrined," "studied," "book," "I formed an idea of my own" (i.e., an image), "glancing," "discover," "hiding place." In the first five pages we find Jane Eyre observed (to be judged) by others, yet at the same time she is not looked at (existentially not seen) by these others; she hides herself so as not to be seen and not to see, but she is sought and discovered; she reads a book and its pictures; she sees an picture-object in the book (the moon) and describes it as seeing (glancing); the book is thrown at her, hitting her above the eye. She also, in the opening page, describes seeing herself—not in a physical mirror, though she will, but in others. She talks of this kind of "seeing" as a "consciousness of"—thus "I was . . . humbled by the consciousness of my physical inferiority to Eliza, John, and Georgiana Reed."

The eyes of the novel have a variety of ranges. One range connects the eye to other organs, as when the eye is said to communicate something to or from the heart. More redundant is the range of transformations the eye is capable of, that is, through linguistic slippage the eye plays the role of other organs, for example, when the eye is said to pierce or nurture: the eye is breast, phallus, womb, belly/tomb. Another range is of what I would call thermal-emotional relations: cold/toxic/murderous eyes; warm/nurturing eyes; fiery/sexual eyes. This range is connected to emotional splittings, for example, we find a bad mother (cold eyes) and a good one (warm ones). In the splittings we can detect a sliding of linguistic markings such that in this example the "eyes" become associated with the "breasts." Another range is developmental. Thus the eyes in the novel span from the symbiotic or narcissistic gazes of infancy to the reading of adults.

So, on a fantasy level in the tale of the eyes, we find a child killed by the cold eyes of the bad mother, nurtured by the eyes of the good mother, seduced by the fiery eyes of the sexual father, empowered to serve the blind father and bear a child with his eyes. And on an adult level, Jane's eyes allowed her to "read" the range of feelings expressed by the eye. In fact, she makes her way in the world in large measure because she reads—reading in some way helped to extricate her from an oppressive and degrading position, it saved her life, allowed her to develop, gave her work (through which she made connections). Indeed, Jane Eyre is the creation of Charlotte Brontë's readings. Finally, there is a dialectical range that spans from seeing to hiding, from seeing to secrets, from sight to blindness, revealing to concealing. This range concerns the psychological politics of information.

We can, on the one hand, classify and categorize the appearances of the eye and the network of visual language in Brontë's novel as I have done above. But there is another aspect of this material which moves toward chaos. Thus several of the underlying psychological states or intensities in the text involve symbiosis, mirrorings, incest, and regressive helplessness (because overstimulated), and in such intensities a person tends to merge distinctiveness; boundaries break down. What Brontë has created also exists on a nonintegrated level: Jane, in some ways, becomes or is all of the characters. Through visual imagery or related networks Jane, for example, is identified as Helen Burns and Mr. Rochester, Mr. Rochester is identified as Bertha Mason Rochester, who in turn is identified with Jane. Or, through a network of names Jane is identified as her mother (Jane Eyre, née Jane Reed) as well as being identified as the nursemaid's child, Bessie's daughter—also Jane; she is referred to several times as "a reed"; she is connected to air (Eyre is pronounced "Aire" by Adele), water (Rivers), earth/plant (Reed), and fire (Eyre). Incest, primal scene and its later embedded adolescent *stade du miroir*, and symbiosis are not only issues of fantasy in the text but have to do with reading and writing literature. This sophisticated—and mirrored—use of language makes use of the eye; what the eye sees in the domains of reading and writing is that boundaries blur and merge. The boundaries of print remain clear enough to see, but inner boundaries are not so clear. One sees the words, but one also is seeing something else, even if one is not fully conscious of doing so, that is, imagining. Moreover, in the domain of literature we are allowed to shift the boundaries: a "willing suspension of disbelief" might be a way of saying that one may drop one's defenses, allow oneself to merge, to enter an alternative mental locus in which to be mirrored, shown scenes, be blind. Thus the formation of the character of Jane, for example, is a merging of past characters awaiting to be merged into the next (for example, Jane is told of Rochester, "he is old enough to be your father"; Lily Briscoe thinks of William Bankes, "he is old enough to be her father"). The self-referencing aspect of the novel, in which the writer (consciously or unconsciously) addresses the acts of reading or writing, shows Jane as a character sprung from other acts of reading, as well as from theater, merged with what the writer sees with her "spiritual eye" (156).

Note on Incest, Symbiosis, and Primal Scene

Incestuous relationships, symbiotic relatedness, the primal scene, and various mirrorings motivate many of the intensities which the eyes radiate. I am not the first to observe incestuous matters in the Brontës' work or in *Jane Eyre* though I do not think other students have seen how extensive it is.4 As I see it, incestuous and symbiotic feelings are also metaphors for reading and writing. In the narrative of the novel the thread of incest can be seen in the following. (1) Jane's aunt Reed hates Jane; as she explains it, she hates Jane because she hated Jane's mother, and she hated the mother (whose name is Jane) because aunt Reed's husband had an especial love for Jane's mother, his sister (Jane Eyre, née Jane Reed). Jane is equated with her mother and implicated—by name and intensity of feeling—in brother-sister incest: she is the child of incest and/or a participant and/or spectator. (2) Bertha Mason Rochester makes an attack on Jane. The attack is nonverbal, pantomime. Bertha's attack comes close to the day that Rochester and Jane are meant to marry. In the text, on at least four occasions, Rochester is identified as "father" to Jane and Jane as "daughter." Bertha Mason Rochester is implicitly the mother. The fantasy level implicates Jane in a father-daughter incest. If there was parental incest (Jane as daughter of incestuous brother-sister), then parent-child incest is a repetition—second-level incest. If literary processes are incestuous, writers are often engaged in deeply embedded incestuous behavior. Brontë's version of literary process would offer a distinctly female layer of reality to Bloom's idea of the anxiety of influence. (3) Expressions of symbiotic feelings are not made in relation to the mother figures but to the father figure. That is, symbiotic feelings are expressed between the lovers, cross-identified as father and daughter, and yet thereby transforming them also into a mother-child pair (with sometimes Rochester as mother and sometimes Jane). Thus in closing Jane tells us: "No woman was ever nearer to her mate than I am: ever more absolutely bone of his bone and flesh of his flesh" (476) Among other things, this is Brontë's hint that Jane and Rochester are one, merged in the imagination, spun from the same yarn, separated only as language. Imagination becomes something like primal incest, original incest, Ur-incest.

In the novel's focus on visual language, the most significant psychological areas are the primal scene and the later, embedded adolescent observation of bodily/sexual change. The adolescent *stade du miroir* embeds within it the excitement, fear, and disgust of the primal scene. The condensation of primal scenes and self-reflections dominates the most powerful scenes in the work—powerful in the sense that Brontë marks the excitement or the degree of stimulation. The following textual scenes exemplify this: the red room scene in which there is a condensation of sexual forces including menstruation (perhaps seen as an attack by the mother on one's insides), erection (an uncle will "rise up"), sexual visitation/incubus. Second, the upstairs chamber scene, described as a "pale and bloody spectacle," in which we see a tableau of Jane mopping the blood from Mr. Mason, who has been bitten by his sister in a vampire-like attack, something psychoanalysis associates with incest. Third is a scene in Jane's bedroom at Thornfield in which just before Jane's wedding Bertha Mason mimes sexuality as somewhat between rape and being attacked by a vampire; and losing one's virginity and being opened is mimed as being "rent"—she tears the wedding veil. (Mrs. Ramsay, in an angry moment, speaks of men: "to rend the thin veils of civilization so wantonly, so brutally . . . so horrible an outrage" (51)). Fourth is the scene of the mock (set up) courtship of Rochester and Blanche Ingram. Jane's emotional response is so roused that ten years later she still gets excited when thinking about it. Rochester stages this primal scene in very much the same way and for the same purpose that Fanny Hill's original seductress stages a primal scene for Fanny—to lure her into the excitement, and in Rochester's case, to make her "madly in love," as he says. The drama of the primal scene either overwhelms Jane (she passes out in the red room and the bedroom), or she is able to master the scene with the help of her Master (as when she tolerates the blood from Mr. Mason's wounds), or the scene pleasurably excites her for years to come. The embedded or impacted primal scene is related to incest—having seen brother and sister (the scene of Mason's wounds, the scene of Bertha's face in the mirror of the bedroom). Or parental intercourse may interpreted, thought of, as incest by a young child. Witnessing the sexuality—intercourse, menstruation, birth—may terrify or overstimulate. In either case, the intensity marks the absence of boundaries: losing boundaries, watching others losing boundaries.

The Cold, Toxic Eye—Incest, Bad Mother, Bad Breast

The toxic eye is a transformation of the bad breast of the bad mother seeking to attack and destroy. The eyes are transforms of the breasts in their structural repetitions—their visual parallels—but also in that the eyes express feelings whose tangible effects on us, especially as children, are akin to and equally important as food. We take in the supplies and they change us: the looks we get from others feed, starve, freeze us, and so on. The toxic eyes offer bad food, or withhold food, while the nurturing ones offer wholesome sustenance. As with other doubles, there is a double bad mother—aunt Reed and Bertha Mason—one appears early in sexual life (menarche), and the other appears at the boundary of an inner sexual readiness. Both mothers behave toward Jane with jealousy and anger. To some extent, these bad eyes are a part of Jane and recur as self-hatred, as when she doesn't want to or is unable to eat. On the whole, however, Jane is seen by enough good, nurturing eyes that her general movement is life affirming.

The aunt's hostility toward Jane is articulated through the eyes Jane sees her as showing. Jane describes them as "cold, composed," "formidable" (28), "devoid of ruth," "eye of ice" (35), "which nothing could melt," "opaque to tenderness, indissoluble to tears" (219), and "eyes of flint" (228). The aunt's emotional frigidity is overtly hostile—she "surveyed [Jane] with a severe eye" and "her glance . . . expressed an insuperable and rooted aversion" (26). Even on the aunt's deathbed, when Jane has long given up bad feelings, the aunt's behavior (and feelings) continue. Thus Jane tells us the aunt "regarded me icily" and turned her face (219) and that her eyes "shunned my gaze" (227). Moreover, the aunt blocks out other information about Jane—for example, she "was blind and deaf [to John's bullying Jane] . . . she never saw him strike . . . though he did . . . in her presence" (10). Mrs. Reed keeps her negative vision of Jane in effect beyond her presence by telling lies about Jane to the man whose school she will be in; he, Mr. Brocklehurst, tells the teachers, "you must watch her; keep your eyes on her movements . . . scrutinize her" (64). Last, and most revealing, the aunt confesses on her deathbed, "I hated it [Jane, as infant] from the first time I *set my eyes on it*" (220). Aunt Reed's cold, withholding eyes/breasts seek to starve Jane out; existentially they murder her.

Aunt Reed's "rooted aversion" to Jane stems from her inability, unwill-ingness, to see Jane. Instead she sees something else: "I had a dislike to her [Jane's] mother always; for she was my husband's only sister, and a great fa-vorite with him . . . when news came of her death, he wept like a simpleton" (220). A psychoanalytic possibility I would derive from this gestalt is incest between brother and sister Reed. The aunt/wife (as individual or as individ-ual's part) is angry because the brother-sister relationship is the "real" love relationship; she punishes Jane for the sins of her husband—Jane is the to-ken and reminder of that relationship. For the aunt, Jane Eyre is Jane Reed (sister-in-law). The incest possibility is stronger for being noticed elsewhere in the Brontës' works (Solomon 1959, McGuire 1988). But also, for a little-noticed piece of information about Jane's family history: *Jane* Eyre's mother was *Jane* Reed Eyre. Thus the daughter (Jane) is the mother (Jane), and the aunt (Reed) is the mother (Reed), and Jane is also identified as a "reed" on two occasions, allowing—linguistically, psychoanalytically—the brother/ uncle (Reed) to be the father in several incestuous permutations. Adding to this case, Jane's parents are also punished by their families for marrying— they disown them—and seem punished by God as well because they both die within about a year of Jane's birth, and they are followed by the death of Jane's uncle Reed (mother's brother) whose last wishes include that Jane be taken care of by aunt Reed.

The memory of incest is one Jane becomes implicated in: the center of her life becomes a married man, a man said to be old enough to be her father (whose child she bears and yet whose mother she seems to become—"the boy had inherited his own [Rochester's] *eyes*, as they once were—large, brilliant, and black" [476]). The incest in the novel is fairly complete: brother and sis-ter, father and daughter, mother and son. Like Robinson Crusoe, Jane is able to pass the punishment onto someone else and have what she wants. But be-fore she (or the writer or the reader) is gratified, she is confronted with the ter-rible eyes of the angry mother—aunt Reed and Bertha Mason.

The culminating moment of the day in Jane's life with her aunt that in ef-fect liberates her from the oppression of the bad mother/family is described thus: "unconsciousness closed the scene" (50). In the famous red room scene Jane sees or envisions something that terrifies her—"some coming vi-sion from another world" or Mr. Reed's "spirit . . . rise before me" (48). Jane is found unconscious, and this little death stirs the aunt to remove Jane to a school for orphans. The scene feels like the scene of first menstruation—all is red, it is a stately bed/sex room, it is connected with punishment and death, and there is isolation upon becoming sexual.

The fainting has a double that clarifies this first "scene." Brontë invites us to think of the two scenes together for the second is marked: "for the second time in my life—only the second time—I became insensible from terror" (270). The second loss of consciousness has also to do with seeing, and this time the seeing is of the bad mother, enraged by incest-to-be; she is seen as evil and looking like "the foul German spectre—the Vampyre." Recall that Bertha Mason Rochester's brother tells us, " 'She sucked the blood; she said she'd drain my heart'" (242). Among other matters, this "spectre" pantomimes a primal scene: a woman with hair "hanging long" and "red eyes and the fearful blackened inflation of the lineaments" and "black eyebrows widely raised over the bloodshot eyes" rips a wedding veil, approaches Jane, and "the fiery eyes glared upon me—she thrust up her candle close to my face and extinguished it under my eyes" (311). Although Bertha is a female, she is later identified as male—"she showed virile force in the contest" (321)—and in this scene performs "male acts" and female ones. Her features seem genital, and the general response calls to mind a line of self-doubt or disgust from Denise Levertov: "our cunts are ugly." Her features are what account for some of Rochester's looks that Jane would like to know about—shame, disgust. In any case, Bertha's features and actions are Rochester's genital in action, ripping the veil/maidenhead, maybe ripping her in half, approaching a "red," "bloodshot," "fiery" eye. And she "thrust up her candle . . . and extinguished it under my eyes." Jane passes out.

Jane is in the red room as a punishment, possibly for menstruating, that is, becoming sexual, thus adult (and more existentially threatening). She passes out from fear of being sexual, of being or having been assaulted. In the later scene, she is in her own bedroom a few days before she is to marry Rochester when she is confronted by a woman who turns out to be Rochester's wife, or in the psychoanalytic tale, Jane's mother. Jane is being punished in the red room in large part because she makes aunt Reed anxious if not paranoid. For example, Jane says to her that uncle Reed "is in heaven, and can see all you do . . . and how you wish me dead" (27); and Mrs. Reed reports on her deathbed of having been distressed by Jane's "continual, unnatural watching of one's movements" (220). Mrs. Reed mis-sees Jane (and plots to have others mis-see her as well); Jane is tainted with incest in the substructure of Mrs. Reed's "rooted aversion." The incestuous strand noted earlier and the paranoid feeling here both speak to a loss of boundaries. The aunt wishes to get Jane out of sight, out of memory, for "no child ever . . . looked as she did," which is "like something mad or like a fiend" (220). Mrs. Reed characterizes Jane the way Bertha Mason will eventually be characterized.

Bertha Mason seems in her primitive way to be protecting a relationship, warning Jane of a violation and in some way attacking her. In the final conflagration of Thornfield, Bertha torches Jane's room. The Bertha Mason aspect of the mother is more fierce than even Mrs. Reed, certainly more primitive, as we retrospectively think about Bertha's savage attack on her brother and the "pale and bloody spectacle" it makes. It is only once Jane meets Rochester that she becomes sexual, hence challenges the mother. Once she sees him and is seen by him, her latent sexual feelings surface—she tells us with a lunar allusion: "my thin-crescent destiny seemed to enlarge; the blanks of existence were filled up" (177). The genital becomes engorged. It is precisely this excitement that the mother must help the daughter resist, frightening her if necessary. The mother/moon keeps an eye/orb on Jane; the moon is eye/I is mother is sexual rhythm.

Benign Eyes

The power of the eye of the other, how it shapes one's vision of one's self, becomes clearer when the toxic eye is contrasted to the benign eye. The benign eye directly nurtures one—it is a good breast—and it oversees one, confirms one's own self-seeing, and fosters consciousness. The world of the toxic eye consists of harsh superego punishment and primitive fears—being entombed in the red room, being violated, ripped open with teeth, bleeding, starving, and freezing under the icy eye. Under the benign eye there is food, growth, learning, and inner seeing. The benign eye is generally maternal, but it is also seen in Jane's sibling relationship with Helen Burns and in her natural relationship with the moon which is usually present—looking at and after Jane—in times of intensity.

Helen Burns teaches Jane about new ways of seeing and looking—looking inward, looking forward—and she helps Jane through some trials by offering her inspirational visual expressions. She is Jane's depressive double—she dies, she swallows her anger where Jane speaks it. In any case, Jane initiates her first conversation at Lowood with Helen; she is surprised she has "the hardihood . . . to open a conversation . . . but . . . her occupation [reading] touched a chord of sympathy . . . for I liked reading" (48). Unlike John Reed, who uses books as weapons, Helen Burns, like Jane, reads them. Jane's identity as a reader is drawn to Helen—a narcissistic pull, a mirroring, a basis for trust. Helen uses her eyes in other ways as well. When she is being punished she is able to focus elsewhere: "Her eyes are fixed on the floor, but I am sure they do not see it—her sight seems turned in, gone down into the heart: she is looking at what she can remember, I believe, not at what is really present" (50). Jane comes to understand that Helen "considered things by a light invisible to my eyes" (54); as Helen says, "I lived in calm, looking to the end" (57). In the face of antagonisms of a similar order to Jane's, Helen looks inward and toward death; her rage turns upon her. She is nonetheless able to see Jane for who she is and this sustains Jane.

Thus when Jane is under duress, Helen's look gets her through the ordeal. Mr. Brocklehurst, carrying forth the toxic feelings of Mrs. Reed, tells Jane's mates to " 'shun her . . . avoid her . . . exclude her . . . shut her out. . . . Teachers, you must watch her . . . scrutinize her' " (64). As Jane sits on a stool in the midst of everyone—"exposed to general view on a pedestal of infamy"— Brocklehurst is going on; she says, "I felt their eyes directed like burning-glasses against my scorched skin." Brocklehurst's harangue is calculated to induce shame, paranoia, alienation, powerlessness, and an awful self-consciousness. As Jane sits on the "pedestal of infamy," Helen Burns goes by and "lifted her eyes" to Jane: "What a strange light inspired them! What an extraordinary sensation that ray sent through me! How the new feeling bore me up." Helen's smile, moreover, "lit up . . . her sunken grey eye, like a reflection from the aspect of an angel." Helen offers Jane some kind of nurturance (breast) in the form of a feeling sent through the eye. Behind Helen's strength is a benign paranoia, a belief that there is " 'an invisible world . . . of spirits . . . [who] watch . . . guard us . . . see our tortures, recognize our innocence.' " Helen, unlike anyone Jane has met, is able to see her. She knows that Jane is innocent of Brocklehurst's accusations " 'for I can read a sincere nature in your ardent eyes.' "

In addition to the self-confirmation, the mirroring, Jane receives from Helen, she receives sustenance from Miss Temple, the chief administrator at the school. Jane tells us that she still retains "the sense of admiring awe with which my eyes traced her steps," and she is particularly drawn to her "brown eyes, with a benignant light in their irids" (46). Because of her positive regard for Miss Temple, she is anxious to retain her good opinion and is concerned for that when Brocklehurst is giving his tirade—"I watched her eye with painful anxiety, expecting every moment to see its dark orb turn on me a glance of repugnance and contempt" (60). Miss Temple, however, does not place undue credence in Brocklehurst and listens to Jane's tale. Jane is relieved at being understood and says she "derived a child's pleasure from the contemplation of her face . . . beaming dark eyes" (69). Jane gazes at Miss Temple's face as an infant would. This is the first symbiotic moment in the text, and it in some respects—along with those "dark eyes"—connects her to Rochester. Jane feels seen by Miss Temple, and the feeling is akin to being fed: "We feasted that evening as on nectar and ambrosia; and not the least delight of the entertainment was the smile of gratification with which our hostess regarded us [Helen and Jane]" (70). And, to complete Miss Temple's gesture, she "embraced us both . . . drew us to her heart" (71). Here, then, Jane is fed physically and emotionally; she gazes in love and is looked at with respect; she is seen for whom she sees herself.

In addition to Jane's earthly companions, the moon often "looks" at Jane, especially at crucial times, and is identified as being a maternal force. There are several moons in Jane Eyre's pictures (157), and she identifies herself with the moon when she speaks of her "thin crescent destiny" (177). It is "by the light of a half-moon" that Jane gets dressed to leave Gateshead. More powerfully, just after Jane's humiliation, when Helen is comforting her and Miss Temple is about to speak with her, the following scene occurs: "Some heavy clouds, swept from the sky by a rising wind, had left the moon bare; and her light, streaming in through a window near, shone full both on us and on the approaching figure, which we at once recognized as Miss Temple" (102). The light of the moon illuminates the three women who illuminate one another—the moon links them. The moon appears again when Jane recognizes that Helen is dying and feels "a necessity to see her"—"the light of the unclouded summer moon, entering here and there at passage windows, enabled me to find [the room] without difficulty" (111).

The moon helps Jane see where she is going and see what is coming as well. Thus on the night she is to meet Rochester for the first time, she first sees "the rising moon . . . brightening momently; she looked over Hay" (143). When Rochester appears and falls, "the moon was waxing bright; I could see him plainly" (143). And when he leaves, she is excited; she contemplates the heavens: "the moon ascending it [the sky] in solemn march, her orb seeming to look up as she left the hilltops . . . and aspired to the zenith, midnight dark in its fathomless depth . . . and for those trembling stars that followed her course, they made my heart tremble, my veins glow when I viewed them" (148). The moon allows Jane to see something new, something she has desired: "I longed for a power of vision . . . which might reach the busy world . . . I had heard of but never seen . . . what I believed in I wished to behold" (140). The heavens become sexually exciting, primal: ascending, orb, look up, aspired, fathomless depth, trembling, tremble, glow, viewed.

The moon not only shines on people, allowing Jane to see them, but it seems to protect and warn Jane as well. On the night Mr. Mason is attacked (by Bertha Mason Rochester, his sister), just before the tumult begins, the following scene is set:

> I had forgotten to draw my curtain. . . . The consequence was, that when the moon, which was full and bright . . . looked in at me through the unveiled panes, her glorious gaze roused me . . . I opened my eyes on her disc—silver-white and crystal clear . . . beautiful, but too solemn. (235)

Just at this moment, there is a "savage" cry, and everyone begins to look out from their apartments. On the night before Jane's wedding is to be broken up, the moon also appears: "the moon appeared momentarily in that part of the sky which filled their [the "cloven halves" of the chestnut tree] fissure; her disc was blood-red and half overcast; she seemed to throw on me one bewildered, dreary glance, and buried herself again" (304). The moon hides again as Jane awaits Rochester's return: "the moon shut herself wholly within her chamber, and drew close her curtain of dense cloud" (305). Again, on the night before Jane is to flee Thornfield and Rochester, the moon appears, but in a "trance-like dream" in which the moon is identified as mother:

> I watched her come—watched with the strangest anticipation. . . . She broke forth as never moon yet burst from cloud . . . not a moon, but a white human form . . . gazed and gazed on me. . . .
> "My daughter, flee temptation."
> "Mother, I will." (346)

Last, on the night that Jane is reconnected to Rochester, the night she hears his call and issues her own, "the room was full of moonlight," and she is able to break from St. John, who is pursuing her to an unloving marriage—"It was my time to assume ascendancy," Jane says, following the moon.

Hide and Seek: Symbiosis and Metamorphosis in the Relationship of Jane Eyre and Edward Rochester

From the very first time they meet, Rochester hides something from Jane—he hides himself, his feelings, his past. In fact, in every encounter before his "disgusting secret" is revealed, he is in disguise. At the same time, he surveys her, scrutinizes her, reads her looks, watches her himself unseen; he disguises himself in manifold ways to see her and to allow her to see him. Jane is an object for this visual epicure: "'I liked what I had seen, and wished to see more'" (341). He watches her as if to take her in, like a breast, and sometimes as if to enter her, his eye as phallus. Jane, on the other hand, although she will confess to enjoying looking at Rochester, will usually hide herself, place herself in the shade, put down a veil, look purposefully away. Nonetheless, when opportunity strikes, she avidly looks at him; she detects "a mystery," a "secret," something "concealed" which she longs to see, and when she does, it will destroy her "vision" and "blind" him. The imagery of the eye in the relationship of Jane and Rochester is most complex. Feelings of symbiosis, sexuality (incestuous), and the terror these bring are shared by both and expressed often in the way they look at and avoid each other.

The nature of their relationship is incestuous. The text is fairly insistent on this: "I am old enough to be your father" (165), Rochester says; he tells her that she "was as dear to him as a daughter" (326). "He might almost be your father" (293), Mrs. Fairfax reminds her. But this is not the only line of the story as told by the eyes—Jane's eyes nurture him, penetrate and master him. Jane is as much his mother as he is her father. At times, he is her mother, feeding her with a glance or a smile. The characters break down as male or female, child or parent. So terrifying is this merging that it must be defended against by withdrawal, hiding, secrets. Indeed, it must be punished—by blindness.

Rochester: Symbiotic Fantasy, Voyeur, Secret Keeper

Rochester falls in love with Jane from the moment he encounters her. At the same time, he hides from her. This tension remains until exploded by the revelation of his previous marriage, at which time she hides from him. In their first encounter, although she "could see him plainly," he is concealed: he says, "'Do you know Mr. Rochester?'" And she replies, "'No, I have never seen him'" (146). He gets her to reveal her identity—"'I am the governess'"— but conceals his own. He will tell her much later that on that first night he "'could not have . . . seen [you] vanish . . . without singular regret'" if he had not known who she was. In fact, he tells her, "'I . . . watched for you. The next day I observed you—myself unseen" (339–40). He confesses: "'I was at once content and stimulated with what I saw; I liked what I had seen and wished to see more . . . I was an . . . epicure and wished to prolong the gratification'" (341). Jane becomes a good breast and he is "content and stimulated." These facts and feelings, however, are not revealed to Jane; they are kept a secret along with Rochester's deeper secret—his marriage—and they emerge only after the deeper secret has been revealed. He tells her about how deep his dependency on her is in the face of being in danger of losing her. This is not to say that Rochester doesn't reveal his feelings, but only that he is generally well defended, very cautious. Indeed, throughout his inverted courtship and on the very occasion of his marriage proposal he behaves sadistically toward Jane before he reveals himself. He loses power in love with her and struggles at the same time to retain it: "'you too have power over me, and may injure me . . . I dare not show you where I am vulnerable'" (246).

He reveals—she has "power over" him—and he conceals—he "dare not show . . . where."

Thus, also in reference to their first meeting, he tells her, after she has rescued him from a fire: "'I knew . . . you would do me good . . . *I saw it in your eyes when I first beheld you: their expression and smile did not . . . strike delight to my very inmost heart so for nothing*" (145, my emphasis). Her eyes have a kind of phallic power—to "strike delight to my very inmost heart"—and he will say of another encounter—"'there was penetration and power in each glance you gave'" (298).

Rochester derives various pleasures from looking at Jane, as he does from being seen by her. He is gratified to find when he looks at her unseen that the "deep reverie" she is in the day after their encounter focuses on him: "'I think those day-visions were not dark: there was a *pleasurable illumination in your eye occasionally, a soft excitement . . . your look revealed . . . the sweet musings of youth*'" (my emphasis). The narcissistic gratification is complemented by a deeper concern, one closer to infancy—he thus "impatiently . . . waited" to see her again and feels "vexed" when she is "out of . . . sight" (297). His symbiotic feelings are revealed in a tale he tells his ward, Adele, about how Jane and he met: "'I never spoke to it, and it never spoke to me in words: but *I read its eyes and it read mine*'" (my emphasis). This "speechless colloquy" gives us an image of the primitive desire to know without language. The regressive pull of this desire—also a defense against being adult and lingual—is one which Jane has to struggle against in both herself and Rochester because it threatens her identity, but it is one to which Jane—as a linguistic artifact—will ultimately capitulate because that is her identity.

Rochester wants to see Jane. He requests at one of their early meetings that she move her chair forward—"I cannot see you" (160). His desire to see her is a hunger for food (breast) and excitement (female)—he wants to suckle her and enter her. He looks at her with lust: he "ran his eye over my dress," "my raiment underwent scrutiny" (146). He desires her in the simultaneous ways we might associate with passionate love—primitively symbiotic, infantile oral-sensory, and adult genital. He senses that she thinks of him as he spies on her the morning after their first encounter, but he is not positive. He sets up several elaborate artifices to give Jane an opportunity to watch him as he has watched her. He stages a courtship ritual with Blanche Ingram, and within that there is a game of charades in which he and Blanche pantomime a wedding. He later explains, "'I wished to render you as madly in love with me as I was with you'" (291). The strategy works: "He made me love him without looking at me" (204).

The visual connections between Rochester and Jane are not totally without verbal communication—metacommunication. Rochester makes explicit to Jane that the eye speaks a language as well as reads it and that it is possible to talk about this speaking and reading, to see at another level. He names the way she looks: her "eyes [are] generally bent on the carpet," "they are directed piercingly to my face," "you look puzzled," "those searching eyes of yours" (162–63). In addition, he responds to a look of Jane's in such a way that it verifies the accuracy of the eye and its vision: he is speaking about some possible "intolerable defects" she might have: "'And so may you,' I thought. My eye met his as the idea crossed my mind: he seemed to read the glance, answering as if its import had been spoken as well as imagined" (166). Last, he says, explicitly what the eye does: "'You would say you don't see it: at least I flatter myself I read as much in your eye (beware, by the by, what you express with that organ; I am quick at interpreting its language).'" (166–67). In all this, Rochester tells Jane that he is watching her— he feels her "examine" him, talk to him—and seeing that she is watching him; he tells her some of what he sees about her looking—that she wants to get into him, that she is afraid. Such communicating is the second stage of Rochester's seduction.

Although Rochester raises the ante at various times, he also retreats—that is the rhythm. He will look unseen, allow himself to be seen, talk about "reading" and seeing and being seen, but he will also disguise himself and his language, concealing what he is revealing. Thus in their second inside meeting, shortly after the dialogue above, Rochester, unable to continue his metalogue, drifts into "a discourse which was all darkness" to Jane about "an angel of light" wanting "entrance to [his] heart," a "disguised deity" who will make a transformation—"my heart was a sort of charnel; it will now be a shrine." He speaks, of course, about Jane and her purifying effect on him: his bowel (with its "disgusting secret") will become a womb; it will become a "shrine," the very place from which Jane's journey began ("shrined" in the window seat reading). To Jane "he spoke to a vision, viewless to any eye but his own." This "invisible being," however, is Jane, but she cannot see herself in his vision just yet, and he cannot tell her just yet.

Jane: Desire

Before Jane meets Rochester, Jane-as-narrator, re-see-er, gives us a map of what is to come in the form of a musing. She tells us that she felt there was more to life than she had experienced, and she longed to see what she had only seen in her imagination, that is, to "allow my mind's eye to dwell on whatever bright visions rose before it—and certainly, they were many and glowing . . . to open my inward ear to a tale that was never ended—a tale my imagination created . . . quickened with all of incident, life, fire, feelings, that I desired and had not in my actual existence" (105). All Jane's seeing has been inward. It has roused her desires and passions but not satisfied them. She longs for sexuality, for procreation: for the eye itself to "dwell on whatever . . . rose before it . . . to open my inward ear . . . quickened with . . . life." In the narrative, she is soon to see exactly what she wants to see—she "could see him plainly" in the "moon . . . waxing bright," and she watches him watch her—"scrutinize" and "examine" her clothes (146). As he sees her, she is seeing him: "he searched my face with eyes that I saw were dark, irate, and piercing" (145). She is excited at this "new face . . . a new picture . . . because it was masculine . . . because it was dark, strong and stern" (111). As she walks onward she says, "I still had it before me . . . saw it . . . all the way home." She resists going into Thornfield to "slip again over my faculties the viewless fetters" of a deadening, nonsexual life. But when she does go in she sees a "ruddy shine" coming from the dining room, which "showed a genial fire . . . glancing on . . . brass . . . and revealing" the room; it "revealed, too, a group." Jane comes to understand that it is Mr. Rochester; she calls for a "candle" and "went upstairs to take off my things." To take off, perhaps, the "viewless fetters."

She has an opportunity to look at him in their second formal meeting; her description reveals her interest in him as revealed by his eyes; Rochester sits, "receiving the light of the fire . . . in his great dark eyes; for he had great dark eyes, and very fine eyes, too—not without a certain change in their depths sometimes, which if it was not softness, reminded you, at least, of that feeling" (126). One feels Jane's increasing interest, excitement, and approval. We see it in the doubled "great dark eyes" and the similarly double qualified, "very fine eyes." We understand, too, how feelingful it is to look so into someone else's eyes that one gets a sense of their "depths" and their "softness." His eyes are female—they "receive the light of the fire." Her look is moving toward symbiotic: while he looks at the fire, "I had been looking the same length of time at him . . . my gaze fastened on his physiognomy" (162)—she would enter him and consume him. Moreover, she is curious about him—there is some "mystery," some "secrets." He wants to let her in—"'you will often find yourself elected the involuntary confidante of your acquaintances' secrets'"—but justly fears that. Nonetheless, some aspects of his secret are revealed, enough to make Jane curious to see more: "Lifting his eyes to its battlements, he cast over them a glare such as I never saw. . . .

Pain, shame, ire—impatience, disgust, detestation—seemed momentarily to hold a quivering conflict in the large pupil dilating under his ebon eyebrow" (136). She feels, seeing this, "as if I had been wandering amongst volcanic-looking hills . . . felt the ground quiver, and seen it gape." The images suggest a primal scene, enthralling but frightening, and will reappear more convincingly. She refers, more longingly, to this eyescape in relation to Miss Ingram, who receives so much "attention" (216–17). Jane observes that this "expression" of Rochester's "that opened upon a careful observer . . . in his eye . . . disclosed" something—and "one day [Miss Ingram] might look into the abyss at her leisure, explore its secrets and analyse their nature." The eye, then, opens into the bowel (as well as the heart), and Jane wants to know everything.

The intensity of Jane's gazing reaches a climax in the section of the novel in which Rochester has set up a complex charade, a mock courtship, for Jane to watch and participate in, demanding her presence: "my particular wish," he says. He starts it and calls it to a close: " ' "the play is played out" ' " (230). He stages a primal scene, this one passionate and exciting, rather than the other dread-inspiring primal scenes (red room, bedroom, and upstairs chamber). The stage is set, the audience is seated ("in the shade," of course), the characters enter, and "He comes in last." The following is from the climax— I have edited five paragraphs (from two closely related sections on pages 203 and 214) to stack up the visual language and its sustained nature:

> I am not *looking* at the arch, yet I *see* him enter. I try to concentrate my *attention* . . . on the work . . . in my hands, to *see* only . . . whereas I distinctly *behold* his figure . . . recall the moment when I *saw* it last . . . and he . . . *looking* down on my face, *surveyed* me with *eyes* that *revealed* a heart filled . . . I had a part . . . without *looking* at me, he took a seat. . . .

> No sooner did I *see* that his *attention* was *riveted* on them, and that I might *gaze* without being *observed*, than my *eyes* were *drawn involuntarily* to his face: I *could not keep their lids under control; they* would *rise*, and the *irids* would *fix* on him. I *looked*, and had an *acute pleasure in looking*—a precious yet poignant pleasure; pure gold, with a steely point of agony: a pleasure like what the thirst-perishing man might feel who knows the well to which he has crept is poisoned, yet stoops and drinks divine draughts nevertheless.

> Most true is it that 'beauty is in the *eye* of the gazer.' My *master's* . . . deep *eyes* . . . full of interest, an influence that quite *mastered me* . . . fettered . . . I had not intended to love him . . . at the first *renewed view* . . .

they spontaneously revived . . . . He made me love him without *looking* at me. . . .

I *saw* Mr. Rochester smile . . . his *eye* grew both *brilliant and gentle,* its *ray* both *searching* and *sweet* . . . I wondered to *see* them [two women] *re-ceive* with calm that *look* which seemed to me so *penetrating: I* expected their *eyes to fall* . . . 'He is not to them what he is to me . . . he is not of their kind. I believe he is of mine.' . . . (203–4)

I did not now *watch* the *actors* . . . my *attention* was *absorbed* by the *spec-tators;* my *eyes,* erewhile *fixed* on the arch, was now *irresistibly attracted* to the semicircle . . . I *still see* the consultation which followed each *scene: I see* Mr Rochester turn to Miss Ingram . . . I *see* her incline her head to-wards him till the jetty curls almost *touch* his shoulder and wave against his cheek; I *hear* their *mutual whisperings; I recall their interchanged glances; and something even of the feeling roused by the spectacle returns in memory at this moment.* (214, my emphasis)

These passages demonstrate how concentrated the visual language can be-come, drawing our attention to it perhaps, to tell us here: this is where the body is, called into existence, set into resonance, by seeing. The earlier pas-sage focuses on the range of Jane's feelings toward Rochester as they are ex-cited by seeing him: she doesn't want to see him—angry, no doubt, that he has neglected her, left her hungry too long. (The anger is never stated—it is enacted: Rochester is later punished but by the "creator" rather than Jane.) But so appealing is the object that Jane can't not look; once doing so, she re-calls his last look—loving and touching and related to and shared with her—via "eyes that revealed a heart."

In addition to being emotionally moved, she feels sexual excitement—"my eyes . . . drawn involuntarily . . . I . . . could not keep their lids under control: they would rise, and the irids would fix on him." The magnetism fluctuates from adult to infantile. In their sexual excitement the eyes become erotogenic, clitoral: "lids [not] under control . . . rise and fix on him." On the other hand, the magnetism seems oral and infantile—the fixed gaze, the initial response of not wanting to look, to deny him as he has denied her.

Jane also sees in the moment as an adult—she sees differences and eval-uates: she looks at the way Rochester looks at other women and the way they respond with their eyes; she knows that it is different than the way she and he interact visually; she understands that the other women fail to see, and consequently, she is more suited to him than they are. Jane will eventually eliminate Blanche Ingram herself by a similar comparison—at first she draws a picture of herself and one of Blanche to remind herself of the differences between them and consequently the impossibility of Rochester's interest in her; but the second comparison, on the basis of how they see (rather than on the surface "look" [i.e., beautiful]) brings Jane to a different conclusion, that "Miss Ingram was a mark beneath jealousy" (215) Why? Because all the defects Jane sees, she sees that Rochester sees: "Other eyes besides mine watched those manifestations of character—watched them closely."

The later passage returns us to other visceral themes—the primal scene: sexual, exciting, infantile. Jane is a spectator (of a charade played by one man on many unwitting players) of spectators (of a mutually agreed-upon game of charade)—we are spectators of it all. And what she is seeing, is "absorbed by," is the spectacle of the spectators. He turns, she inclines, jetty curls touch him, wave against his cheek; they mutually whisper; glance at each other. Jane will not name the feeling—"something even of the feeling roused"— just as she would not tell us on recognizing that the man she had met on the road, who had excited her, was the man now in the house, the master. But in the very next sentence she speaks of her "love" for Mr. Rochester.

Who Is Jane Eyre?

On one level Jane is the name of a spectator-narrator of a story about herself, Jane Eyre, now retrospector. This retrospector often marks her tale as theater, drama, staged, acted: "A new chapter in a novel is akin to a new scene in a play; and when I draw up the curtain . . . reader, you must fancy you see" (125). Brontë names intense moments in Jane's life as "scene" or "spectacles." To her aunt, "I was a precocious actress in her eyes" (49). She says of the ordeal in the red room that the "scene closed" with unconsciousness; the time spent with Mr. Mason is described as a spectacle (238); Bertha is a "spectre" (311); the fire at Thornfield—and its attendant suicide, rescues, and disasters—is a "terrible spectacle" (451). "Spectacles" are also used to see something, to read. So although a "spectacle" may be disturbing, such "spectacles" may be "spectacles" through which one can read ordinary life— which begins to sound like a "justification" for the "spectacles" of novels. A spectacle is something we can look through and with which we can see better. (This semantic-phonetic connection is made by way of Mrs. Fairfax— the only person who wears spectacles—when she offers her advice to Jane after being told by Rochester that he intends to marry Jane.) Brontë insists, in other words, that the eye and seeing and reading and all their relations in the semantic network—observation, notice, glared, gazed—that this immense grid, dominated by the eye, is central to the experiencing of the text. One has to be able to *see* at all the levels that Brontë shows; she seems to want to enable the reader to see as she does, as she has been enabled. And in the psychoanalytic scheme of things, Brontë's insistence on seeing leads us to think of seeing something one finds emotionally distressing, maybe overwhelming—one's own sexual body, incest, parental sex.

One thing Brontë tells us about her character Jane is that she is who Brontë has read, combined with her own visions and imaginings, following her "inner eye," for example. She has heard and read fairy tales and ballads, *Gulliver's Travels, Rassleas*, Bewick's *History of British Birds* (40), Goldsmith's *History of Rome*,(43), Richardson's *Pamela* (41), the Bible (65), Arabian Tales (70). To be read to is to be fed—Bessie "fed our eager attention with passages of love and adventure taken from old fairy tales and older ballads; or (as at a later period I discovered) from the pages of *Pamela*, and *Henry, Earl of Moreland*."

The character of Jane is her mirrorings. She is who she sees in the red-room mirror—"half fairy, half imp . . . appearing before the eyes of belated travellers" (46). This identity is corroborated by Rochester, who comes to her as "belated travellers" (143) do and says to her the next day, "I thought unaccountably of fairy tales" (153) when he saw her the night before. She is who she sees in the red bedroom mirror; who she sees in the mirror of Helen, the reader; who she sees when she draws a portrait of herself and one of Miss Blanche Ingram to compare herself, as she also does in the second paragraph of the novel when speaking of being "conscious of" a difference that degrades her; and she sees herself in the mirror of her lover's eye, sees as he says "her likeness."

Another mirror is that which the imagination creates. Jane talks about imaginings in relation to her painting. She says the images had "risen vividly on my mind," and she "saw them with the spiritual eye, before I attempted to embody them . . . but my hand would not second my fancy . . . it had wrought out but a pale portrait of the thing I had conceived" (156). Speaking of her response to painting, she says, "To paint them . . . was to enjoy one of the keenest pleasures I have ever known." In painting one can create a mirror of the interior; it is a different sort of mirror from that on the wall or on the face of the Other. In imaginings one creates yet another visual domain: "my sole relief was to walk . . . and allow my mind's eye to dwell on whatever bright visions rose before it . . . and . . . to a tale . . . my imagination created . . . quickened with . . . life, fire, feeling" (141).

These multilayers of visual referencing are dizzying and dazzling. Freud speaks of condensation as one mode of representation in dreams; one element in a dream represents more than a single corresponding element. Melanie Klein spoke of splitting in which a single object—the Other—is perceived as two separate beings, one good and one bad, nurturing and attacking. I would add another mode of representation, certainly occurring in the long strings of aesthetic works: *faceting*, a multiplying of perspectives and refractions. Faceting is akin to mirroring and splitting and is in some dialectical tension with condensation. In Jane Eyre, for example, the mother is faceted through many different figures, as are siblings and the father. The mother is many figures:

1 A young rebellious woman whose family disowned her when she married and who dies not long after Jane is born. As fantasy: the withdrawn mother who abandons the child because the child is so awful or so awful a reminder. The child feels rejected by its mother, as its mother was rejected by her mother.

2 The mother is aunt Reed—Jane's mother's maiden name, and ascribed to Jane twice in the text, where she is described as like a "reed." The aunt is frigid, unyielding, the bad breast, the witch.

3 There is Bessie who complies with the aunt on several decisions and thus treats Jane poorly, but she also reads to and sings to Jane; she gives Jane language and narrative—she has a "remarkable knack of narrative" (61); she does offer Jane positive mirroring when Jane grows—she confirms the change—and she has a daughter named Jane.

4 Miss Temple, whose eyes feed Jane.

5 Mrs. Fairfax, who warmly greets Jane and welcomes her, and who offers Jane a moment of painful, good advice.

6 Bertha Mason, who presents Jane with a pantomime of sex, losing virginity.

7 Mr. Rochester, who feeds her a new vision of herself, seen through his eyes.

Jane "is" who she sees herself to be, who she has read herself to be, who she sees imaginatively she is, who she has been seen as, who she is identified as being through semantic networks. Jane is Brontë's artifact, a conclusion to and variation on the reading she has done. We merge with what we see and we make what we see discrete again. Laing speaks of this as a matter of being both separate and related, and D. W. Winnicott says we are always negotiating our boundaries.

Coda

The novel is a complex of vision. That the tale is told through the eye and that the eye and its manifold activities are so omnipresent make me think of all the trees Defoe has Crusoe plant in front of his fortress. That is, the eye is an obsession; it must be protecting something as well as announcing it, perhaps some "disgusting secret." Something is being revealed, staring you in the face—as Mr. Rochester is on the road—but that something is concealing.

I sense a variety of "disgusting secrets"—a sense of a sexual self coming from the mirrors into which Jane has looked: thus eye/I see myself; eye/I see vulval eye (for her Vulcan lover); I see my blood/ menses, I see my pubic hair. We may, like William Blake, learn to see the beauty of the genitals, but we can also understand and know their relative ugliness, particularly as they "mature" in adolescence. In the red room is a "great looking-glass" which "repeated the vacant majesty of the bed and room." The "scene" of the red room is doubled, the gap and the bed. Into this "vacant majesty" enters Jane:

> I had to cross before the looking-glass; my fascinated glance involuntarily
> explored the depth revealed . . . the strange little figure there gazing at me
> with a white face and arms specking the gloom, and glittering eyes of fear
> moving where all else was still, had the effect of a real spirit; I thought it
> like one of the tiny phantoms, half fairy, half imp . . . coming out of lone,
> ferny dells in moors, and appearing before the eyes of belated travellers.
> (46)

Jane is presented to us as an innocent. In this vast red room, bedroom, death room, punishment room—they threaten to tie her down if she does not stop fighting—Jane is fragile, fearful, vulnerable. She thinks of "never eating or drinking more, and letting myself die." Jane enters the room innocent. It is she, however, I think the fantasy runs, who makes the room red, who screams and faints at the sight of her own blood. She can later look with relative equanimity at Mason's blood because she is prepared. The second major mirror scene involves Bertha Mason, for it is in the mirror that Jane sees Bertha's ambiguously male-female genital-like "discoloured face" with its "hair hanging long down" and its "red eyes"; the one who rends the veil and "thrust up her candle" in Jane's face. This scene follows the budding of Jane's sexuality—"my thin crescent destiny seemed to enlarge; the blanks of existence were filled up" (177). And it precedes by hours the consummation of those desires in a marriage bed. This second mirroring is, then, a representation of sexual fears, sexual terrors. Such fears are part of the first mirror scene since there Jane is afraid of something that might "rise before" her, and when she sees a light and thinks it a "vision from another world": "My heart beat thick, my head grew hot; a sound filled my ears . . . I was oppressed." She is overwhelmed by overstimulating thoughts. She is overwhelmed by the processes of her own body. In the second scene, she is also overcome, but this time by interior thoughts. The scenes are reversals, mirrors: in the first, she *thinks* she sees something but realizes later it was just a flicker of light from a passing lantern; in the second scene, she has evidence in the ripped veil that someone else was there, though she allows herself to be persuaded by Rochester that she saw someone she knew. As I read it, she does see something in her first mirroring—menses—whereas, in the second scene there is no one, only her fear and disgust. These *stade de miroir* mirroring scenes mirror primal scenes that mirror sexuality from more distant spaces and times.

The matrix of eyes, if factored out of the narrative, would begin to merge and blur boundaries between characters. Odd connections are made: Adele is the charge whom Jane is given at Thornfield and whose origins, as Rochester explains it, have nothing to do with him but whose mother he had loved (and had sexual relations with), and he took pity on her when her mother died. She is not his daughter with someone to whom he was not married. Jane herself is orphaned and taken in by a kindly avuncular man. Adele is described as having "large hazel eyes." Rochester, the day after he proposes to Jane, praises Jane's "radiant hazel eyes." Jane, no Freudian, simply notes that she has green eyes, and "you must excuse the mistake; for him they were new-dyed, I suppose" (287). Why the connection? The only mentions of hazel eyes in the book are Adele's and the ascription of them to Jane. Adele is the daughter of an illicit relationship; does Rochester's Freudian slip suggest that Jane's is, too, or that she might be the parent of one? Or that he is her father, illegitimate, and now he will father another level of incest—as in Roman Polanski's *Chinatown*. The issue of illegitimacy might be one of the ways Brontë's doubts about her work would surface. In any case, two orphans, two benefactors, merged. Rochester is to Adele as uncle Reed is to Jane Eyre. Rochester says his mistress says Adele is his daughter, "and perhaps she may be, though I see no proofs of such grim paternity written in her countenance" (176). Is it possible, then, that uncle Reed is the father of his sister's child?

Jane's name deconstructs in a fireworks of possibilities that may clarify this issue of merging and dispersing: ire (48), fire (127), eye, ear, hear, hair, eerie (309), eerie and dreary (53), aerial (288), Aire (133) (Adele's mistaken pronunciation), fairy (135), eyrie (235). Eyre is a bundle of odds and ends, body parts, parts of the universe, feelings, mythology. The deconstruction of the name, which has its own linguistic logic in phonetics and semantics, is important to the general idea that seeing, reading, writing, also have a less narrative, more unconsciously whimsical, perverse, incestuous, boundariless, spontaneous, impulsive side. We make a neat distinction of two axes of reading—between diachronic (history/narrative/chronology/surface structure syntax)) and synchronic (cross-sectional/time, semantic network, deep structure syntax). But there is another distinction, between the "chronos" of both axes and the absence of "chronos," achronic—a less rational axis in the usual sense of that word—perhaps it is a right brain affair. And in this realm Jane Eyre is Jane Reed Eyre is aunt Reed is Bessie is Mrs. Fairfax is Miss Temple is Helen Burns is Bertha Mason is Celine Varens (Rochester's mistress), is Rochester, and so on. I am who I see, who I read, what my eyes read in those of others, and finally in my own as well. This seems to be part of Brontë's existential understanding—one is autonomous, different, individual, but in no way simply discrete and utterly separate. The terrific fear that Defoe's hero manifests—being merged, swallowed—though threatening in Brontë's work is also cultivated, idealized, and mocked.

6

Syntax
and
Sexuality
in
Virginia
Woolf's
To
the
Lighthouse

"some deep, some
buried, some quite
speechless feelings" (123)
"It was one's body feeling,
not one's mind" (265)

In Woolf's work the bodily focus is genital, gendered, engendering. Brontë's focus on the eyes/seeing and Defoe's on eating/food are something like statistical facts about the linguistic surface of those texts—nouns and verbs relating to the focus form the densest clusters, just as cities would be seen to have the densest clusters of lights, roadways, housing, and pollution. In Woolf's work, the focus on the genital—sexual, endangered, procreative, mysterious—is more elusive and protean; there are no overt genital references. But there is a semantic cluster focusing on procreation—barren, sterile, fertile, birth, empty, fecundity. Likewise, there is a cluster of "male" movements—protrude, intrude, pierce, break in, plunged into—and of "female" structures and movements—middle, center, sealed, concealed, locked up within, secret, vise, dome, wedge-shaped, cleavage, circle of life, embraced, surround. The semantic networks are complemented by a redundant syntactic image/structure—something in the middle of something else—whose syntactic action seems to mime the structures and movements indicated by the semantic clusters. The focus on interiorness in Woolf extends to her mode of narration, an interweaving of various interior thoughts and translations of feelings. Finally, the focus on the interior, the vulnerable genital, is a matter with some biographical relatedness.

Syntax

In the opening two-sentence paragraph of Virginia Woolf's *To the Lighthouse* (1955 [1927]), we find a rhetorical pattern of syntax which initiates a repeated structural motif. The organizing pattern of this paragraph is found in other guises throughout the novel, for example, in the three-part format both of Lily Briscoe's painting and of the novel itself. Moreover, the pattern has roots in Woolf's general way of perceiving and in several particular traumatic experiences, both of which she describes in her autobiographical writings. The pattern gives the novel its striking aesthetic cohesiveness. Equally important, it carries a series of "statements" about male and female behavior and relationships. Thus the formal pattern we will examine transforms personal experience, elaborates the overt concerns of the novel, and serves to articulate though not necessarily to resolve conflict. The pattern encodes two basic messages: the male intrudes and destroys, and the female intervenes and harmonizes. These messages are no secret to the reader; we recognize that issues of maleness and femaleness are of thematic concern and importance in the novel. What has amazed me as a reader is how deeply embedded the messages are—indeed, that these issues are somehow replicated syntactically. The novel "talks" about men and women (to marry, to have children, to be without children, to take care of parents, to have a sense of what is right for men and women to do, think, say, and so on). At the same time that it "talks" about such matters, it "does" something—it structures an environment for experimenting with emotion. The following analysis will explore the various conflicts, anxieties, and wishes these "facts" give rise to.

Abstractly, the pattern concerns SOMETHING IN THE MIDDLE OF SOMETHING ELSE, schematically: [A [B] A]. At issue are the possible relationships of the middle to the frame. Given the many variations this thematic motif can create, it is best to look at the first concrete example in the text, its opening statement by Mrs. Ramsay: "'Yes, of course, if it's fine tomorrow,' said Mrs. Ramsay. 'But you'll have to get up with the lark,' she added" (9). It may take the reader several pages and perhaps a rereading to grasp the import of Mrs. Ramsay's remarks. Reference is being made to something that may or may not take place tomorrow, depending on the weather; if it does take place, it will require getting up early. We might put the remarks in the context of the title and speculate that the reference is to a trip — to the lighthouse. This hypothesis gains some footing in the next sentence with its reference to "expedition." If we are busy trying to construe the reference or preoccupied with puzzlement, we might miss out on the other dimension of meaning embedded in the syntax of Mrs. Ramsay's statements. The structure of the sentence is not linear and static; it is a dynamic linguistic action that loops around its central clause in a manner similar to Mrs. Ramsay's knitting. This linguistic action, in any case, is a key to one facet of Mrs. Ramsay's interpersonal interactions.

The statement begins with a strong affirmative — " 'Yes, of course.' " A quick turn of events occurs in the phrase that follows — " 'if it's fine tomorrow.' " The conditional introduces the potential negation of whatever has just been affirmed. The final move of Mrs. Ramsay's speech is a remark that is "added" — " 'But you'll have to get up with the lark.' " That the narrator characterizes this portion of Mrs. Ramsay's utterance as "added" indicates that Mrs. Ramsay, consciously or not, felt something was not just right. The importance of the new portion of her sentence is that it returns our attention to the original affirmation and directs us away from the potential negative. In all, Mrs. Ramsay succeeds in embedding a potential negative inside a positive frame.

In this particular case, the middle of the structure, a conditional clause, very concretely represents a male intrusiveness from which Mrs. Ramsay wishes to protect her son James. Mr. Ramsay, that is, insists not only that " 'it won't be fine' " (10) but that his children must confront such " 'facts' " directly. Mrs. Ramsay softens Mr. Ramsay's "fact" or "truth" first by making it conditional and then by embedding it in an affirmative frame. The argument that ensues between Mr. and Mrs. Ramsay is not so much about the weather or about the truth as it is about male and female modes of presenting the truth and how children assimilate truth. Although Mrs. Ramsay has ambivalent feelings about her husband, at this moment she is angry: "To pursue truth with such astonishing lack of consideration for other people's feelings, to rend the thin veils of civilisation so wantonly, so brutally, was to her so horrible an outrage . . . there was nothing to be said" (51). For Mrs. Ramsay, civilization is tenuously constituted of feelings; she is displeased by her husband's violation of this fragile system.

Let me offer two more images of Mr. Ramsay's intrusive nature. First, the narrator, looking through James's eyes, describes him as "lean as a knife, narrow as the blade of one, grinning sarcastically" (10). And second, in a silent interaction between Mr. and Mrs. Ramsay, his consumption of sympathy from her is described thus: "into this delicious fecundity, this fountain and spray of life, the fatal sterility of the male plunged itself, like a beak of brass, barren and bare" (58). When we read back the gist of these images—their prepositional and verbal direction—to the original sentence under consideration, the male intrusiveness of its middle clause resonates more completely. The male is consistently depicted as entering a space ("plunged" "into") only to "rend" it; whereas, the female is capable of enveloping this male negativity and protecting others from it. The opening sentence can be read as a symbolically sexual interaction—male entering female—much like the image above of the "beak" that "plunged" "into . . . life." Mrs. Ramsay absorbs the thrust of Mr. Ramsay, which is partly aimed at the son, and thus allows James to keep his anger to a wish for he "would have gashed a hole in his father's breast and killed him" (10). In other words, Mrs. Ramsay comes between father and son to prevent oedipal mayhem from surfacing any more than it is. Thus, in the material examined so far, the middle emerges as a significant space. We see it in syntax, images, and mis-en-scène: Mrs. Ramsay embeds a potential negative in a speech act and thereby acts to mediate (to be a positive center) between father and son; both Mrs. Ramsay and her son perceive the father as having a negative, damaging center; and James wishes he could destroy his father's negative center with one of his own. Given these examples of the basic pattern, we can go on to examine the variations it develops.

Mrs. Ramsay: The Emotional Center

Although Lily Briscoe is in some respects the heroine of the novel, Mrs. Ramsay is its emotional center. As we have seen, she can wrap the negative (male) in her own positive frame, and she can enter the middle to prevent the frame from exploding. In addition, she brings people together and creates a unity, however tenuous. Because of her warm center, others seek her out—Lily, in particular, expresses a desire for a symbiotic union with her, but Lily is not alone. Mrs. Ramsay also has a more private center to which she periodically withdraws, and she has a wish for gratification that mirrors her own way of giving. We can speak of Mrs. Ramsay as a "phallic woman" in that she not only gives and absorbs, but she also moves directly between others. As we look at Mrs. Ramsay's perceptions and actions, and particularly the language and images associated with her, these ascriptions will be refined.

Mrs. Ramsay's ability to contain negativity and intervene in the service of unity appears in a scene in the children's room. Mrs. Ramsay goes to the children's room after dinner to check on them; she finds them still awake: Cam and James are quarreling about a skull hung on the wall. The children are in a bind because the skull casts a shadow that frightens Cam and prevents her from going to sleep, but James refuses to sleep if the skull is removed. "'Well then,' said Mrs. Ramsay, 'we will cover it up'"(172). This is the perfect solution because the skull remains hung but no longer casts a frightening shadow. The skull has come between James and Cam; Mrs. Ramsay mediates the dispute and embeds the negative. The gesture is completed when Mrs. Ramsay, unable to locate something with which to cover the skull, "quickly took her own shawl off and wound it round the skull, round and round and round." The structure of the image of the shawl-covered skull is precisely that of the opening utterance of Mrs. Ramsay's—[A [B] A], [yes [if] but]. In that first example, the negative is wrapped with reassurance or distraction; here she wraps the negative up with the source of her own comfort—the shawl. We see from this example that the middle is also associated with death (in addition to intrusion). It is striking that the skull is structurally associated with male intrusion—Cam feels it "branching at her all over the room." The parallel form of the opening utterance and this scene in the children's room thus makes an equation between Mr. Ramsay's negativity and death.

The basic pattern is also replicated in the mise-en-scène—that is, in the imagined scene Mrs. Ramsay physically comes between the two children, as she earlier comes between James and Mr. Ramsay, and mediates. In contradistinction to male intrusiveness, we have female intervention; Mrs. Ramsay promotes cooperation, Mr. Ramsay, divisiveness. The imagery associated with Mr. Ramsay would be called phallic—the "beak of brass," for example—and as such we understand its intrusive quality. What are we to call the imagery associated with Mrs. Ramsay? Certainly it must be gender specific. Mrs. Ramsay is associated with such images as these: she is seen "holding her black parasol very erect" (19) or just "erect" (25). She herself is often seen in the same configuration: the "torch of her beauty; she carried it erect into any room that she entered" (64). As she is giving emotional solace to Mr. Ramsay, we get a picture of her "flashing her needles, confident, upright," and of James "standing between her knees, very stiff" (59). Or we see Mrs. Ramsay in the face of Mr. Ramsay's "demanding sympathy" (58): she "seemed to raise herself . . . and to pour erect into the air a rain of energy, a column of spray." And "this delicious fecundity" is meant "to be drunk and quenched" by Mr. Ramsay. Once he is "filled," he becomes "like a child who drops off satisfied" (60). Mrs. Ramsay is associated with images that have been associated with the phallus (erect, upright, standing very stiff), but that association does not seem entirely appropriate in a novel by Virginia Woolf. Organs other than the phallus—clitoris and breast—also become erect and stiff; and the breast, as well, can "pour erect into the air a rain of energy, a column of spray . . . a delicious fecundity." One power, then, of Mrs. Ramsay is that of the breast—it is the breast which intercedes, mediates, soothes warring factions.

There is yet another facet to Mrs. Ramsay's powers—her genital center. In the case of her statement to James and in her wrapping up the skull, we see her as actively harmonizing an interpersonal situation by negating a negation. She is the positive middle (breast) entering a negative interpersonal situation, and she engages the negative middle by surrounding it. In the situation with Mr. Ramsay, she is seen as a center of sustenance, a "delicious fecundity." In connection with this, she also has a creative center, a womb, and others desire to be in a symbiotic relation with her in this respect.[1] Mr. Ramsay wants "to be taken within the circle of life, warmed and soothed"; he wants to be "in the heart of life" (59). Lily Briscoe's symbiotic wish is even deeper or perhaps more powerfully regressed: Sitting "on the floor with her arms around Mrs. Ramsay's knees . . .

> she imagined how *in the chambers* of the mind and heart of the woman who was, physically, touching her, were stood, like . . . *treasures* . . . tablets bearing sacred inscriptions, which . . . would teach one everything. . . . What art was there, known to love or cunning, by which one *pressed through into those secret chambers?* What device for becoming, like waters poured into one jar, *inextricably the same, one with the object one adored* . . . it was not knowledge but *unity* she desired . . . *intimacy* itself. (79, my emphasis)

Lily sees people as being "sealed," and one comes to know them "only like a bee, drawn to some sweetness . . . one haunted the dome shaped hive" (80). Sadly for Lily, "Mrs. Ramsay would never know the reason of that pressure" and thus, "nothing happened. Nothing. Nothing." When we examine Lily, we will see how she resolves her frustrated wish to be "inextricably the same." For the time being, it is enough to see that Mrs. Ramsay is a center to which others are drawn—for nurturance, sustenance, for "the dome," "the fountain,"—with "one wanting this, another that" (51).

Mrs. Ramsay expects and solicits such responses—"they came to her, naturally, since she was a woman" (51), and she boasts of her "capacity to surround and protect" (60). Nevertheless, giving depletes her and she needs to withdraw to restore herself. Thus the "rapture of successful creation" she experiences in relation to giving to Mr. Ramsay brings her to "fold herself together . . . the whole fabric fell in exhaustion upon itself" and she feels "exhausted in body" (60–61). The images suggest an implosion—giving creates a vacuum that then collapses the structure. Although she feels a "rapture," it is one-sided; she gets only what she gives. Moreover, her "successful creation" makes her feel guilty. More technically, the pride she takes in her aggressive mothering turns on her, and she takes on a narcissistic defense of self-abnegation.[2] In light of Mr. Ramsay's infantilization, she says "she did not like even for a second, to feel finer than her husband"; or again, "he was infinitely the more important, and what she gave to the world, in comparison . . . negligible": she "feels herself convicted of unworthiness" (62). One suspects that her self-accusations amount to an anger turned inward. She doubly protects Mr. Ramsay—once from his own despair by giving to him and opening herself for him, and once again from the anger she feels at the lack of reciprocity. In the end, the best she can do to express her anger is to withhold something he wants: he "wanted the thing she always found it so difficult to give him; wanted her to tell him that she loved him. And, that, no, she could not do" (184). The most she can win is an empty victory—"she had triumphed again. She had not said it; yet he knew" (186).

Mrs. Ramsay's need to withdraw is grounded in her feeling of receiving too much without getting enough. Thus she "often felt she was nothing but a sponge sopped full of human emotion" (51), and yet "there was scarcely a shell of herself left for her to know herself by; all was so lavished and spent" (60). In her withdrawn state, Mrs. Ramsay can indulge in a narcissistic fantasy of freedom and can obtain a disembodied sexual satisfaction. She first of all feels "relief" when she is alone: "All the being and the doing, expansive, glittering, vocal, evaporated; and one shrunk, with a sense of solemnity, to being oneself, a *wedge-shaped core of darkness*, something invisible to others" (95, my emphasis). In this state, the "self having shed its attachments," she is "free," and "the range of her experience seemed limitless." She "could go anywhere," "losing personality," "things came together," there is a "summoning together." Thus reducing herself to a "wedge" or "core of darkness," she is able to reintegrate. The imagery here suggests that while Mrs. Ramsay gives out and takes in from her center, there is a still deeper center—the one Lily seems to know and long for—which she reserves for herself and finds "this rest, this peace, this eternity." Moreover, in her meditative state she experiences an orgasmic pleasure of a disembodied or narcissistic sort—her center is deeply touched by what she perceives as a reflection of her own self.

Her experience begins with the forepleasure of watching "that stroke of the Lighthouse, the long steady stroke, the last of the three, which was her stroke" (96). She feels an "irrational tenderness" (97) toward the lighthouse beam; there arises in her mind the image of "a bride to meet her lover" (96). Yet she explicitly identifies herself with the lighthouse. The "third stroke" "seemed to her like her own eyes meeting her own eyes, searching as she alone could search into her mind and her heart. . . . She praised herself in praising the light, without vanity, for she was stern, she was searching, she was beautiful like that light" (97). The self-reflecting penetration leads her to a deeper pleasure; she feels "as if it were stroking with its silver fingers some sealed vessel in her brain whose bursting would flood her with delight. . . . And the ecstasy burst in her eyes and waves of pure delight raced over the floor of her mind and she felt, It is enough! It is enough!" (99–100). Intense and significant as her withdrawal is, it is short-lived. Mr. Ramsay is waiting for her; he feels her "distant, and he could not reach her." She senses his presence — "he wished, she knew, to protect her" — and so she goes off to him, to feed his ego.

Mr. Ramsay is not the only one whom Mrs. Ramsay feeds. Indeed, the culmination of the day represented in the novel's first chapter is the *boeuf en daube* dinner to which Mrs. Ramsay gathers her family and guests. It is an important event for Mrs. Ramsay because she acts as a center of social cohesion as well as of emotional and nutritional giving. One facet of this role as social mediator comes out in a form that Lily refers to as "this mania of hers for marriage" (261). For example, we see Mrs. Ramsay looking at Lily and Mr. Bankes and having the "admirable idea" that they "should marry" (42). Or she thinks "Minta must, they all must marry" because "an unmarried woman has missed the best of life" (77). Last is the forthcoming marriage of Paul Rayley and Minta Doyle, which Mrs. Ramsay helped to organize; as Paul thinks to himself when the engagement is certain, he will tell Mrs. Ramsay right off "because he felt somehow that she was the person who had made him do it" (119).

What is the mania about? There is a hint given when Paul, arriving almost too late for dinner, explains why he and Minta were delayed; he begins the explanation with "we" — "'We' — that was enough," thinks Mrs. Ramsay (150). The pronominal transformation signifies a new symbiosis (lovers), which will yield in turn yet more such relations (mother-child). Mrs. Ramsay thinks to herself, "what could be more serious than the love of man for woman . . . bearing in its bosom the seeds of death" (151). On the one hand Mrs. Ramsay's mania is a narcissistic wish that others act as she has. But on the other hand, she believes in the value of people trying to be together. Mrs. Ramsay's thoughts on this matter are not simple-minded. She is well aware "of the inadequacy of human relationships. . . . The most perfect was flawed" (62), and she knows this through her ambivalent feelings toward Mr. Ramsay. Moreover, she recognizes in the romantic aura around Paul and Minta that they are engaged in a narcissistic "illusion" (151), as indeed all lovers are. It is perhaps because death is so omnipresent that love—in marriage and with children—is necessary; love surrounds death though it cannot surmount it.

Mrs. Ramsay's motives for bringing people together are complex—selfish and altruistic. She wants to exercise her power as a woman to feed others, to make them converge, to get them outside of their abstract mind-sets—their preoccupations, their books, and their work—if only to revitalize their selves; and she wants to be admired and partaken of. By themselves, Mrs. Ramsay "felt, as a fact without hostility, the sterility of men" (126); they "lacked something" (129). And the men, in part, verify this—one feels he must prove he is not "just a dry prig" (131), and another "felt rigid and barren" (135) in her presence. Only by merging can such feelings be dissipated, but there is great resistance, which Mrs. Ramsay contends with and for a time succeeds in dispelling. Before dinner there are many private selves—"all those scattered about . . . on perches of their own" who must "assemble" (125). Once they are physically together, there remains emotional distance to contend with: "Nothing seemed to have merged. They all sat separate. And the whole effect of merging and flowing and creating rested on her" (126). Her sense is verified particularly by Bankes and Tansley. The former "preferred dining alone" (135) so as to be "free to work"; he "wished only to be alone." He wonders why "does one take all these pains for the human race to go on" (134). For Tansley the situation "was all in scraps and fragments" (136); "if only he could be alone . . . among his books" (131) for then he might not feel as now so "isolated and lonely" (130).

Gradually Mrs. Ramsay is able to orchestrate some harmonious interactions from her reluctant ensemble. For example, she sends Lily a "glance" loaded with meaning to say "in effect . . . 'I am drowning . . . say something nice'" to Tansley or "'life will run upon the rocks'" (138)—and Lily does so. Or, when she sees Lily is "out of things" she says something and "she drew her in" (156). She applies some pressure to Mr. Ramsay, who also responds; he, who had previously excluded Augustus Carmichael, "had drawn him in" so as "to make it all right" again (165). Lily thinks to herself that Mrs. Ramsay has "put a spell on them" (152). Once things begin to merge and flow "all her beauty opened up again" (152). Knowing full well that "this cannot last" in the short run, Mrs. Ramsay pauses to look "at them all eating" and feels "she had reached security. . . . An element of joy . . . filled every nerve of her body fully and sweetly" (157). The moment "partook . . . of eternity"; she feels "there is a coherence in things, a stability . . . something immune from change" in spite of the "flowing, the fleeting." In sum, "of such moments, she thought, the thing is made that endures" (158). Part of her pleasure in this "party round a table" (146) is that "here, inside the room seemed to be order and dry land," whereas outside is more threatening—"things wavered and vanished, waterily." Thus "making a party together in a hollow, on an island," they are making "common cause against the fluidity out there" (147). Her orchestration pleases her; she has created an enduring moment in the middle of eternal flux.

Much of Mrs. Ramsay's role is summarized by "a yellow and purple dish of fruit" appropriately placed "in the middle" of the table, which, to Mrs. Ramsay, is a "trophy" associated with Neptune and Bacchus. It was, she thinks,

> like a world in which one could take one's staff and climb hills . . . and go
> down into valleys, and to her pleasure (for it brought them into sympathy
> momentarily) she saw that Augustus too feasted his eyes on the same plate
> of fruit, plunged in, broke off a bloom. . . . That was his way of looking,
> different from hers. But *looking together united them.* (146, my emphasis)

Asked, toward the end of the meal, if she wants a pear, she says no. "Indeed she had been keeping guard over the dish of fruit (without realising it) jealously, hoping nobody would touch it." Although it is pleasurable to look at it and share it with Carmichael, touching it is another matter:

> Her eyes had been going in and out among the curves and shadows of the
> fruit, among the rich purple of the lowland grapes, then over the horny
> ridge of the shell, putting a yellow against a purple, a curved shape against
> a round shape, without knowing why she did it, or why, every time she did
> it, she felt more serene; until, oh, what a pity that they should do it—a
> hand reached out, took a pear, and spoilt the whole thing. (164)

The particular twinge Mrs. Ramsay feels about the end of the fruit bowl's integrity is similar to her feeling at the end of the party around the table. As she leaves with Minta, she takes "one last look" at the room—"already the past." As Lily observes from within the room which Mrs. Ramsay has just left, "And directly she went a sort of disintegration set in; they wavered about, went different ways" (168). The fruit bowl, in any case, seems like a mirror for Mrs. Ramsay and her efforts. It is in the center—as the table is in the center of the room and the room in the center of an outer darkness—it draws others into it, and this drawing together unites them, "brought them into sympathy momentarily." Moreover, the bowl has its own center, which holds a sensuous landscape one can plunge into or climb up and down in, or feast on. The landscape in the bowl has its own harmony, the interfacing of colors and shapes. And last, like all composed forms, something gets taken away and the form is no longer intact.

To bring some closure to these observations on Mrs. Ramsay, we might review the role that the middle plays in them. The sense of a center emerges in syntax, images, symbols, and mis-en-scène descriptions and interactions. The psychological meaning of the middle varies—it represents the breast, the genitals (female and male), and an existential core. It is a place of nurturance, of security and merging, as well as of potential destruction. That which frames the center often represents antagonistic pairs or a negative surround, but it can also be a positive force—an outer circle that contains and can withstand an interiorized force of destruction. More specifically, Mrs. Ramsay opens herself to others and takes them in; she is a center of great attraction—others desire to feed from her and merge with her. As a result, she sometimes feels filled with others' feelings. She also feeds others from her center and thus sometimes feels empty, but at other times filling others fills her with pleasure. For her men are often empty (barren, sterile) and/or destructive, and she can neutralize them—either fill them or contain them. Alone, she can empty herself of others and become reduced to an inner core; she can take in satisfaction from a benign if disembodied light that reflects her self-image. With others, she promotes merging; she tries to bring harmony or at least neutralize hostility between Cam and Andrew, Paul and Minta, Lily and Tansley, Mr. Ramsay and Mr. Carmichael, Mr. Bankes and Mr. Tansley, herself and Mr. Carmichael. And last, she brings cohesion to the group by bringing all the separate individuals to a central place to feed them in body and spirit. And thus between a beginning time of separateness and fragmentation and a closure of re-disintegration, there is a time of cohesion, which, though it dissolves in the present, becomes a significant, enduring moment and so stands out. Finally, in the space-time of cohesion, there is besides feeding, filling, merging, and flowing, a center of protection, like the lighthouse itself, against the forces of the night.

Mr. Ramsay: The Arid Scimitar

The male role in the novel is more limited, less complex, and generally more negative than the female. The male center—primarily represented by Mr.

Ramsay—intrudes, shatters, explodes, castrates, and sometimes greedily devours. Psychologically, the male is phallic and sadistic and sometimes oral sadistic as well. We have encountered some of these qualities in Mr. Ramsay's interactions with Mrs. Ramsay. The more positive "phallic" powers seem reserved for association with women in such symbolic representations as Mrs. Ramsay's knitting needles, her umbrella, the spurting fountain of her energy and of Lily's, the lighthouse as it reflects Mrs. Ramsay (and to which Mr. Ramsay makes an expedition in homage to her), and Lily's paintbrush. Such configurations are, of course, not necessarily phallic, but rather breast-like or clitoral. Nonetheless, there are some positive qualities to the male's energy—Mr. Ramsay's mind has penetrated some important problems; as Bankes says, Ramsay has "made a definite contribution to philosophy" (39). And Ramsay is willing to confront a surround of negativity. In all, he is a difficult character because of his contradictions: "so brave . . . in thought" and "so timid in life," at once "venerable and laughable" (70), and one might say, so hard and so soft.

The negative aspects of Mr. Ramsay are felt most keenly by those who are threatened by him—James and Lily. The anger Ramsay evokes in James (10, 58–60, 273–77) is basically oedipal in nature—Ramsay "disturbed the perfect simplicity . . . of his relations with his mother" (58). The images of Mr. Ramsay as he comes between mother and son are most unbecoming. He is seen as taking Mrs. Ramsay's energy: "the fatal sterility of the male plunged itself, like a beak of brass, barren and bare" into the "delicious fecundity" of Mrs. Ramsay. Or, "the arid scimitar of the male smote mercilessly, again and again" as her energy is "drunk . . . by the beak of brass" (59). These are images James retains; they return to him a decade later—"the wings spread, and the hard beak tore" (274). James feels something "darkened over him—something arid and sharp descended . . . like a blade, a scimitar smiting . . . that happy world and make it shrivel and fall" (276). Another part of James's anger is from his sense of his father's "cutting off" one's "right to speak" (274). His father, in other words, in addition to having his mother—engulfing her, entering her, severing James's relations with her—is castrating. In retaliation, James not only calls up denigrating images but has a violent fantasy: "had there been an axe handy, or a poker, any weapon that would have gashed a hole in his father's breast and killed him there and then, James would have seized it" (10). The fantasy is a mirror of the aggression that James feels from his father.

Lily also feels threatened by Mr. Ramsay, though her response is to try to withdraw. Her anger is more subdued. She sees Mr. Ramsay as intrusive and voracious—infantile. In a scene in the last section of the novel Lily sets up her canvas, hoping it will act as a "barrier" however "frail" (221). Of Mr. Ramsay she says, "he *permeated*, he prevailed, he *imposed* himself" (my emphasis). He "never gave" and she "would be forced to give" (223); he is "greedy, distraught" (224), with an "insatiable hunger" (226). She feels under immense pressure (228) to give. She wonders if she can't "imitate" the "rhapsody, the self-surrender," the "rapture of sympathy," "the most supreme bliss" that she has seen in other women (224–25). She is virtually engulfed by him—"his demand for sympathy poured and spread itself in pools at her feet," but all she can do is draw "her skirts a little closer" (228). Lily seems to feel she is close to an emotional rape; that Mr. Ramsay is surrounding her, will invade and consume her; and that she cannot respond appropriately to this sexuality or need for mothering. Somewhat later in the section, Lily recalls an incident of some humor which nonetheless brings out similar characteristics of Mr. Ramsay: "How Prue must have blamed herself for the earwig in the milk! How white she had gone when *Mr. Ramsay threw his plate through the window*" (298). Mr. Ramsay becomes fairly infantile, raging at his spoiled milk; he explodes, shatters a window. It is just such underlying rage that Lily must be wary of in her desire to retreat.

Mr. Ramsay is not the only aggressive male; there is Charles Tansley, a protégé of his. At the dinner table he sits "precisely in the middle" of Lily's view out the window (128). He feels "extremely, even physically uncomfortable" because he wants "a chance of asserting himself" (136). Lily sees him, in her own sarcastic from, "as in an X-ray."

> The ribs and thigh bones of the young man's *desire to impress* himself, lying *dark in the midst of his flesh* . . . his burning desire to *break into* the conversation . . . why should I help him relieve himself?
>
> There is a code of behavior . . . it behooves the woman . . . to help the young man . . . expose and relieve the thigh bones, the ribs, of his vanity, of his urgent desire to assert himself. (137, my emphasis)

We learn something from Lily's method of dealing with anger, as well as of her perception of male aggression. She is, rightly, angry at Tansley's oppressive male consciousness as it surfaces in his judgment that "women can't paint, women can't write," for it annihilates her. Lily is angry at the contradiction: the man needs me but does not want to recognize my self. Tansley denies women a sum of generic intelligence, just as Mr. Ramsay does—"the folly of women's minds enraged him" (50). If the female is so worthless, the male who absolutely craves her cannot be much better. In any case, Lily's anger is expressed in her sarcasm and her resistance to behave according to the code—she will withhold and frustrate. Here she is not denying him the breast, as she does Mr. Ramsay, but her whole body as a stage for him to perform on. At the silent request of Mrs. Ramsay, Lily gives in and says the right thing. Mr. Tansley gets to relieve himself: "Mr. Tansley raised a hammer: swung it high in the air . . . he could not smite that butterfly with such an instrument. . . . He could almost pity these mild cultivated people, who would be blown sky high . . . one of these days by the gunpowder that was in him" (138). Mr. Tansley's desire to "expose" himself, to "break into" the conversation, and to see people "blown sky high" by his forcefulness points to his intellectual exhibitionism and aggression; his mind is phallic and sadistic. But because he is a peripheral character, a voice of the male chorus, he is less threatening than Ramsay.

Although Ramsay is a leader, he will not accomplish as much as he had wanted to in his life: "His own little light would shine, not very brightly, for a year or two, and would then be merged in some bigger light" (56). As his contribution to philosophy is "merged" into others, so his life will merge into darkness. Ramsay looks out to sea and thinks; he has

> come out thus on a spit of land which the *sea is slowly eating away*, and there to stand, like a desolate sea-bird, alone. It was his power, his gift, suddenly to shed all superfluities, *to shrink and diminish* so that he looked barer and sparer, even physically, yet lost none of his intensity of mind, and so to stand on his little ledge facing the dark of human ignorance, how we know nothing and the sea eats away the ground. (68, my emphasis)

Mr. Ramsay here reduces himself and thereby gives us a male parallel to Mrs. Ramsay's dissolution to a wedge of darkness. Instead of becoming a core of darkness stroked by the beam of the lighthouse, he sheds his body, "to shrink and diminish," and becomes focused as an "intensity of mind" which faces "the dark." The image recalls the one above—"eyes fixed . . . to pierce the darkness." Putting the Ramsays' separate visions together, we see a sexual relation—she is the darkness he penetrates, he is the light to which the sealed vessel of her mind opens. The darkness is comfort, physical and psychological, for Ramsay. He looks toward it without gloom—he longs to merge with it. Thus he sees himself like the land which "the sea is slowly eating away." And, as above, he sees his work "merged in some bigger light." Mrs. Ramsay is somewhat puzzled by his negative tropism—"how strange it was that being convinced . . . of all sorts of horrors seemed not to depress him, but to cheer him" (107). For Mr. Ramsay the negative center, the en- gulfing sea/darkness/womb/death is a source of physical pleasure and men- tal solace. We see him repeatedly attempting to achieve a merged state—"to be taken within the circle of life, warmed and soothed" (59). He knows, of course, that "the whole of life did not consist in going to bed with a woman" (181), but it certainly is a part. In a different way, he achieves a symbiotic state in the process of his work—he is "hung round with solitude," "wrapped up," and "in a dream." He is wrapped up in "himself" in some sense, but in him- self is a large store of external information, the knowing of others. Death, then, is simply the most radical form of merging, and it happens to be an ul- timate fact from which there is no escape. What gives Ramsay particular "cheer" about death is his very logical sense that since nothing lasts—not Shakespeare, not the land itself—there is therefore no need to be unsettled by the failure to achieve a certain goal, however important it is to try.

At the same time that Mr. Ramsay is facing the sea, Mrs. Ramsay is look- ing at him; she sees him "as a stake driven into the bed of a channel upon which the gulls perch and the waves beat inspires in merry boat-loads a feel- ing of gratitude for the duty it is taking upon itself of marking the channel out there in the floods alone" (69). He is not quite a lighthouse, but he is im- portant nonetheless. It is significant that Mrs. Ramsay is willing to grant Mr. Ramsay some positive status for his maleness because she often views men as castrated and impotent—as "dried up" or "sterile" or "missing some- thing." She attributes other positive qualities to the "admirable fabric of the masculine intelligence," which is "like iron girders . . . upholding the world"—indeed, "she let it uphold her and sustain her." She can "trust her- self" to the grid "which ran up and down, crossed this way and that" (159). The image that emerges is of being held by a father—and she does compare the situation with being "a child." The male knits things of a different order than those Mrs. Ramsay knits, but they also provide comfort. Finally, to fol- low up on the positive male center, there is Mr. Ramsay's daughter's recol- lections of him. Cam recalls "the old gentlemen in the study" and how "she strayed in from the garden" to watch and listen to them. She feels that "one could let whatever one thought expand here like a leaf in water; and if it did well here, among the gentlemen . . . it was right." In specific regard to her father, she thinks he is "not vain, nor a tyrant, and did not wish to make you pity him." In fact, "if he saw she was there, reading a book, he would ask her, as gently as any one could, Was there nothing he could give her?" (282). In other words, in the center of the male domain, the study, there is nurturance, too, and things can grow.

Lily's Painting: The Moment Made Permanent

Lily's painting—as both active process and object—is one of the central thematic motifs in the novel. The painting, as form, recapitulates the basic pattern—a center-frame tension—and resolves, in some respects, male-female conflicts. As a work of art, the painting is also representative of the novel itself; it is a metaconstruct, a self-referential monologue about the process of transforming and sublimating. The resolution the painting offers involves bringing male and female together—amalgamating Mr. and Mrs. Ramsay—into what can be called an abstracted androgyny. The process of making the painting demonstrates the personal work involved in overcoming negativity from others and from within. In all, the painting shows us how Lily changes those psychological defenses that prevent relationships from becoming creative.[3] What Lily is unable to achieve in contact with direct experience, she is able to realize on a different level of experience—the aesthetic.

The first time we get a sense of the overall structure of Lily's painting occurs when she shares the unfinished canvas with Mr. Bankes. She is uncertain about how to proceed; the problem is "how to connect this mass on the right hand with that on the left." As she thinks of tentative solutions, she worries—there is "the danger . . . that the unity of the whole might be broken" (83). A solution to the structural problem of the painting comes to Lily as she simultaneously wrestles with two issues while at the dinner table with the Ramsays and their guests. She is trying to separate her personal response from her social responsibilities in regard to her interactions with Tansley; and on another level of consciousness, she is seeking a solution to the aesthetic problem her painting poses. "I must move the tree to the middle; that matters—nothing else" (130). She succeeds in being socially correct with Tansley, and "then her eye caught the salt cellar, which she placed there to remind her . . . she would move the tree further toward the middle" (140). Lily's resolve is stated one more time: "For at any rate, she said to herself, catching sight of the salt cellar on the pattern, she need not marry . . . she was saved from that dilution. She would move the tree rather more to the middle" (154).

Her solution is to remove herself from the realm of social forms or to comply with the rules of day-to-day behavior but no more and to concentrate instead on aesthetic ones—to transform the former into the latter. Her resolve in the aesthetic realm is to place a symbolic object, a tree, in the middle of two masses and thereby maintain "the unity of the whole." Her aesthetic problem, though as abstract as the work Mr. Ramsay does, has a solution similar to the one used by Mrs. Ramsay—enter the middle and harmonize the rest by so doing. The psychological step she takes to accomplish this solution is by "subduing all her impressions as a woman to something more general" (82). That is, she splits from the physical world. As we will see, however, the aesthetic world becomes imbued with sexuality.

On her return to the Ramsays' summer house after a decade's absence, Lily revives her idea of the painting she "solved" but never finished. As she recalls the aesthetic problems, her psychological and physical activity—her aesthetic meditation—is interrupted against her will by Mr. Ramsay himself and by her memories of and feelings about Mrs. Ramsay, now dead. Although she feels that "any interruption would break the frail shape she was building" (220), it is actually only by facing the interruption that she can complete her work. She fears the intrusions, tries to defend herself against them, but she needs them. She must open herself to these others before she can see what is before her—her "white and uncompromising" canvas (233), her self—and give it shape and meaning. On one level, the two masses of the painting are Mr. and Mrs. Ramsay, and they are finally connected by a stroke down the middle—Lily herself, her consciousness, her vision. Lily thus "gets" both of them, but only at a distance—of time (Mrs. Ramsay) or of space (Mr. Ramsay).

Even before she begins work, she is conscious of and anxious about Mr. Ramsay's presence and Mrs. Ramsay's absence. Without Mrs. Ramsay she feels "cut off," as if she "had no attachments here, she felt, no relations with it . . . as if the link that usually bound things together had been cut" (218–19). On the other hand, there is Mr. Ramsay, with his "imperious need" and his "penetrating" gaze (219). She tries to protect herself against him by using her canvas as a "barrier" to "ward off" Mr. Ramsay (223). She also feels "anger rising in her" against Mr. Ramsay because "he permeated, he prevailed, he imposed himself," and against Mrs. Ramsay because "Giving, giving, giving, she had died" (223). Lily seems to be at a double disadvantage—the central "link" is missing, the one who can make "of the moment something permanent" and can find "in the midst of chaos there was shape" (241). And the intrusive male—"like a lion seeking whom he could devour" (233)—is before her. The positive center is gone, the negative one is present—and her own canvas is blank.

Lily is angry because she seems to think that she is meant to give Mr. Ramsay sympathy; she resists this demand, as she had resisted Tansley: "She could say nothing" (227). In a sense she is mirroring what she feels is his negation of her. There is a break in the tense, silent struggle between them: "he noticed that his boot-laces were untied. Remarkable boots they were too, Lily thought . . . 'What beautiful boots,' she exclaimed" (228–29). She feels her comment, though genuine, is off the mark, but Mr. Ramsay responds very positively. He has strong feelings about the quality of his boots and enjoys sharing these feelings. At this point, the interaction is virtually over; Mr. Ramsay is ready to depart with Cam and James for the lighthouse. Lily now seems to understand something, and she thinks of "her callousness . . . she felt her eyes swell and tingle with tears . . . she felt a sudden emptiness; a frustration. Her feelings had come too late; there it was ready; but he no longer needed it" (230–31). When she begins to paint again, she is "driven by the discomfort of the sympathy which she held undischarged" (241), and "the sympathy she had not given him weighed her down" (254). In this episode, Lily's feelings become a center: she is filled with anger, then empty, and then filled with sympathetic tears.

What allows Lily to resolve some of her feelings about Mr. Ramsay is her identification with him—as someone who works hard, as someone who abstracts, and as someone who loved Mrs. Ramsay. She comes to realize that Mr. Ramsay, like herself, has doubts about the value of his work. She appreciates what he does; it was

> something visionary, austere; something bare, hard, not ornamental . . .
> Mr. Ramsay kept always his eyes fixed upon it, never allowed himself to
> be distracted or deluded, until his face became worn too and ascetic and
> partook of this unornamented beauty which so deeply impressed her . . .
> he must have had his doubts . . . whether it was worth the time . . . whether
> he was able after all to find it. (233)

Having reached this moment of understanding, Lily will follow Ramsay's progress to the lighthouse as she works on her painting; and she will complete her work simultaneous to his arrival there, thus bringing closure to her identification with him. Lily also sympathizes with Mr. Ramsay in advance of getting in touch with her own grief for Mrs. Ramsay, whose loss she has not completely assimilated. Her initial anger at Mr. Ramsay is a mirror of her own anger for being ungiving and unsympathetic. In a sense she is jealous of his grief, for it openly speaks to his human dependency and his love. When Lily's anger shifts to sympathy, when she sees in Mr. Ramsay what is missing in herself—including his male center, "something bare, hard"—she can turn to reflect on her loss and complete her work.

In describing Mrs. Ramsay and Lily's grief, the images Woolf uses are those of centrality. Mrs. Ramsay is a center who joins others together, and Lily is depicted as being at once empty of feeling and filled with pain. As with Mr. Ramsay, so with Mrs. Ramsay, Lily feels points of identification. Mrs. Ramsay "brought together this and that and then this . . . like a work of art" (239–40). Moreover, she is capable of "making of the moment something permanent (as in another sphere Lily herself tried to make of the moment something permanent). . . . *In the midst of chaos there was shape* . . . 'Mrs. Ramsay! Mrs. Ramsay!' she repeated. She owed it all to her" (241, my emphasis).

Mrs. Ramsay is a center of cohesion; she brings order "in the midst of chaos." As Lily continues to paint, scenes with Mrs. Ramsay come to her mind, and she critically analyzes her, particularly her emphasis on marriage. But as she continues in that vein, she realizes that she finds it hard to "express that emptiness" she finally feels in Mrs. Ramsay's absence. As she says,

> To want and not to have, went *all up her body a hardness, a hollowness*, a strain . . . that wrung the heart, and wrung it again and again . . . suddenly she put her hand out and wrung the heart thus. Suddenly, the empty drawing-room steps, the frill of the chair inside, the puppy tumbling on the terrace, the whole wave and whisper of the garden became like curves and arabesques *flourishing round a center of complete emptiness*. (266, my emphasis)

Under the weight of these feelings, Lily's "eyes were full of a hot liquid," and as she cries, she wishes for a miracle — "*the space would fill; those empty flourishes would form into shape* . . . Mrs. Ramsay would return . . . the tears ran down her face" (268; my emphasis). Once the "pain of want, and the bitter anger" decrease, Lily is freed to complete her work. Lily has had to feel the impact of the external emptiness — Mrs. Ramsay's death — on her own internal state; she has had to feel the emptiness there which, once recognized, becomes filled with genuine grief and can be released. The process is much the same as her recognizing the sympathy she has for Mr. Ramsay. In both cases, the release of feelings is akin to birthing something.

In the process of understanding her feelings about her relationship to the Ramsays, Lily comes to fill the "hideously difficult white space" of her canvas (237). Her "clean canvas" (220), which at first "seemed to rebuke her with its cold stare," begins to give "her mind a peace" and then an "emptiness" (234) requisite for her to recall the aesthetic problems she wants to resolve. The canvas reflects her feelings. As to the activity of painting, the movement of her brush on canvas, it seems broadly sexual—male, female, orgasmic, conceiving, and birthing. There is a consciousness that the activity is a sublimation or transform of sexual energy in which Lily "exchanged the fluidity of life for the concentration of painting" and becomes "an unborn soul, a soul reft of body" (237). Her hand "stayed trembling in a painful but exciting ecstasy" as she decides her "first quick decisive stroke" (235). She continues, "so pausing and so flickering, she attained a dancing rhythmical movement," until her strokes *"enclosed . . . a space"* (236). Lily's interaction with the painting reaches an intense pitch in the following:

> For the mass loomed before her; *it protruded;* she felt it *pressing on her eyeballs.* Then, as if some *juice necessary for the lubrication of her faculties* were spontaneously *squirted,* she began precariously dipping . . . moving her brush . . . it had fallen in with some *rhythm which was dictated to her . . .* by what she saw, so that while her *hand quivered with life,* this rhythm was strong enough to bear her along with it on its current. Certainly she was *losing consciousness of outer things . . .* her mind kept throwing up from its depth, scenes, and names, and sayings, and memories and ideas, like *a fountain spurting up over that glaring . . . space.* (237–38, my emphasis)

The canvas seems masculine—it "loomed before her; it protruded"—and feminine—white space to be filled. So Lily also seems both masculine—with her brush in hand and her mind "like a fountain spurting"—and feminine—responding to the protrusion—"as if some juice necessary for the lubrication of her faculties were spontaneously squirted." In addition, the finished painting has both characteristics. Lily completes her work with "a sudden intensity . . . she drew a line there, *in the centre. It was done; it was finished.* Yes, she thought, laying down her brush in extreme fatigue, I have had my vision" (310). The three-part configuration of the painting is overdetermined: it is male and female and oedipal. The line down the center fills the empty, enclosed space and serves to unite the masses on either side of it. Lily unites the mother/female and the father/male through the medium of her own consciousness.

"Time Passes": Some Cleavage of the Dark

The middle section of the novel, "Time Passes," is a major authorial gesture pointing to the ambiguity of the center. This middle space, more lyrical than narrative, depicts both fearful negativity and hopeful rebirth in space-time. As such, "Time Passes" joins the various visions of Mrs. Ramsay, Mr. Ramsay, and Lily, first threatening to shatter the frame with death and darkness, then unifying it with birth and light. On one side of this chapter, night comes to the Ramsays' house; on the other side, ten years later, the dawn comes. Between this frame is the night and the dreams therein. The decade-long night is filled with images of collapsing centers—decay, death, war, and threatening sexuality. The negation is ultimately stayed as we witness a "rusty laborious birth" (210) which salvages the wreckage of time on the Ramsays' space. As much as the trip to the lighthouse, this voyage of time in the center of the novel is the perilous journey. The destruction taking place in the long night threatens to undo all the relationships we have come to know; the redeeming labor that reconstitutes the summer house allows the survivors of the decade to complete their various journeys and understandings.

The opening segment of the middle chapter sets the tone and predicts the whole. Images of darkness abound as all the house lights are "extinguished" save for Mr. Carmichael's—he "kept his candle burning rather longer" (189). There is a dialogue ostensibly between several characters—Bankes, Andrew, Prue, and Lily. But their speeches seem directed as well at the reader. Thus Mr. Bankes says, "we must wait for the future to show," as indeed we will. Andrew says, "It's almost too dark to see," and Prue adds, "One can hardly tell which is the sea and which is the land." These remarks recall the fear of engulfment which both Mr. and Mrs. Ramsay give voice to; they prepare us also for the darkness to follow and the loss of boundaries that takes place upon entering sleep and dreams. Once "'everyone's in'" and "the lamps were all extinguished," the nighttime journey can begin.

The house is presented as a space, "empty" (202) and "deserted" (206) of people. The night engulfs it—in a "flood," a "downpouring of immense darkness"—and intrudes—"full of wind and destruction" (193). Together with other forces of nature the "long night . . . seemed to have triumphed" over the house: "The saucepan had rusted and the mat decayed. Toads had nosed their way in . . . a thistle thrust itself between the tiles in the larder. The swallows nested in the drawing room . . . rafters were laid bare; rats carried off this and that to gnaw behind the wainscots" (207). Woolf compares these forces to the "wanton lust" of whales—"the amorphous bulks of leviathans whose brows are pierced by no light of reason . . . mounted one on top of another" (203). We see this destructive sexuality—"the fertility, the insensibility of nature" (207)—taking over the Ramsays' house and garden: "Poppies sowed themselves among the dahlias . . . giant artichokes towered among the roses; a fringed carnation flowered among the cabbages" (207). The decay reaches a critical point: "One feather, and the house, sinking, falling, would have turned and pitched downwards toward the depths of darkness" (208).

The long symbolic night brings with it more than the decay of house and garden. During the decade several of the Ramsays' die, and there is a war. The deaths of Mrs. Ramsay (194), Prue Ramsay (199), and Andrew Ramsay (201) are announced in bracketed sentences. The brackets make the narrative facts stand out and intrude into the reader's consciousness. The facts themselves make one feel as empty as Mr. Ramsay's arms as he reaches out for Mrs. Ramsay (194). The war is also an intrusion, and Woolf presents it with a violent image of a sunken ship: "There was a purplish stain upon the bland surface of the sea as if something had boiled and bled, invisibly, beneath" (201).

All the negativity in the center of the novel is countered by an old woman, Mrs. McNab, who "tearing the veil of silence" (196) at the house begins to restore it. Although life for her is "one long sorrow and trouble," she has "some incorrigible hope." Woolf depicts this hope as a center of light— through the "cleavage of the dark . . . some channel in the depths of obscurity through which light" issues (197). Through her work she "stayed the corruption and the rot." She "rescued" much of the house and its contents "from the pool of time that was fast closing over them" (209). This is the "rusty laborious birth" that takes place and allows Lily and the Ramsays who remain to return and complete their own particular tasks.

The Overall Pattern: The Male-Female Model

The configuration of a middle and its surround dominates the novel as a pattern, a syntax. I have demonstrated some of the meanings of this pattern by exemplifying the various relationships between the middle and its frame. The ubiquity of the pattern makes it difficult to perceive its complexity. Below, I have reduced the pattern to its primitive configurations so that we can see the pattern of the pattern (Bateson 1972, 128–56). It will not be as successful as the sonnet Mrs. Ramsay is reading and describes as "beautiful and reasonable, clear and complete, the essence sucked out of life and held rounded here" (181), but it moves in that direction. The major variants of the basic pattern are reviewed, in any case, with an eye to interrelating them. When that integration is completed, we can explore some of the significant roots of the pattern in Woolf's autobiographical writing. These writings will confirm and clarify the significance of the pattern and of pattern making, as well as the interpretation of them.

First, I would like to clarify the way meaning has been derived from the pattern. The assumption I have been working with is that the syntax of the pattern, in conjunction with the choice of specific language chosen by the writer, becomes another unit of meaning, that is, the syntax acquires semantic significance. By the phrase "the choice of specific language" I mean that Woolf chose, consciously or not, a set of words with linguistic markers that direct the reader to a concern with centers and middles: for example, prepositions that give directions and locations in, out, into, within, between, and around; verbs that specify actions of moving into and out of, of enveloping, wrapping, engulfing, of invading, intruding, penetrating, damaging, and rending; nouns that name the states of being in the center, core, or middle or of spaces that have centers—canvas, house, body, heart. This specific language has a parallel in syntax that reflects its concern. Thus we find an abstract pattern that is constructed to have a middle and a frame. To derive meaning, we have to watch the relationship between the two sets of relationships: first, we watch the relationship between the elements of the pattern, the frame relative to the middle—call it the syntactic motion—and then we watch the relationship of the language choices to the syntactic motion. Doing this double watching, we can offer interpretations of the abstract pattern. The reading of the pattern given here is that the relationship between the elements of the pattern concerns the relationships between and within male and female, between men and women, between women, within individual men and women. Given the interpersonal and intrapsychic relationships, the interpretation of the relationships offered here is psychological.

The Male Model

The male is almost never seen as a container; indeed, he is often viewed as empty and barren; thus he is not regarded as having seed, being fertile. Most often he is depicted as an invader and consumer. He is rarely seen as allowing someone in or as giving something out. Schematically, we see the male in the following ways:

1. [female [male] female]
2. [father [son] father]
3. [solitude/self/darkness [male] solitude/self/darkness]

The male enters and takes from the female (1); the son desires to gash a hole in the father (2); the male wants to pierce the darkness, to be wrapped in solitude (3). To develop such a model of man is one way to express hostility toward the male; Woolf's anger on this score will be further explored. There are some grudging acknowledgments of the male, though one is likely to feel Woolf undercutting some of this with sarcasm and mock heroics — Mr. Ramsay's polar expedition fantasy, for example. Man does make a "contribution" to civilization, and he does construct structures and networks that function and seem to Mrs. Ramsay at least to be admirable and trustworthy. Mr. Ramsay is capable of giving, so Cam feels. And there is recognition of the aesthetic and value of the male form. Thus Lily praises Mr. Ramsay's boots; she appreciates his "bare, hard" form; and Mrs. Ramsay sees him as a channel marker, a "stake," for which one can feel gratitude.

The basic hostility to the male stems from his destructiveness to the female and thus to the relationship possibilities between male and female and their development. As we will see, the destructiveness of the male has roots in Woolf's experiences of male violation at a young age. The message that seems to be here is something like this: "I feel empty in part because the male has violated/stolen/damaged my insides;4 I will say he is empty, barren, and sterile as a way of expressing my anger at his negation of me." The violation that leads to Woolf's anger is one of the greatest sources of personal contamination she experienced.

The Female Model

The female, in contrast, is virtually always a positive force; she is both frame and center. She opens to others, gives out to others, embraces, internalizes, and withstands negativity, and is a powerful centripetal force. The female pattern has one negative variation in association with it — when the outside frame is depicted as engulfing darkness or as the encroaching sea. And yet to Mr. Ramsay, even this is not seen as hostile so much as a final merging with the female force. By way of demonstrating the positive force of Mrs. Ramsay, we might recall the movement of the pattern as it is played out in the children's room. Schematically, the movement looks thus:

1 [Cam [death/skull] James]
2 [Cam [Mrs. Ramsay] James]
3 [Mrs. Ramsay/shawl [skull] Mrs. Ramsay/shawl]
4 [Mrs. Ramsay/sleep [Cam and James] Mrs. Ramsay/sleep]

The figure of death creates contention between the children, preventing them from being enveloped by sleep; Mrs. Ramsay replaces the negative figure and wraps it up and thereby brings harmony and allows the children to sleep. Or recall the opening sentence and the situation in which the configurations are embedded:

[James—	[Mrs. Ramsay]	Mr. Ramsay—
gash a hole		accuracy]
yes/positive	if/softened negative	but/positive

The opening sentence characterizes the conflict between male and female and demonstrates Mrs. Ramsay's way of framing the negative; and the situation puts Mrs. Ramsay between the feuding males. She frames and mediates negativity. The role Mrs. Ramsay plays in the novel seems to be a carryover from Woolf's life—the love, frustration with, anger toward, and loss of her mother at the age of thirteen all work their way into the novel. Woolf's descriptions of her mother show how Woolf assimilated and transformed the power and the patterns she recognizes in her mother. The generally positive nature of the female model might also raise some suspicions along the lines of "protesting too much." I suspect an underlying anger at the mother for failing to protect the daughter from the destruction of the male and perhaps for being "too good" at times.

The Structure of the Novel

I see the center of the novel as symbolically representing Woolf's bodily center—the genital and existential core which the darkness of male sexuality has invaded. The fearful negativity of the middle chapter is the anxiety of an empty womb, damaged or destroyed by external (male) forces. What saves this center from complete devastation is Mrs. McNab—a disguise for some aspect of Woolf's self, perhaps the internalized "good enough mother."[5] It is this aspect of her self that carries "some incorrigible hope." It is in her self that she finds "some channel in the depth . . . through which light . . . issued." The restoration of the house, the "rusty laborious birth," is a reperceiving of the self—from a biological to an aesthetic creator. The center of the novel, then, plays out the consequences of both the male and female models—the male damages, the female repairs.

The Structure of the Painting

Lily Briscoe's painting carries forward the birthing made possible by the restoration of the novel's center. In the painting's abstract form, we can see a fantasy of symbiosis, the merging of many patterns, of all forms of relationship in harmony. It is in that sense a "vision," a powerful summation of patterning. If we think of the stages of the painting schematically, it looks something like this:

1. [mass/Mrs. Ramsay [empty] mass/Mr. Ramsay]
2. [mass [tree] mass]
3. [mass/color/iron bolt [butterfly] mass/color/iron bolt]

The first stage is the "empty female" position, or the childless parents, depending on whether the frame is seen as being the Ramsays or Lily's self. The second stage, when Lily decides to move the tree to the middle, is the "phallic male" position, and it is taken up in the heat of Lily's anger at Tansley and men in general—a displacing: they deny Lily her power, she asserts it. The third and final stage is the richest and most overdetermined. Some of the possibilities can be outlined thus:

1. [Mrs. Ramsay [Lily] Mr. Ramsay]
2. [female [male] female]
3. [breast/thigh [vagina/womb/child] breast/thigh]
4. [buttock [anus] buttock]
5. [testicle [penis] testicle]

The picture contains and unifies; it brings together the family, male and female; it brings the body together and is itself a creation, a birth depicting birth. The symbiotic desire here is also expressed in Woolf's autobiographical writings. And there she explains the salvation that pattern making gave her. In her ability to make these complex patterns, and to construct the particular pattern of this novel, we can see a connection to Woolf's mother and her ability, in Woolf's eyes, to create such structures though in different forms—much like Lily's perception that she and Mrs. Ramsay "make of the moment something permanent."

The Psychological Story

Having explored these four pattern variants, a relationship among them can be posited. I would explain the relationship for the moment in the form of a psychological story: There is an anxiety about opening to the male for fear of being damaged or an anger for having been damaged. Refusal to take the male in makes it impossible to become pregnant and bear children. This, in turn, creates feelings of emptiness and failure, and perhaps a wish to die, to merge the sea and the land in the darkness of "Time Passes." By way of association to a negative merging comes a regressive wish to merge with the mother—to return to the womb or the postnatal relation with the mother. In the warmth of that environment one might be healed. Perhaps even to get in touch with this wish, to wish it, is an antidote to despair and is the "cleavage" through which light emerges. Thinking of this positive merger seems to allow Woolf to be reborn, and reborn she can give birth. Both of these processes are, however, fraught with anxiety—Lily tells us she feels the "passage from conception to work as dreadful as any down a dark passage for a child" (32). But she surmounts her anxiety, gathers her courage. And Woolf, like Lily before she begins her painting, is an "unborn soul," a "soul reft of body." But through the completion of her work, she is embodied and born. However it arises, Woolf gathers a powerful creative surge that converts pain into harmony and beauty. By transforming conflict into pattern, Woolf achieves her autonomy—her own way of opening, making, and giving.

Moments of Being

We can see from Woolf's autobiographical writings—published under the title *Moments of Being* (1976)—that the idea of a "center" is important to her. It is enmeshed in her way of seeing experience; she explains and describes people, events, and relationships in terms of it. I believe the primary reason the center is such an important intellectual and aesthetic construct to her is grounded in a devastating and damaging series of sexual attacks she suffered at the hands of Gerald Duckworth. These attacks on her genital center had lasting psychological consequences for Woolf, one of which was the formation of an abstract gestalt in the form of the pattern we have seen in *To the Lighthouse*. The physical configuration of the body, in other words, became a model for a pattern. Through the autobiographical writings we can roughly trace some of the stages Woolf is likely to have gone through to make the transformation. First, the rage she must have felt over these attacks was not directly expressed but rather internalized, and there it gnawed at her in the form of self-attack. In addition, the attacks seem to have caused her to split body and mind, divorcing the body and living in the mind. In spite of the physical attacks and the damaging psychological defenses they called up, Woolf managed to transform the negative into psychological, aesthetic creativity. The positive energy she needed to make this heroic transformation may well have had its source in the power of her mother, whom Woolf repeatedly describes as "central" to her. Whether this is directly the case or not, it does seem that by making patterns Woolf achieves a measure of control over negativity and of integration of self. And finally, by making patterns Woolf fulfills her desire for a symbiotic relationship with others. In what follows, we will examine the general form of the basic pattern as seen in Woolf's way of perceiving experience; the development of internal negativity as a result of external (male) attacks; the foundation of a positive center; and the significance of pattern making as a means of transforming negativity.

The General Form

The most general case of the pattern of embedding is found in Woolf's description of day-to-day life. Her perception is that there are, now and again, "exceptional" but "separate moments of being" and these are *"embedded in many more moments of non-being"* (70, my emphasis). As she says, one might have a good day, but "goodness was embedded in a kind of nondescript cotton wool." In other words, the moments of being are times when something enters one's field of perception with enough energy that one becomes conscious of it. Consciousness comes in the midst of routine—"a great part of every day is not lived consciously." So, for example, in thinking about what she recalls from childhood, Woolf gives us a "rough visual description" of colors, sounds, and people "all *surrounded by a vast space*" (79, my emphasis). Or, she notes, "I still see the air-ball, blue and purple, and the ribs on the shells; but these points are *enclosed in vast empty spaces*" (78, my emphasis). Memory, then, is composed of just such moments that stand out of the nonconscious cotton wool of daily life.

Woolf offers us another image to describe this process of being or becoming aware of something; she tells us of an "instinctive notion," "the sensation that we are sealed vessels afloat on what it is convenient to call reality; and at some moments, the sealing matter cracks; in floods reality" (122). This statement describes how various scenes of life become "something comparatively permanent" in Woolf's mind. The images are far from neutral. They give us a clue to the possible psychological significance of these moments of being. The image here describes the basic pattern—something being within something else in a more active and intrusive way than those above where the intense moment is depicted as "embedded," "surrounded," or "enclosed." In other words, the emphasis changes from the "nondescript cotton wool" frame to the action of an impinging reality. The "sensation" Woolf tells us about has two parts: in the first, one is both self-enclosed and surrounded by a larger body—a sea of some kind. In the second part, one becomes opened to the larger body, "reality." The image of the first part— "sealed vessels afloat"—is one of symbiosis; it describes interuterine life, as well as the comfort of sleeping, being held, or feeling safe at home. The second part of this narrative image carries several suggestions of aggression— something cracks and is flooded. It feels as though some outer force has eroded the seal, that there was resistance to being opened and flooded. In comparison to the first image, this second seems dangerous; to carry out the metaphor, the vessel will become too heavy and sink (as did she die). The second image (being flooded) is implosive-intrusive and could suggest forcible feeding (infantile period) or sexual aggression directed at her (in childhood and adolescence). However one sees these images, it should be clear that Woolf's moments of being are neither neutral affairs nor airy intellectual insights, but rather derive from visceral experience.

The Negative: Aggression, Sexuality, and Death

Most of the moments of being Woolf describes lead her to a "state of despair" (71); they come to her with a "sudden violent shock; something happened so violently that I have remembered it all of my life" (70). Some of her earliest recollections focus on aggression and death. One such moment occurs as she and her brother, Thoby, were "pommelling each other with our fists."

> Just as I raised my fist to hit him, I felt: *why hurt another person?* I dropped my hand instantly, and stood there, and *let him beat me.* I remember the feeling. It was a feeling *of hopeless sadness. It was as if I became aware of something terrible*; and of my own *powerlessness.* I slunk off alone, *feeling horribly depressed.* (71, my emphasis)

Another of these negative moments occurs when she learns that a family acquaintance, Mr. Valpy, "had killed himself." After learning this, she is in the garden at night, where, staring at an apple tree "in a trance of horror," she tells us, "I seemed to be dragged down, hopelessly, into some pit of absolute despair from which I could not escape. My body seemed paralyzed" (71). These two moments are recalled in association with each other and are interrelated. In the first incident we see, step by step, the internalization of anger and its immediate consequence. The anger, however playful it may have been, is first enacted, but then she stops her aggression and "let him beat" her, and finally, she embeds it—"alone, feeling horribly depressed." As she says, "I was quite unable to deal with the *pain of discovering that people hurt each other*" (72, my emphasis). In fact, she does "deal with" the discovery by making the "pain" her own and thereby protecting the other: after all, if "people hurt each other," there may be people she wishes to hurt (who may have hurt her). The second instance—Valpy's death—complements the first. Woolf experiences a moment of identification with Valpy which ties in with the earlier internalization of anger. She recognizes in Valpy's suicide something of herself—the "logical" extension of internalizing anger

and of self-attack is suicide. The realization paralyzes her, and she is engulfed in a "pit of absolute despair."

Another description of a negative moment focuses on death and presents
us with a vivid image of a center in a negative frame. In speaking of death —
her mother's, Stella's, and Thoby's — she recognizes the paradoxical fact that
death, a "mutilation of feelings," in fact "sensitizes" one "to be aware of the
insecurity of life" and thus to respect the "force" of death all the more (117).
In trying to evaluate the pain of these deaths, Woolf asks, rhetorically, "But at
fifteen, to have that protection removed, to be tumbled out of the family shel-
ter, to see cracks and gashes in that fabric, to be cut by them, to see beyond
them — was that good?" (118). Caring relations have been destroyed with a violence that cuts the survivors — the images here recall ones cited above — "the
sealing cracks; in floods reality [here, death]." Equally forceful is the "visual
way" Woolf uses to describe the contest between life and death: "I would see
(after Thoby's death) two great grindstones . . . and myself between them"
(118). When she reports this, she seems to feel adequate to deal with the pressure. But the image is disquieting — that one needs to suffer, to "wince" and
feel "ground between grindstones" in order to perceive and appreciate life.
She knows it would have been more benign to have remained "surrounded"
by the "rush and tumble" of life with her family. In the first image, Woolf is
inside a space, "surrounded" by family life, but death destroys that Eden —
she is thrown out and "cut." In the second image, she is the positive, life energy, center struggling against the enclosing forces of death.

In the preceding paragraphs we have examined a number of "moments":
(1) Woolf takes abuse without retaliation and turns aggression against herself
(depression); (2) she is paralyzed upon confronting the ultimate consequence of self-attack (Valpy's suicide); (3) she wishes for a symbiotic relationship (to be within, surrounded, afloat, sealed); but (4) is thrown out and
separated (because of death) and imploded ("in floods reality"). The image
of Woolf between grindstones is perhaps the most succinct statement of
these various moments: she tries to remain a life force as she struggles between the pain of realized death (her mother's and others) and the possibility of self-imposed death (given her tendency to self-attack). The grindstone
image does not give us a neat clue as to the inception of Woolf's self-hate or
its ramifications. But the next set of images and experiences examined will
help us see some of the roots and branches of Woolf's self-hate.

Woolf graphically describes a sexual attack that she succumbed to when
she was six years old. This attack was the first of many — she was sexually
abused by both of her half-brothers until she was in her teens and, appar-

ently, even after her first psychological breakdown following her mother's death.[6] Beginning at the same time as the first attack, Woolf began to evidence the consequences of the sexual abuse—self-hatred, sexual repudiation, and a dividing of body from mind. Certainly these episodes of sexual abuse played a large role in Woolf's self-attacks, frigidity, depression, and suicide.

Let us look at Woolf's description of what seems to be the first sexual assault on her, when she was six:

> There was a slab outside the dining room door for standing dishes upon. Once when I was very small Gerald Duckworth lifted me onto this, and as I sat there he began to explore my body. I can remember the feel of his hand going under my clothes; going firmly and steadily lower and lower. I remember how I hoped that he would stop; how I stiffened and wriggled as he hand approached by private parts. But it did not stop. His hand explored my private parts too. I remember resenting, disliking it—what is the word for so dumb and mixed a feeling? (69)

This moment of being, like the one involving the fight with her brother, arose out of intense bodily contact, which in this case was focused in the genitals, the bodily center—the sealing of the vessel that cracks. Being molested in this way is a frightening event and a sensitive one to analyze. At the moment Duckworth was "exploring" her, and on subsequent occasions, Woolf expressed no overt anger—she recalls "resenting, disliking it." She "hopes" he will stop but does not tell him to. There are a few angles from which to see the absence of overt anger. Perhaps anger is even more taboo and dangerous than sexuality. If this is the case, the narcissistic defense was well in place—the anger was directed at the self, thus Woolf came to fear and hate her own sexuality. In her revelation about aggression in the episode with her brother, we saw a similar inversion of anger. There is another side to the absence of anger. By failing to fight him off or report him to her parents, Woolf in some measure collaborated with him in her destruction. There are, sadly, good reasons for compliance in such situations—fear of greater danger and harm that might come from escalating the fight. She may have felt that she was participating and equally guilty.[7] The displacement of guilt (from Duckworth to herself) is a complementary note to the turning inward of anger.

There are several experiences Woolf describes, from the same period of time, all of which focus on mirror images. These experiences document a link between the sexual assaults and her repudiation of sexuality and her self-negation. In discussing herself at "six or seven," she tells us of a "habit of looking at my face in the glass" about which she feels "shame" and "guilt" but nonetheless continues her habit (68). As Woolf explores the feelings she had about looking in the mirror, she first connects it with a "tomboy code" which she shared with her sister, Vanessa. Looking into a mirror was seen as a female habit and thus against the tomboy rules. She seems caught in a double rebellion—first against being female, and second attempting to repudiate her male envy and appreciate the feminine (her half-brothers, after all, seem quite fascinated by it). Unsatisfied with the tomboy explanations, she senses that the issues "went a great deal deeper." She recounts an anecdote about a grandfather "who once smoked a cigar, liked it, and so threw away his cigar and never smoked another." The anecdote suggests a family precedent for giving up pleasure, though it does not explain Woolf's sexual repudiation, as she herself recognizes. Yet the anecdote, told in association with her feelings about looking in the mirror and her experience of being molested, does suggest an element of libidinal interest. In other words, the narcissistic enjoyment she secretly took in looking in the mirror—"I only did this if I was sure that I was alone"—like the pleasure her grandfather felt in his cigar, indicates that she may also have had erotic feelings in connection with Duckworth. As we see, however, a much stronger current washes back on that and destroys it. And thus she explicitly connects her negative feelings of "shame" and "guilt" over her self-enjoyment to the sexual assault.

A further connection between the sexual attacks and her sexual negativity comes from a dream that "frightened" her: "I was looking in a glass when a horrible face—the face of an animal—suddenly showed over my shoulder" (69). Here guilt turns to anxiety. The dream seems to say that if one takes pleasure in one's body, one will be assaulted. One more encounter seems related to these issues: "There was the moment of the puddle in the path; when for no reason I could discover, everything became unreal; I was suspended; *I could not step across the puddle*; I tried to touch something . . . the whole world became unreal" (78, my emphasis). Here Woolf becomes paralyzed, and the outside world no longer seems tangible. Although she cannot offer an explanation, we might suggest that the puddle would have acted as a mirror and thus if she stepped over it, she could have seen her reflection—her "middle," maybe the "face of an animal," might have been exposed. As a defense against the anxieties raised by sexuality, even to an awareness of it, Woolf freezes. She is one step ahead of Narcissus—he killed himself by becoming entangled in the mirror; she obliterates herself at the very thought of looking. Thus, on a minor note, she tells us, "I cannot now powder my nose in public" (68).

In addition to internalizing anger and feeling guilt, shame, and anxiety over sexual matters, Woolf seems to divide her body and mind; technically, she employs a schizoid defense. This defense is a further way of "protecting" herself both against the onslaught of external forces—the Duckworths—and against any residual erotic (or autoerotic) feelings she might have. Thus she tells us, "my natural love for beauty was checked by some ancestral dread. Yet this did not prevent me from *feeling ecstasies and raptures spontaneously and intensely and without any shame or the least sense of guilt, so long as they were disconnected with my own body*" (68, my emphasis). Her notion of "ancestral dread" of bodily pleasure seems a rationalization. That is, in spite of her more or less public revelation of the Duckworths' sexual abuse—which revelation is an expression of anger, a just act that resembles revenge—she is still hesitant to express outrage fully. In any case, the above quotation points to one of the ways that Woolf, after being attacked, defends herself— by making the mind a space for erotic pleasure. The split is also rationalized by parallels she sees in her family. On the one hand she tells us that "femininity was very strong in our family" and that "we were famous for our beauty"—this gives her "pride and pleasure." But she feels an opposing thread in her makeup—the "puritan" grandfather and, closer to home, her own father: "My father was Spartan, ascetic, puritanical. He had I think no feeling for pictures; no ear for music; no sense of the sound of words" (68). This family division seems to give Woolf a way to manage, though not resolve, her own split. She becomes sexually ascetic, identifying with her paternal side, and aesthetically sensuous, identifying with her maternal side (and this goes together with Lily's painting).

The Positive: Mother, Symbiosis, and Separation

Woolf also experiences positive moments of being which leave her "in a state of satisfaction," although she does not mention many of them. One comes as an epiphany of wholeness as she is "looking at a flower bed" at St. Ives: "'That is whole,' I said. I was looking at a plant with a spread of leaves; and it seemed suddenly plain that the flower itself was a part of earth; that a ring enclosed what was the flower; and that was the real flower; part earth; part flower" (71). Two natural elements become unified and encircled. The image suggests a perfect symbiosis—mother/earth and daughter/flower—in which one element grows from and is nurtured by the other. Hence the affect of "satisfaction." She tells us, moreover, that "in the case of the flower I found a reason . . . I was not powerless" (72). In other words, her perception of wholeness is a "discovery" (71), an understanding which is "enclosed" by the "ring" of her consciousness. And for Woolf, being able to understand something gives a measure of power and control which she quite clearly lost under many of the other circumstances we have examined. Her understanding, however, also represents a wish—a wish for symbiosis, integration. It is to the images of her mother—Julia Duckworth Stephen—that we need to look to see if we can find the crux of this desire.

The reading I would make of Woolf's relation to her mother is that it was at first, as an infant, deeply satisfying. This would give Woolf a feeling for, and later a yearning for, a whole relationship. Yet the symbiotic phase did not last long enough and separation was perhaps difficult for Woolf. Her brother Adrian was born a year after her. Such a reading simplifies matters, but the images Woolf supplies us with seem to indicate this general pattern. What should be stressed is that however ambivalent Woolf may sometimes feel about her mother, there seems to be some deep strand of positive feelings to which she returned in times of psychological distress[8] and which gave her the strength to reshape the negatives she encountered. One of the first images Woolf offers us is this: "Certainly there she was, *in the very centre* of that great Cathedral space which was childhood; there she was from the very first. My memory is of her lap; the scratch of some beads on her dress comes back to me as I pressed my cheek against it" (81, my emphasis). Her mother is also described as "the creator of that crowded merry world which spun so gaily *in the centre of my childhood*" (84, my emphasis). These images, with their insistent focus on centrality, emphasize a preambivalent state: it is holy, omnipotent, primary, and connected with being held and in touch with the heart and breast. The image of centrality here is a far cry from the aggressive and sexually intrusive ones that generated Woolf's feelings of "despair." The picture Woolf paints, sitting on her mother's lap, suggests peace, closeness, and security. It is a feeling state one would rightly long for, especially under the stresses Woolf was subjected to. One other significant aspect of the image—as well as those that follow—is that the center is outside of Woolf. That is, Woolf is not described as being in the center, nor is her own center at issue; rather it is her mother who is the "centre of that great Cathedral space which was childhood." I think that Woolf, like Lily Briscoe in her desire for Mrs. Ramsay, would like to have been in that center more than she was and that she reached it by realizing it symbolically through her work.

Another description of Woolf's relationship raises a more ambivalent sense, though the image of centrality remains:

> And of course she was *central*. I suspect *the word "central" gets closest to the general feeling I had of living so completely in her atmosphere* that one

never got far enough away from her to see her as a person . . . she was the whole thing; Tailliard House was *full of her*; Hyde Park Gate was *full of her* . . . I see now . . . why it was that it was impossible for her to leave a very private and particular impression upon a child . . . I see now that she was living on such an extended surface that she had not time, nor strength, to concentrate, except for a moment if one were ill or in some child's crisis, upon me, or upon anyone—unless it were Adrian. . . . Can I remember being alone with her for more than a few minutes? Someone was always interrupting. (83)

Here we find notes of distance, jealousy, and perhaps oppression and suffocation. On the one hand, the mother is all-pervasive—at once the center and the whole. And on the other hand, she is too distant and spread out to know. The image of the mother as center seems more threatening and distant than the one above. We get a paradoxical sense of her as dominant and omnipresent—"living completely in her atmosphere" and spaces being "full of her"—and yet inaccessible—"she had not time . . . to concentrate . . . upon me." The mother is the center of the child's perception, and the child would like to feel herself in the center of the mother, but the dynamics of this center are such that the child feels herself on the periphery of her mother's consciousness. She seems stultified, tantalized, and unsatisfied.

Woolf indicates that she had several defenses against this paradoxical force. For one, she "enclosed that world in another made [by her own] temperament" (84). And for another, she distanced herself from that world—she "went far from it; and kept much back from it." Thus to keep from being engulfed and to keep herself away from the tempting union she desired but could not attain, she removed herself. Nonetheless, her mother's death makes itself felt: "and *she was the centre*; it was herself. This was proved on May 5th 1895. For after that day there was nothing left of it . . . everything had come to an end" (84). The "common life of the family" disintegrated. Woolf became haunted by her mother: "The presence of my mother obsessed me. I could hear her voice, see her, imagine what she would do or say as I went about my day's doings. She was one of the invisible presences who after all play so important a part in every life" (80). Although Woolf felt somewhat deprived as a child, she felt even more so when her mother died. Thus she internalized her mother's voice as a way of keeping her alive in fantasy where she could sustain her.

The way Woolf managed to wean herself from her mother was through writing *To the Lighthouse* when she was in her mid-forties, some thirty years after her mother's death. She tells us that "when it was written, I ceased to be obsessed . . . I no longer hear her voice; I do not see her" (81). Thus aesthetic action creates a transformation; it releases Woolf from her inside mother; she allows her mother to die. She wonders, "Why, because I described her and my feelings for her in that book, should my vision of her and my feelings for her become so much dimmer and weaker?" (81). My sense of the answer is that Woolf, without consciousness, assimilated that aspect of her mother's being in the world which thwarted her as a child, that is, her mother's present absence. She resolves that paradox by becoming it, or symbolically enacting it, through Lily (and all the characters) in her art. And beyond that, in *To the Lighthouse*, Woolf explores all the dimensions of the center—positive and negative, male and female—and becomes the very center she desires, not only for herself but for others, for her readers.

The Transformation—"I Make It Whole"

In the days following her mother's death (and before her funeral), Woolf experienced a moment of being, a unifying experience with a poem. She tells us that "my mother's death unveiled and intensified; made me suddenly develop perceptions, as if a burning glass had been laid over what was shaded and dormant" (93). With this heightened sensitivity, she feels, "It was as if I became altogether intelligible; I had a feeling of transparency in words when they cease to be words and become so intensified that one seems to experience them; to foretell them as if they developed what one is already feeling" (93). In the Woolf household reading and writing are very much a part of daily life, but this experience is a breakthrough. She says she has difficulty explaining the gist of her feelings—"no one could have understood from what I said the queer feeling I had in the hot grass, that poetry was coming true." But, she tells us, the feeling "matches what I have sometimes felt when I write. The pen gets on the scent." The description of her experience with this poem is related to her perception of the flower-earth unity. Here, however, the merging is not between two external objects but between herself and the consciousness/patterning/language of the other. The symbiotic feeling is mental, not physical. In time Woolf learned to reverse roles, to become the poet with whose consciousness others can merge. In a description of her writing, she tells us of "the feeling of the rapid crowd of ideas and scenes which blew out of my mind, so that my lips seemed syllabling of their own accord" (81). As a young reader—the central figure in whose life has just died—Woolf experiences a new kind of merging, with language; and as a mature writer she finds her experience emerging.

In one powerful passage Woolf describes her need to write:

> It is only by putting it into words that I make it whole; this wholeness means that it has lost its power to hurt me; it gives me, perhaps because by doing so I take away the pain, a great delight to put the severed parts together. Perhaps this is the strongest pleasure known to me. It is the rapture I get when in writing I seem to be discovering what belongs to what. . . . From this I reach a . . . philosophy . . . that *behind the cotton wool is hidden a pattern; that we—I mean all human beings—are connected with this*; that the whole world is a work of art; that we are parts of the work of art. *Hamlet* or a Beethoven quartet is the truth about this vast mass that we call the world. But there is no Shakespeare, there is no Beethoven; certainly and emphatically there is no God; we are the words; we are the music; we are the things itself. (72)

The passage is a fairly complete description of Woolf's creative transformations of pain into beauty. The impulse to create comes from feelings of "hurt," "pain," and being "severed." I have discussed some of the particular life crises that formed these feelings—the sexual assaults, the absence of protection, the death of mother, sister, brother, and neighbor. She accomplishes several psychological feats through her writing. First, she neutralizes the pain and anger she feels; more, she expresses the pain and anger verbally. She gains some mastery over these feelings—she can "take away . . . [the] power . . . [and the] pain" of them. Second, she obtains a form of sexual gratification from her aesthetic activity—it is a "great delight," "the strongest pleasure," and a "rapture." Third, she takes the "severed part" and finds out "what belongs to what" and re-creates a "wholeness." That is, she can bring fragmented pieces back to a state of union. In her assertion that she can "make it whole" there are several underlying wishes—to return to a symbiotic state in relation to others (not so far removed from the desires of Mr. Ramsay or James or Lily), to become whole within herself (body and mind), and to create in a biological sense. Finally, we see in the last sentence of the quote above her vision of merging—that we all belong to a "hidden . . . pattern," "the work of art" that is language and living.

Coda

In the opening sentences of the novel we find a syntactic pattern that makes a statement about the female center—it is strong enough to withstand the negativity of the male. Indeed, the center does "surround" (Mr. Ramsay's negativity) and "protect" (James from his father and his father from him). Later images ascribe other powers to this center—it is a "vise," it can make things "be clamped together with bolts of iron"; it is a "fountain" that "spurts" creative energy. The middle chapter of the novel, like the opening sentence, also says something about the female center, and particularly about Woolf's own center: this center has withstood the ravages of the long night—sexual abuse and loss through death; it has been damaged and it has encountered death. But in spite of this pain, the center remains creative; although some aspect of it has been denied, some aspect of it will assert it. The last image of the text—the completion of Lily's picture—is yet another statement of the powers of the female center, genital and existential, to bring together and to bring forth. Since the completion of the painting (and the completion of the trip to the lighthouse—Mr. Ramsay's completion of a promise) coincides with the completion of the novel, giving the ending an orgasmic quality, we are not only in touch with Lily's completing her work but with Woolf's as well. The reciprocity here takes us to similar moments of high conjunction: Mrs. Ramsay's with the lighthouse as reflection and Lily's with her painting as the canvas protrudes and her juices start flowing. We have seen much of what the painting brings together for Lily and thus some of what it brings together for Woolf. The culmination is also a statement of Woolf's to the reader: "I, Virginia Woolf, by completing the writing of the completing of the painting, have myself completed, summed up and transcended the patterns herein." Woolf has indeed, consciously or not, taken a motif, of center and frame, embedded it in many ingenious ways, and brought it to a Bachian end. All of this development and resolution of the motif tells us of the power of the female—her consciousness, her genital. There are fears and anxieties, there is a hidden rage, issues are resolved only at some distance, but the ending does fulfill a wish to "merge and flow."

The novel has, then, a kind of female bravado about it. It proclaims the power of the female center to surround, protect, nurture, and create; the ability to withdraw from others into a deeper level of self and there to surround, protect, nurture, and re-create the self; and last, the resilient power of the female to surmount the male force. When we turn to Woolf's life, we see the pain that she had to work with to transform; we see her conscious concern with and belief in pattern making; and we see the particular pattern examined in the novel. Living is a series of striking moments inside the routine of "cotton wool," each of these center-entering-frame moments is like a chord, and the series of them, aesthetically ordered, a quartet. These various moments—often frightening, shattering, fragmenting, and paralyzing—lend the basic form to the pattern Woolf metamorphosed from the vulnerable body and sensitive feelings into an aesthetic whole, a "vision."

7

◇◇

The
Chaneysville
Incident
by
David
Bradley:
The
Belly
of
the
Text

The bodily locus in Bradley's novel is the belly—the hero, John Washington, has a feeling of cold in his belly. The feeling of cold threatens, in dreams, to envelop him. I trace the formation—history, content, motivation—of that pain (the cold, frigidity) and its subsequent deformation or reformation. The cold is a bodily condition under tension, and in this case the tension is at least five generations old. The hero is offered and internalizes a sustained history of pain—slavery and its aftermath. He studies diligently, thoroughly, and extensively to find some missing piece of information, but he is off the track and he fails, which deeply grieves him. He suffers for what he does know as well as what he does not. He carries both the pain of history and the pain of failure in his belly, the locus of his coldness. What he eventually finds, he was not looking for; it provides a warmth that in turn allows him to understand something deeper than he could have anticipated, and it allows him be creative as a man and an artist.

The Belly—Separation from; Torn Apart; Repository of Shit, Grief, and Rage; Freezing/Frozen/Frigid; Long Birthing Labor—Introduction to the Novel

The belly manifests itself in various ways. First, it is named (on the average of once every twenty pages). Second, we can establish interrelated semantic networks; for example, one semantic cluster is of varieties of drink—coffee and alcohol, particularly hot toddies—which are also coded for gender. In the novel, drinking is always done for the purpose of making some change in the system (e.g., to warm Washington), so even if the belly is not mentioned, it is present. Third, there are symbolic spaces—interior, community—that work like the belly, holding things in. Last, there are syntactic gestures that interplay with the semantic redundancies: in the belly of the text, dead center, is a funeral. On some level the novel centers on the belly—the pain and its resolution therein. Within the belly is both a personal history and a multigenerational political history—and these, untold and unsettled, freeze John Washington. The novel tells the tale of the nine days (nine months of pregnancy) during which Washington conceives and gives birth to the tale for which he has been searching and conceives a child with his lover. The frozen, sterile, shit-filled belly is warmed, emptied, filled with fertility.

David Bradley's *Chaneysville Incident* (1981) won the PEN Faulkner Award in 1981 and is a major novel by a black American male. My interest in the novel is with its particular visceral representation, its transformation of belly from bowel to womb. There are many layers built upon this bodily configuration, many "reasons" why the belly is the center of this novel. Before exploring the work, I would like to introduce it because it is relatively new.

Bradley's novel builds on central themes in our separate and related American literary traditions; he creates a new dialectic both between and within the black and white traditions. We can see Bradley's relation to Faulkner's "Bear," Melville's *Moby Dick*, and Hemingway's "Old Man of the Sea" in his use of the hunt as a way to explore the relation of man and nature and man to man. Bradley's hero, John Washington, a professor of history, is a contemporary descendant of Faulkner's Ikkemotubbe; he knows the primal relation of man and animal, hunter and hunted. As Faulkner writes in the opening page of "The Bear": "It was of the men, not white not black not red but men, hunters, with the skill and hardihood to endure and the humility and skill to survive." But Bradley's hero also embodies a broader consciousness from other learning systems. Moreover, Bradley does not exclude women from his universe. And, of course, Bradley's metaphoric view on hunting has the perspective of historically being hunted. Bradley's hero, finally, wants more than what is considered in "The Bear" "the best of all listening, the voices quiet and weighty and deliberate for retrospection and recollection and exactitude among the concrete trophies." For John Washington, the telling and listening to the telling of tales is a matter of life and death.

Bradley is also thematically related to black writers—James Baldwin, Ralph Ellison, and Alex Haley—in his hero's quest for identity as a black man in America. John Washington's situation, however, is complicated by his mixed genetic heritage, whose roots include African black, American Indian, and Anglo-Irish white, and his mixed education, apprenticed as a youngster to a black backwoodsman and later becoming a professor of history. John Washington confronts the issue of racism (white and black, external and internalized) through the family history he reconstructs and in his intimate relationships with his childhood mentor (a dying father) and the white woman with whom he has been living for five years. Bradley creates greater complexity than earlier writers (black and white) in his hero's search for identity. Bradley's hero endures new forms of alienation but gains new perspectives and offers new possibilities.

◇◇ Since the story is contemporary and its plot complex, an overview will be helpful. The novel is built on several temporal planes: a present time frame of nine days and a past that includes the hero's history and the five-generation history of the hero's paternal family line. As we move forward in the present, we also return to various dimensions of the past. For example, at the beginning of the novel, John's present life as a history professor and lover of a white woman is interrupted; he is asked to return to his rural place of growing up to take care of his dying mentor and longtime friend of his father, Jack Crawley. The spatial return—university to country—sets John up to recall various aspects of his own growing up, especially his earlier search into his family history and his failure to resolve several problems in his historical reconstruction. This failure follows John around in a painful, symptomatic way.

He began his historical researches in high school, working from documents his father, Moses Washington, had amassed over his lifetime and from the tales Jack Crawley had told him about his father and the black community. He had put together a basic outline of the family history in America that went back to the Cherokee brave and the black slave woman who began it.

There was, however, one crucial individual, John's great-grandfather, whose death John could not account for. The great-grandfather was a daring anti-slavery fighter who seems to have disappeared without a trace, although he left much documentation about his life. John senses that the great-grandfather's death is linked to the death of twelve runaway slaves—the Chaneysville Incident—that occurred at the time of his disappearance. But the connection is unclear, and John is left with a "gap" in his history. He feels like a failure. His sense of failure provokes psychological symptoms—a coldness within, a kind of male frigidity, and a fear of the dreams that come with sleep. He stopped working on the history when he went away to college, and he kept his distance through graduate school and into his present career work—but the symptoms persist.

In the present time of the novel, John is living with Judith, a white woman, a psychiatrist; they have been together for five years. In the nine-day period of the novel, John's relationship both to Judith and to the unresolved history undergo radical changes. When John goes to take care of Jack Crawley, he begins retracing the history he has been avoiding. He opens up the psychological wound of his failures and fears. His psychological pain increases with the recognition that his father committed suicide—the death was not a hunting accident as the official story had it. In his pain, he withdraws from Judith and regresses into a suicidal state. Judith senses the danger and goes to him, arriving shortly after Jack Crawley's funeral. Her presence and love allow John to confront the "gaps." This time, he is able to take a "creative leap."

The fleshed-out version of the story sketched here is fascinating, and Bradley's way of developing it is even more so. The novel is epic—it has thematic concerns in common with the *Iliad* and *Odyssey*—the anger of Achilles and the necessity of Telemachos's search for his father. Bradley's mode of storytelling is also related to Homer's—it is highly embedded. The novel unfolds one new dimension after another—historical, political (micro and macro), linguistic, interpersonal, intrapsychic, spiritual. There is also an integral, unintrusive, and illuminating consciousness of the process of "making" with language. There is the history John tells us but also the histories of the history. Indeed, assembling and telling the history is what constitutes John's heroism. John's task involves all the processes of writing history—gathering and sorting information, reconstructing sequences and simultaneities, and confronting the gaps. The task also leads him to another modality of knowing, though to get there, he must drop his scientific/obsessional ways.

The focus of the history itself is on racial conflict from slavery to the present as seen through the microcosm of one line of descent—that of John's father, Moses Washington. A central concern of the history is with black heroism, rebellion, and subversion—the fight to be seen as autonomous. At the interpersonal level, the novel focuses on the tensions between generations, races, and sexes. The history and present moments of John's relationship to Judith has its own distinct tensions; and these tensions are brought up against the origins of John's side of the antagonism and ambivalence: Jack Crawley, John's surrogate father, the last father in the line. Jack teaches John many invaluable skills; he tells two or three of the best stories in the novel (about the great trickster, Moses). At his funeral—in the belly of the text—we learn how generous he has been to the community. But he also prohibits John from the white world and the sexual world. John has entered both.

The world John grew up in, the one he now lives in, and the one he returns to are fraught with tension. The focus of this chapter is on how that tension manifests itself with the character, particularly how it is inscribed in the body and mapped out in the language. I specifically focus on the symptomatic pain in the belly of John Washington. The conflicts generating the pain and anxiety are rooted in the hero's historical quest, in the history he discerns, in the primal rage developed within his family with its rage, and in his fear of the gaps of history and relationships (and women). The resolution of the pain, the interpersonal knots, and the historical problems emerge almost simultaneously, interdependently, precipitated by one another. The ending brings us to the birth of the narrative, the possible inception of new life, a new paternity, and an understanding of heroic suicide and spiritual birth. The hero, at least for the moment, succeeds in leaping the gaps between male and female, black and white, stories and history, past and present.

The Belly

My working hypothesis is that in the present John is frigid, unable to "imagine" the resolution of the mysteries, unable to procreate; he is disabled by untold grief and the prohibitions of the father. When Jack dies, John's mourning of that death—like Lily's for Mrs. Ramsay—effectively releases the grief embedded in the novel. For John, it stops the voice of prohibition and clears the way for the dissipation of symptoms. John is then free to love; he is able to procreate with Judith. His ability to love allows him to have a vision from which he creates the tale that resolves the mysteries.

In Bradley's novel the most striking, redundant, bodily referent is to "the belly" of the narrator/hero, John Washington. Although the motif appears only eighteen times in a quarter of a million words, it is central to the layers of psychological patterning in the novel. The belly is the organ in which the hero's body, experience, and generational history is inscribed; it reflects pain, need, and desire. The belly is the locus of a symptom, a self-attack — as John says, "the place at the base of my belly . . . never seemed to get enough warmth" (5). Whenever John comes close to his particular pain, he experiences a wave of cold in his gut — "a sudden chill at the base of my belly" (24). We will track the symptom to its primal and generational roots, its crystallization, and its resolution. We will examine the "internal empire of the belly"[1] — the establishment and creative transformation of the "glacier in his guts" (430).

The belly is a dual location: a bowel and a womb (linguistic inversions, too). The belly is a place of excremental buildup — deaths, grief, failure — and a place of creative ferment — generation, babies, tales. This duality is "syntactically" represented in one of the narrative's structures.[2] That is, the privileged loci in the novel — beginning, center, and end — have this schema: [birth [death] birth]. The novel opens and closes with elements related to birth — umbilical cutting, conception, and the like. And right in the middle of the novel is a death and funeral — that of the symbolic father. The strategic placement gives the dual thematics of the belly a significant redundancy: death and birth are inscribed spatially by the privileged loci and temporally by the narrative. Death is in the belly of the novel as well as of the hero; but in the end, there is birth, as there was in the beginning.

We will examine the "internal empire" in a chronological fashion reconstructed from the narrative sequence. The chronology of John's life, like the narrative, carries its own syntax. In this case, we see another dual development — of primary relations, repeated twice, or taking place on simultaneous planes. From age one to age nine, John has a good enough mother and a mad father; beginning at adolescence, the mother becomes bad; at age nine, he acquires a good father and at age twenty-six, a good mother. John's integration of good and bad allows him to tell his story. The narrative shows the resolution of historic conflicts taking place in a relationship which could become a repetition but instead evolves into maturity. In other terms, the oedipal configuration is played out twice — John with his mother and father, John with Jack and Judith. When the two configurations are superimposed, seen as from the same temporal zone, we recognize splitting (that is, good and bad mother and father); when seen as occurring successively, we recognize maturation and integration.

Birth, Weaning, and Transitional Object

We can now turn to watch the evolution of the symptom. We begin with John's primary pain, represented in fragments of early bodily feelings of separation, shock, and loss. The opening paragraphs are laden with images and sensations of separation—birth, umbilical cutting, weaning, death. There is a phone call from John's mother telling him that Jack Crawley is severely ill and wants to see him. The mother hangs up on John before answering all his questions; she will have nothing to do with Jack beyond conveying the message to John. And John is equally resistant; he does not wish to hear her or respond to her. The connection between mother and son is cut. While they are connected, the message concerned death. The narrative spirals from one separation to the next into a chasm five generations deep. As the hero gets deeper into the mysteries of the family, he actively withdraws from his intimate connection with Judith and moves into a suicidal position, a generational repetition.

Below the narrative surface of the opening are more primitive forms of similar thematics. The language asks us to hear, see, and feel an older story, a conflation of fragmented moments. We are asked to feel the body—its cold, its shock. The sensory information intimates separation at birth and weaning. We feel, initially, an intrauterine space: "the night is deep and the room is dark." Into this comes the ringing of the phone, "slicing through . . . sleep." This brings a shock to the sensorium—there is "shivering," "the rasping of . . . breathing . . . and the hammering of . . . heartbeat." Most prominent is the image of "the wire" (the phone lines) stretched between mother and son—the umbilical cord[3]—the image recurs five times, is represented pronominally three times, and is the implicit/deleted head of nine other deep-structure sentences. The image is associated with inarticulate (preverbal) sound—"crying, panting, humming, moaning like a live thing." The symbiotic connection breaks loose; we hear sounds of pain and struggle, the distress of waking into, being born into, the cold, the announcement of death. The voice of the mother is characterized by John, projectively, as having a "little bite in it" and then a "real bite." She cuts the connection: leaves him with the scar of separation, omphalos; she withdraws the breast at his bite.

The primary pain of birth and separation from the mother is extended to the limits of John's tolerance by his father, Moses. Moses exploits the rage of John's frustration by manipulating John's "transitional object." The transitional object, delineated by Winnicott, is a something—blanket, piece of string, doll—the infant/child takes as not-me; it allows the child a bridge between self and other, helps to separate and clarify.4 The interaction of child and transitional object is a gauge of the mother-child interaction as felt by the child. Here is John as an infant/child, described by his mother: "'I'd make you a toy and you'd . . . look at it for a long time . . . and then you'd pick it up and poke it and squeeze it and then you'd go to work and tear the stuffing out of it. And when you'd torn the thing to pieces, you'd sit there and giggle'" (202). She says he would "go crazy" when he could not figure out how to solve the puzzle. There is a disturbance in John's interactions with his toy. The fantasy of his action is one that Melanie Klein would recognize as a desire to open up the mother and tear out her insides—for example, mother is pregnant when John is fifteen months old—(1981, 186–98; 1975, 128). It is a rageful fantasy, with sadistic pleasure—he giggles at the fragments—recalling the cannibal feast in *Robinson Crusoe*. The motive for the rage is indicated by the separations noted above—from the body and the breast of the mother.

The rage and anguish expressed in relation to the transitional object could be soothed, but in fact they are encouraged by the father, whose mother died giving birth to him. The father "used to love" to watch John tear things apart; he gives him objects increasingly difficult to tear:

> And one day he . . . got one that was too hard . . . and he sat there all day watching you while you tried to tear that thing apart. *You'd beat it and you'd bang it* until you were tired, then you'd go to sleep, and then you'd wake up and *you'd beat it and bang it more.* . . . And when it finally dawned on you that you weren't going to be able to tear that stuffing out of it, he sat there and laughed while you cried. . . . It almost made me wild, *the sound the two of you made, him laughing and you crying.* (203, my emphasis)

The hostility toward the bad breast, the unyielding breast, is deepened by the father, who teases the child into more sustained aggression and greater frustration. The father's sadism is partly motivated by his past—the death of his mother. To turn Winnicott's phrase, the child functions as the father's transitional subject to whom he can transfer his historic frustration and rage. He wants John to repeat his history and get through it; he is teaching John a kind of crazy endurance.

The mother's desire to separate father and son stems from her intolerance of the madness of the scene—it seems a primal scene with masturbation

overtones ("beating it"). The scene is sadistic, primal, maniacal, diabolic—
"crazy making" as John says of another encounter with the father. The father's desire is to separate mother and son (a repetition) for a higher purpose
of solving the problem of family history. The theme of hostility to, and fears
of dependency on, women is a strong one in the text and given clearest voice
by Jack Crawley. Jack conveys to John how Moses felt about women and particularly how he feared John's reliance on them, for example, Moses "'was
afraid your mamma would do for you so much that you wasn't never gonna
be able to do for yourself . . . an' end up the kind of fool that can't go to sleep
lessen he knows 'xactly where he's gonna get his pussy an' his next pay'" (35).
Moses weans John from the comforts of the breast/mother to focus him on
tolerating frustration and confronting failure and death. Moses encourages
the game of deconstruction to prepare John for his later life tasks. He is proud
of John's development. Jack Crawley tells John that what Moses "'liked
best'" was the way John "'hated him'" (36); Moses saw potential in that rage.
The novel is the mark of John's success—the climactic moment resolves the
puzzle, brings together the fragments, and fills in the gaps. John breaks the
repetition of madness and makes reparation to the torn-up breast.[5]

History and Environment: The Negative Internalized

The primitive feelings of loss, separation, and rage stay with John through
his childhood. Thus he describes some photographs of himself: "I could look
at a fading image of myself . . . at age seven or five or two, I had to be angry.
No; furious" (137). In his adolescence the complex of feelings finds a focus
in history. Specifically, his father leaves for him a set of historical documents
and problems concerning his line of descent. John intently studies the documents and maps out the history, but he reaches an impasse, as did Moses.
There are "too many gaps" (152), and the problem, like the transitional object his father gave him, is "crazy making." The intensity of the history cul-
minates in a nightmare, the genesis of John's symptomatic inner cold. John
looks into the history; it replicates and amplifies his own primitive pain. He
embeds it; it becomes impacted. In addition to internalizing the history,
John is affected by his environment, another layer of redundancy. The environment, like John, is filled with death and excrement.

The negativity of John's history can be shown schematically in a ge-
nealogical sentence:

> [John Washington loses his father, Moses, at age nine; he also loses his
> brother, Bill, at age twenty; and

[Moses lost his mother, Cora Alice O'Reilly Washington, at birth; and
[Moses' father, Lamen, lost his wife (Cora), and his father, C.K. Washington, at age three, and
[Lamen's father, named Brobdingnag but called C.K., lost his father at age eight, his mother at eighteen; he subsequently lost his wife (seven months pregnant), and after her a woman he loved deeply, and finally he loses his own life—in the service of the antislavery movement; and
[Zack, father to C.K., lost his life for trying to raise a rebellion against slavery; and
[Zack's mother, an unknown slave, lost her entire family and homeland; and his father, a Cherokee brave, belonged to a people who were being displaced in their own land.]]]]]]

As John studies history, he internalizes it; he becomes the bearer of five generations of loss. His primitive rage is compounded by historic grief. He acquires "cold facts, and more cold facts" (152), but they seem only to build up within—nothing is born from them.

In addition to his embedded grief, John grows up in a house marked by death. His father built the house from stones cut like the graveyard markers in the Chaneysville cemetery that John will eventually have to explore to fill in the gaps of his history. The triangular stones of Moses' house are iconographic hints to John. John eventually discovers the graveyard, the scene of his father's suicide and the burial site of John's great-grandfather and twelve runaway slaves whose untold tale awaits John's hearing. Moses' house is a tomb for the living, a monument for the dead. John's mother has a domestic habit that complements the father's concern with death. She buries things—things pile up in the house such that no space "went . . . unfilled . . . until one day there wasn't any space . . . and the original shape of anything that had been there was lost under the piles" (128). If the house is a symbolic body, the interior of John's is a constipated bowel—things piling up within, burying them.

John is surrounded by death at home; the outside environment is also presented as psychologically toxic. For example, in the locale where he grew up, one would have "smelled a hundred and fifty years' worth of . . . shit"— the smell of the history of poverty created by slavery and racism. The excremental is strongly associated with death: corporeal, spiritual, or moral decay, as we see from John's description of his feelings for the rural hollow where he grew up: "This place stinks. It makes me choke . . . a stench, like somebody buried something, only they didn't bury it quite deep enough, and it's somewhere stinking up the world" (288). The external appearance of excrement in the "atmosphere" as well as in the literal pile suggests an internal dimension—the grief, the cold, the death, and rage are all a form of withheld, piling up excrement. Excrement is the physical analogue for unrelinquished generational grief.

Adolescent Nightmare of Cold

The fragments of pain—primitive, environmental, and historic—crystallize in a nightmare of cold, leaving John with the symptomatic cold in his belly. The nightmare occurs when John is about seventeen and has been working for four years on the historical documents Moses left. The dream leaves John with an "all-encompassing sensation of icy coldness, and a visual image of total white . . . the coldness and whiteness growing to envelop me, like an avalanche of snow . . . covering me, smothering me" (154). The dream is precipitated by John's perception that he has failed to make something of all his labor on the puzzle of the family history. At the moment he senses his failure, he feels the cold of the attic where his father's study was—this is the first attack of coldness. One frightening thing about the dream is its similarity to those reported by schizophrenics just before they experience major episodes (see Laing 1960, 51–53). The fear the dream engenders is not only maddening; it lasts for the next fourteen years. It is a fear to sleep perchance to have the nightmare and suffocate in the cold.

John's analysis of his failure is that he has all the facts "but . . . could not discern the shape that they fill in" because there are too many "gaps." He concludes that he "could not imagine," hence he could not solve the problem. Without being able to imagine "you will never know the truth." He will end up with something "full of cold, incontrovertible logic, never any of the burning inductive leaps that . . . let you really *understand* anything" (152). The primitive problem is that there is a hole he cannot fill, whose shape is beyond him (mother). He will fill himself up with cold things (excremental autocreation, akin to Crusoe's), until he matures enough to be creative, master the gap. The adolescent problem is more existential—focused on death, guilt, and the failure to make reparations. John says that "what a man's dying really means [is] his story is lost" (49). Hence if he cannot create the tale and tell the story, he has failed to keep Moses and C.K., in particular, alive, spirited through the language.

In John's nightmare, he is initially "burning"; his mother soothes him with "ice water." The fever turns to chills; he asks her to stop, "but she kept on bathing me, and I realized she was trying to kill me." He escapes and she pursues; he reaches the crest of a hill and sees a "giant gorge, a hundred feet deep, with a stream of frothing white water." The gap in history, the gap of the mother, becomes "a giant gorge," which we meet again in the climactic tale John is eventually able to tell. Here the gorge appears as the cold womb ("giant gorge") and breast ("frothing white water") of certain death.

The image of death appearing in the second part of the nightmare in which the father makes his appearance echoes the image in the mother's and translates "frozen" from coldness to stuckness, Sisyphean repetition. John see Moses "naked to the waist despite the driving snow and horrible cold, building a cairn of giant triangular boulders." After he builds it, he kicks it down. John approaches the rocks, and he builds them into one form, takes them down, puts them back, takes them down, and so on. He knows "it would go on like that. Then I had tried to wake. But I could not. Something had shackled me in the dreaming state" (154). In the mother's sector is the womb of death, here in the father's is the phallus of death—erected and deconstructed endlessly without creative power. John is frozen at the gap and shackled into narcissism. As devastating as the dream itself is the feeling of being stuck in its very universe—falling into some gap of the mind and going mad.

From the time John has this nightmare, he is unable to "take the risk to sleep" because he fears he won't awaken. He did not awaken spontaneously when he was living at home; his brother would wake him, "touching me lightly and waiting until the cries had stopped." Later, he sets his alarm clock to wake him at half-hour intervals. And when he begins living with Judith, she takes the role of his brother—she "slept with her hand on me, to feel the first shivering, and then . . . waking me and holding me." But as loving as Judith might be, she is tainted by the bad mother and proscribed by the father. John says he "could never really trust her. Because some night she might not feel the shivering, and there would be nothing to wake me, and I would freeze" (154–55). John's adolescent nightmare haunts him into adulthood; the cold it engenders in his belly cannot be dispelled until he can accept the warmth of the other.

The Warm Belly—Good Objects and Creation—Jack Crawley: Nurturing Phallus, Paternal Breast

Had John only internalized negativity—cold, death, grief, and failure—he could not have begun to formulate the history he does, let alone resolve its conflict. He may live on the edge of madness, of being frozen from within or smothered by the cold outer world, but he does not go over the edge—

there is something good inside as well. The person identified with the good inside, the warm belly, is Jack Crawley who replaces Moses in John's life on the very day of Moses' funeral. John acquires a mentor who is a *good enough father*, a master of tracking, nature, local history, and telling tales. Jack teaches John a "know how" that goes beyond having skills to having a wisdom necessary to create.[6]

In contrast to Jack, Moses knew a great deal but withheld everything. What Moses did not know was how to interrelate as a person. Moses releases what he knows when he dies—he collects. He leaves what he knows in writing—documents and diaries he had collected in his search of the past. When John is growing up, the father spent much of his time in the attic, a *mad man* in the attic: "we knew that whatever he had been doing up there was bizarre and probably unfathomable and almost certainly crazy-making . . . a mystery" (143). Moses is always intense, demanding instant attention, saying very little, making visceral assaults (e.g., as in his role with the transitional object).

From Jack, John obtains a good inside which is symbolized, metonymized, by a cup filled with hot toddy—this is the paternal breast, the nurturant phallus. During their first meeting, Jack makes a toddy in a cup for John: "In a minute," John says, "I could feel the *warmth growing in my stomach*" (34, my emphasis). With his second cup, he says, "All I knew was that the taste was strong and sweet and good, and that the *warmth of it moved through me like joy*" (38, my emphasis). Here is the first good breast of the novel, an antidote to the symptomatic cold engendered by John's toxic history. The antidote has an increased value for its association with Moses and C.K., both of whom had made and drunk "'shine" to support their antislavery and antiracist activities.

Jack teaches John how to order life space but also indicates when rational order breaks down and one lets go of narrow intellect to assume a state of meditative action (hunting) or contemplation (listening to the voices in the wind). The paradigmatic lesson in ordering space is simple: "'Always put things back where you found 'em so you'll know where they are when you need 'em again'" (39). The lesson is important to John for when he enters his father's inner (and upper) sanctum, he is able to recognize the order. Where John's brother sees only "a mess of old papers and books," John says "that 'mess' of things . . . put me in mind of Paradise." He has a profound respect for the order: "I realized that what I was looking at was perfect, and that anything I did, one false step, would destroy that perfection, would probably obscure whatever message might be in the scene" (144–45).

John's reconstructive activities are obsessively ordered in comparison to

have a hunting accident but committed suicide; he discovers as well a host of new documents left to him in his father's will and held back from his knowing by his mother. He writes to Judith that he will not return. She decides to go to him, sensing that he is in danger. He is not at Jack's shack when she arrives. When he comes in later from hunting, he is frostbitten. The first interaction they have is symbolic of those to come: she warms him up. On previous occasions Judith tried to warm John up by "cupping" his belly—he says, she "slipped her hand inside by waistband . . . cupping my belly" (74). But the belly never seems to get warm. On the day she arrives at Jack's shack she warms John's frostbitten hands: "She . . . thrust my hands into her armpits . . . I . . . felt the sensation come back, felt the warmth and pressure from her, the swell of her breasts against my wrists" (266). Here the symptomatic cold is close to what it was in the nightmare, but there is a good enough breast to warm him. He wants to feel that warmth in his belly as well and makes a toddy (daddy), but it fails him: "I wanted the toddy hot . . . so hot it would burn." But having drunk it, he says, "The warmth hadn't made a dent on the cold in me" (306).

After his body is thawed out, she pushes him to talk and he resists. Although he begins to talk, her counterresistance intrudes. Finally, she owns it: "'All the way up here I was waiting to talk to you. I was worried and I was scared, but what I wanted was to talk to you. So I get here and all I can do is yell at you and badger you and act . . . like a Southern belle who can't have everything nice and neat and clean'" (307). She was not prepared for all the "shit" she encountered on the hill and in the hollow. Moreover, she is ambivalent about hearing his past with all the "dirt" of the place; she sees her defensiveness; and she declares her love by being loving. Her revelation is emotionally comforting to John—it warms him up; he feels loved—"'It's good to see you,'" he says in response.

John becomes trusting enough to tell her that he came to understand (on the day he wrote to her) that his father committed suicide, and he decided to stay at Jack's to try to understand that act of madness. Moses, it seems, was driven crazy by his inability to understand—or by his understanding of— what happened to his grandfather, C.K. Judith is no closer to understanding why John had to "walk away from everything to come set up housekeeping in a one-room shack with a dirt floor" (268). The revelation of Moses' suicide transforms them both, even though they do not understand it.

At the moment of John's revelation to Judith, she becomes very powerful and he becomes very childlike: "She . . . pulled me up . . . undressed me quickly, efficiently, as if she were undressing a child. I did not resist her"

(319). She puts him to bed, undresses, and joins him. In bed, she continues to hold him like a child—she "pulled me to her, her arms strong . . . holding me immobile . . . her body . . . unyielding." It is as if she had wrapped him in swaddling. He struggles, but she whispers and soothes him "until the keening of the logs . . . became a lullaby." Out of this quiet, mother-child intensity comes an active intimacy. A symbiotic moment becomes a sexual one—the only one between them depicted in the novel and likely to be a procreative one. Judith and John had talked of having a child shortly before he knew he was going to take care of Jack; Judith said, "'I think I would like to have your child'" (249). But she feels he would not: "'You as much as admitted that if I were pregnant, you'd leave me'" (250). In the shack, now, she takes his seed; he yields it.

Their intimacy occurs the night after Jack's funeral—the father is dead, all the fathers are dead. In the intimate moment between John and Judith, the biological fathers are to be regenerated. When John is in Judith's embrace, he notes: "I thought I would fall asleep, fall away from her. And then, *just when I would have,* she gave one deep sigh and her breathing quickened, and I felt her thighs move, slipping around me below and above, and I *felt her belly against me* and then the softness and heat and moistness that lurked below" (320, my emphasis). Judith "makes" him a child—follows him to Jack's out of love and concern, warms him with her breasts, listens to his pain, undresses him, holds him in swaddling, merges with him ("just when I would have")—and then she makes a child with him in her belly. Her inner warmth, her creativity, her good insides, become his.

The regenerative act is powerful beyond the moment; this order of intimacy has not obtained in the family for long years. John's mother, for example, explains her marriage to Moses as a kind of deal: "'He wanted two sons . . . after your brother was born, that was the end of . . . that part of things. Because he had what he wanted, and I had what I wanted'" (322). C.K. had conceived a child with a woman he loved, but she was killed in a white-inspired race riot. He has a son, Lamen, with a woman he does not marry or particularly love as he loved his wife and later another woman, Harriet Brewer. Moses' mother dies in childbirth. Generative, emotional love carries with it a great danger in the family—the men are shocked by loss and thus fearful of contact. John becomes frozen, suffering from a kind of male frigidity which Judith resolves. In loving her, he has managed to fill the gap, to cross the gorge.

The day after Judith and John are sexually intimate, they visit the graveyard where Moses killed himself and, John concludes, where C.K. and the runaways are buried. As in Moses' attic, John is able to read the scene of the graveyard—the layout of the stones tells who is related to whom. When they return to the shack, John begins explaining his hypothesis about Moses' death. It is a spiritual idea—Moses killed himself, not to die but to be with his relatives—and Judith finds it "crazy." But she stops resisting the idea, as she had the day before. She brings John a hot toddy while he is talking; it is the first time she was willing to do so: "'You don't think I understand. You're right; I don't understand. But I can believe in you. . . . And if you say you need something that I can't give you, something you need a toddy to get, then I'll make a toddy for you'" (407). John gets what he wants and needs from Judith—basic support, belief, warmth from the female breast, and a sense of creative potency. With her good insides coming into him along with the good insides of the ancestral figures, he is intoxicated and enabled to follow Jack's tracking/hunting instructions: "Quit tryin' to figure where he's at an' just follow him'" (410).

John begins to hear the wind, as he heard the wire in the opening paragraph of the novel: he has a new symbiotic tie. In the wind he hears the breathing of the runaways. He is able to envision C.K. and reconstruct the two-day ordeal he and the twelve runaways endured before dying. It is an important matter for him to tell the tale because of "what a man's dying really means: his story is lost" (49). When Jack is close to death, John says the "stories were breaking up inside him; he coughed out fragments." John offers reparation, becomes a progenitor, and fulfills his promise.

By telling the tale, he also communicates with Judith: he tells her that her love for him has allowed him to leap the gorge and has thawed him out. His metacommunications occur through the medium of the story. He tells her about a gorge, "'a jagged gash in the mountainside,'" which C.K. will have to cross two times in order to shake his pursuers. This is the gorge of John's nightmare. It takes courage to jump, so C.K. "'reached down *into his guts* and found a little more will, a little more determination'" and he "'leaped'" (422–25, my emphasis). Having shaken the bounty hunters, he reaches the runaways among whom is his lost love, Harriet. John pauses in the tale to note something auspicious about his insides: "And then I realized that something strange was happening. Because I was no longer cold." The tale is resumed:

> "He was warm now," I said. "He was warm, and the feeling was strange.
> Because he had not realized how cold he had been. He had known that
> his hands and feet were cold . . . so numb he had lost the feeling. . . . But

> he had not known about the other cold, *the cold inside, the glacier in his guts that had been growing and moving, inch by inch, year by year, grinding at him freezing him . . . he could feel it melting. The heat that melted it did not come from the fire; it came from her arms . . . the warmth of her hand that cupped the base of his belly.*" (430–31, my emphasis)

Before Judith's arrival, John was on the brink of repetition, of suicide, of jumping blindly into the gorge. Unable to speak, he would enact, reenact. What John figures out, or lets himself discover, is that C.K. and the twelve runaways were trapped by white slave catchers but died rather than be taken. The song he imagines they sing when the slave catchers move in—the same sung at his father's funeral—tells the story: "'And before I'll be a slave I'll be buried in my grave, and go home to my God, and be free'" (448). Moses, enraged much of his life, is not able to love, is maddened, and repeats the death he doesn't fathom. John is released from reenacting by telling the tale. He is free enough to risk living. In the quotation above, we see that the cold in the belly is dissipated, and it is the "mother" with good enough breasts and insides who has helped dissolve the ice. Judith brings John into new life; he brings Jack, Moses, and C.K. back to life; and together Judith and John bring a new generation to life.

Coda

This chapter has traced the history of a symptom portrayed as a part of a character's psychological makeup. It has examined the evolution and transformation of the personal and transpersonal rage engendered by racism. It is the rage of the American black engendered by the external white world and internalized by the black self, occasionally used against the Other in violence but invariably moved against the self, sometimes to the point of revolutionary or spiritual suicide as the only escape from enslavement—I think of Richard in *Go Tell it on the Mountain*, Okonkwo in Achebe's *Things Fall Apart* or Sethe's baby in Morrison's *Beloved*.

The novel is a quest to complete history and to continue life. Although arduous and painful, the quest is successful and liberating: the tale is told and the future becomes possible. The hero descends into the darkness of the past—slavery, postslavery racist destruction, and the fight for political freedom—carrying with him the psychological pain of five generations. He emerges with a new understanding that enables him to be freed of psychological symptoms and to be generative as an artist and a man.

In the course of the quest, the racial frame that surrounds life for blacks in America is confronted but is not addressed in a simple fashion: white people enslaved blacks and systematically cut off and destroyed routes of escape, physical and psychological; but white people also fought against this system, and black people, including John's own mother, sold out to it at great cost to others. Most significant to the present time in the novel is that John Washington has a long-term relationship with a white woman whose family history is implicated in slave dealings, and this woman, Judith, helps John reach the understanding he is seeking. The rage that consumes John from within is the internalized bad object of racist (and sexist) perceptions, prescriptions, and proscriptions. The intimacy offered by Judith neutralizes the rage and frees John's energy to focus on creation.

Resolution of racial conflict on a political level is not generalized. That John has an intimate relationship with Judith, that they might have an interracial child, does not suggest racial conflict is at an end. But on the aesthetic level and in the realm of creativity, there is a generative synthesis of Western white ways and African ways, for example, scientific methodology and spiritual in-touchness. We see the synthesis of narrative tradition and linguistic strains in Bradley's embedded way of telling the mesh of tales and the ways he tells the individual tales. That is, Bradley gives us a range of voices—Jack Crawley's tales about Moses; C.K.'s various diaries and accounts; John's tales to Judith and his monologues on such matters as the class analysis of toilet facilities in public transportation, the history of street names in his town. It is in this range of voices that integration takes place.

Bradley sees it is possible for a black man to make the synthesis of black and white—he has done so. It is as Jack says of Moses several times, he can "talk like a white man." Knowing this other language allows an edge in the conflict as well as in creative and moral development. The question is whether a white man can do likewise—it will only be at that point that racial conflict will diminish because racial difference will be creatively appreciated instead of defended against out of fear, anxiety, or guilt.

8

Coda

The body is the center of culture. There is very little human effort that does not in one way or another emanate from or return to the human body. The body acts — gathers, hunts, cultivates, and fabricates — and interacts to obtain and ensure its comforts, to protect it against harms, and to relieve its pains and wounds. It has been remarkably successful and prolific; it has been maddeningly destructive as well. On its own, however, the body would not have attained the powers it has achieved. Only by coevolving with human language has it been able to generate such a reach and range. Language codifies our cultivations and fabrications and thereby ensures their independent survival and modifications in the manner that all things coevolve or become extinct. DNA is the code of our genetic body; our more imperfect but more flexible and mutable verbal language is the language of our human body. This language spirals with the body — it invents, voices, and stirs the very desires it helps to satisfy by cultivation, fabrication, and destruction.

We see the body transformed in various ways. We recognize in machines, for example, extensions of our bodily functions; machines are specialized part-functions that perform for us more effectively and precisely than we could alone (though, as Illich [1977] recognizes, not without cost). We recognize our bodies, also, in symbolic artifacts — fabrications that do not have a visible function, which in Morse Peckham's phrase exhibit "nonfunctional stylistic dynamism" (1967, 69–73) — paintings, novels, fashion (clothing, automotive), and the like. We have recognized, from Freud on, the presence of the body in the images, symbols, and syntax of our dreams. In this book, I set out to illustrate how deeply the body is embedded in linguistic artifacts. I have shown how one detects, reads, and articulates the presence of the body through a mixture of feelings and responses, linguistic analysis, and psychoanalysis.

The body is by no means the only thread in the linguistic complex of the novel, but I see it at the core. That is, the body embeds the conflicts it encounters and transforms them into symptoms (internalized politics), interpersonal behavior (externalized politics), or symbolic language (aesthetic, theoretical, and so on) with its own political subtext (Laing 1970, Millett 1969). Scholars of the subjective (e.g., Bleich 1979 or Stolorow and Atwood 1979) have identified how theory is formed (informed and deformed) by personality, family history, and conflicts. I sense that the preverbal, the nonverbal, the shut-up—that which happens to the body without benefit of language—is at the core of one's subjectivity. Having suffered to the point of or beyond its threshold of tolerance, the body seeks relief, perhaps for all of its days, as post-traumatic stress syndrome suggests. The body might enact that suffering and reenact it, it might simply die, or it might, through language, transform it, shift its energy from negating the other or the self to affirming the other, the self, and the negative, and thereby take the negative out of the realm of the unspoken, the repeated.

Maxine Hong Kingston's story "White Tigers" in *The Woman Warrior* tells a tale of Fa Mu Lan, the woman warrior. She is trained as a soldier-warrior in the mountains for years by an elderly couple. When she returns home, in part to lead an army to right various injustices, her parents are eager to see justice done and to make sure all know the injustice, the following takes place:

> "We are going to carve revenge on your back," my father said. "We'll write out oaths and names."
>
> "Wherever you go, whatever happens to you, people will know our sacrifice," my mother said. "And you'll never forget either." . . .
>
> My father . . . brushed the words in ink, and they fluttered down my back row after row. Then he began cutting; to make fine lines and points he used thin blades, for the stems, large blades.
>
> My mother caught the blood and wiped the cuts with a cold towel soaked in wine. It hurt terribly—the cuts sharp; the air burning; the alcohol cold, then hot—pain so various. I gripped my knees. I released them. Neither tension nor relaxation helped. I wanted to cry. If not for the fifteen years of training, I would have writhed on the floor. I would have had to be held down. The list of grievances went on and on. (34–35)

It is my sense that most people have such experiences—having the grievances of the Other metaphorically carved into one's back, embedded in one's body. Writers transform such matters by carving on paper—recall Blake's "corroding fires." The transformation is of great consequence because it takes the realm of action/reaction (our DNA body) into the realm of language and defuses the potential for destruction while exercising the feelings of it. Writers do one of the most human things one can do—they put something into language and thus out of action.

It is understandable that a writer may work out pain through language. But what happens for or to the reader of the writer's journey? Aristotle's idea that we experience a catharsis in relation to aesthetic works (specifically, tragedy) points the way by suggesting a bodily response. Aristotle's metaphor of catharsis suggests that something enters the body and then leaves the body taking impurities with it, hence "purifying" and "purging." The interaction between reader and text, in addition to this product, this cleansing, is a process, an "exercising" that may well be the major agent in the purifying process. That is, the interaction reminds—perhaps rebodies—the reader of more of his or her feelings than he or she is generally aware. This exercise of feelings, responses to representations, seems to have something to do with our species' survival; we would not find so much of it otherwise.

Gregory Bateson has suggested in various places in his writings that art is crucial to our survival. For example, he speaks about flexibility being a key to a system's survival—flexibility, "defined as uncommitted potentiality for change." Specialization, a formidable aspect of modern life, tends to undermine flexibility. It is the loss of perspective and consequent rigidification which he feels are restored by exercising the subjective: "Mere purposive rationality unaided by such phenomena as art, religion, dream and the like, is necessarily pathogenic and destructive of life; and that its virulence springs specifically from the circumstance that life depends upon interlocking circuits of contingency, while consciousness can see only such short arcs of such circuits as human purpose may direct." D. W. Winnicott in his explorations of play has said something that speaks to the environment the arts create and the function they serve: "It is assumed here that the task of reality-acceptance is never completed, that no human being is free from the strain of relating inner and outer reality, and that relief from this strain is provided by an intermediate area of experience which is not challenged (arts, religion, etc.). . . . This intermediate area is in direct continuity with the play area of the small child who is 'lost' in play" (1958, 241). Morse Peckham has suggested something else about the relation of audience and art: that "art is the reinforcement of the capacity to endure disorientation . . . [a] rehearsal for the orientation which makes innovation possible" (314). Putting these remarks together, we find that staying alive, surviving on a large scale, requires flexibility. When our arteries—actual or metaphoric—get rigid, the system will fail. For a system to be and remain flexible, it must exercise that flexibility. Art provides that exercise, it exercises the inner body, and it does so because the inner body is inscribed through the language on the page. Art also provides a space outside the usual realm of life tasks which must be carried out appropriately or one will be fired, divorced, locked up, or committed. The space is, as Winnicott suggests, relatively free of the judgment of others or the demands though it is by no means without constraints, rules, and demands. It is a relatively safe place in which to exercise a different order of stress, a dynamic stress, an essential tension.

If we become locked into the objective mode, Bateson's "mere purposive reality," we will become pathogenic. Winnicott says there are some people "who are so firmly anchored in objectively perceived reality that they are ill . . . being out of touch with the subjective world and with the creative approach to fact." Paulo Freire, in another context, suggests the need for a dialectic; otherwise one has objectivists who make up a world without people and subjectivists who make up people without a world (1972, 35). Winnicott suggests a tension between self and other, inner and outer. Bateson points to rebalancing out-of-balance systems by ensuring communication between levels of mind. Art is effective in teaching us something about the balance, the dialogue, the dialectic of you and me, in that it represents the body and resonates with the body—it exorcises, excoriates, exercises.

I do not mean to suggest that literature is a savior. Virtually any aspect of reality can be turned. We learn from the brilliant analyses of such transformations in Nazi Germany by Bruno Bettelheim (*The Informed Heart*, 1960) and Robert Jay Lifton (*The Nazi Doctors*, 1986) that the right set of negativities can take even the Hippocratic oath and invert/subvert it, creating a moral black hole. Literature has a force, and having one, it can be bent, shifted. The force is related to a primitive quality, one with which we might well resonate because it is physical, bodily. The literary artist uses the primitive to give force to culture, that is, to continue the possible, the "infinite game" (Carse 1986). The writer finds a way to contain aggression in language and hold fragmentation together in form. As such, literary artists are the polar opposite of terrorists, who use the sophisticated tools of human culture to give force to the primitive, to act in reality in such a way as to destroy it.

Literature may well be a gift, but as feminist criticism has amply illustrated, there are politics in the gift—there is power vested, power taken, and power withheld; social myths are perpetuated, even propagandized. Thus in the excerpt from Maxine Hong Kingston we see that language is also part of the pain of the tale, for it is language which is carved into the back.

◇◇ In the analysis of the novels here, the body has emerged through a linguistic exploration grounded in Chomsky's notion of transformational-generative grammar. The vision that arises by seeing the language of a novel through that lens is akin to something my computer program allows, that is, to see all the commands embedded in the text, for example, tabs, page numbers, running heads, margins, line spacing, and so on. Imagine, then, being able to see the distinctive features of each word in the text. Such a display would make it clear that the text is organismic—not only in terms of its vast networks of connections but also in terms of its motility, as the words flow and permeate one another. More concretely, our imaginary display would let us see what words were marked <+body>, and we could then trace, name, and analyze their various pathways. In addition, we could discern another range of words; in these words we would find shared distinctive features with words marked <+body>—and by the action of linguistic slippage, this range of words often comes to represent the body. So the body is directly present— named (nouns) and implied (verbs)—and it is shaded in by the cross-hatching of other layers of reference—the linguistic slippage of spatial images and syntactic images.

I have approached and explored this body, emerging from the linguistic complexity, with a psychoanalytic perspective. In fact, it was because I had been reading psychoanalytically that it occurred to me that a linguistic analysis would make the body all the more palpable. The imaginary linguistic display makes clear that the body is present, but linguistics is a discipline that, like all disciplines, reads only what it reads. Psychoanalysis allows us to read, to talk about, the cohesion and chaos of the body, its boundaries, terrors, and desires. It seems to me that no other discourse has focused so clearly on the interface of body and language.

The separate discussion of each novel has brought their different emphases; I would like to emphasize that they also share some deep connections to the body. Analogically, our fingerprints all differ, but they are all found on an organ that shares particular functions. I would observe the following, as a beginning: All the novels present virtually the whole body along with its history; and all the novels are versions of life myths—inception, conception, birth, symbiosis, separation, wounding and breaking apart, growth, generation, death. At the same time, or in the same space, we do not always perceive the body's presence while we are in (or "into") the narrative, and yet it communicates feelings to us, to our bodies. Finally, when we do perceive the body, it is both coherent and not coherent, stable and mutable, firmly defended and permeable, primitive and mature.

We might note, more concretely, some aspects of the body shared by the works examined. All the novels have a concern with eating—thus the mouth and the breast:

1 Crusoe's focus of energy on defending himself against being swallowed and on ensuring himself ample supplies of necessities;

2 Jane Eyre's fantasy of not eating as a way to die; her later experience of being without food and almost dying; her various shifts in appetite; her emotional feedings from Miss Temple and Mr. Rochester; and her bringing Mr. Rochester a glass of water at the moment of rapprochement;

3 Mrs. Ramsay's dinner which nurtures the visitors and family as food and feeling;

4 John Washington's attachment to, history of, and need for hot toddies.

The characters take something inside to make something, for example, Crusoe "takes everything" from the ship; Jane and Rochester take in each other with their eyes; Mr. Ramsay drinks from the fountain Mrs. Ramsay offers, Mrs. Ramsay takes in the lighthouse beam, Mr. Carmichael takes a second bowl of soup; John Washington drinks the drink made by his father and his great-grandfather and his great-great-grandfather—to get a good enough breast (food, feelings, money, drink, supplies). The characters are also confronted with bad insides—having messy insides, vomiting something bad, or being eaten by others (Crusoe), being eaten or frozen from within (John Washington's "glacier in his guts"), being intruded on and damaged (Lily Briscoe), being empty or ripped open (Jane Eyre). We find pile-ups of shit (Bradley), corpses (Defoe), blood (Woolf), secrets (Brontë); we find death and mutilation—cannibals, slavery, war, suicidal/homicidal fire, sexual abuse).

As if to counter such terror, all the novels present a desire to be in a safe space—a womb or embrace: Crusoe's deeply embedded fortress or his richly fecund island omphalos; several of Jane Eyre's beds and bedrooms (e.g., sleeping with Helen, being safely in bed at her cousins'); Mrs. Ramsay's wedge-shape core of darkness, and also, for most of the characters, their very own consciousness, their very own spaces; Moses Washington's study, indeed his house. All the novels express a desire for excitement, adventure, stimulation—phallic, clitoral, vaginal—to penetrate, to open. All the novels have hands that create by writing, painting, drawing, knitting, weaving, potting, building (homes, walls, boats, stills). And all the novels present the death of the body—sacrificed, risked, aged.

Out of the struggles come more struggles because only through differ-ence, tension, is life life—chaos and cohesion, narrative and its disintegra-tion. The novel reaches to the primitive body, which knows no boundaries—where men have breasts (the "table in the wilderness" God sets for Crusoe, the hot toddy Jack gives John, which warms him) and women phallus (Jane's penetrating eye, Mrs. Ramsay's umbrella, fountain, beauty, and knitting nee-dles, Lily Briscoe's paintbrush); where the eyes and mouth metamorphose; where bowel and womb shift into one another. And from this primitive body, the novel reaches back up into language telling us a tale, carrying us along on a journey in time, space, and mind.

Notes

Chapter 1

1. Thirty years ago Starobinski said that once we begin looking into the issue of the body "it becomes apparent that we are far from being the first discoverers of bodily reality. That reality was the first knowledge to enter human understanding: 'They knew that they were naked' (Genesis 3.7). From then on, it has been impossible to ignore the body" (1989 [1964], 353). A look into Barbara Duden's "Repertory of Body History," a hundred-page bibliography/index of modern/contemporary works on the body, allows one to see one part of the library on the body. Every mode of discourse has a continuing focus on the body—expressive, literary, scientific, metalinguistic. Within all the major disciplines of the physical, social, and human sciences the body is examined: historical, social, psychological, anthropological, medical, biological, chemical. We have reached a remarkable point of reading the language of our own genes.

2. Gregory Bateson defines coevolution as a process of interaction in which changes in one element "set the stage for the natural selection of changes" in another element whose changes in turn set the stage for "more similar changes" in the first (1979, 46, 227).

Chapter 2

1. Morse Peckham (1967), Gregory Bateson (1972), and D. W. Winnicott (1971a) all argue, in their own ways, from their own disciplines, that the arts and the particular tensions they allow us to experience and exercise are salutary and necessary in the same way that dreams are necessary to health and survival.

2. A new piece of research (Beardsley 1989) confirms Spitz's findings from a converse perspective: handling premature infants increases their growth—the contact of hand to body stimulates actual growth and increases the number of neurotransmitters and hormones necessary for it.

3. Miller's observations are not singular; see, for example, Anny Katan's "Children Who Were Raped" in which she notes, "Some of my patients showed a repetition compulsion even more dangerous than that described by Oxman. They had the tendency to expose their own children to the same experience, mostly by not protecting them when they should have been protected. Their own overwhelming excitement severely hampered their capability for mothering" (1973, 220).

4. See, for example, Dorothy Bloch (1978). Bloch's work does for fantasy what Piaget's work does for perception—she allows us to see the process of the transformation of parental patterns as they become distorted into fear by the child's way of reading the patterns.

5. One can find numerous examples of bodily fantasies in Klein's work; it is the ground from which she works. See also *Love, Guilt and Reparation, and Other Works, 1921–1945* (1981).

Chapter 3

1. I would mention Ronald Finke's essay "Mental Imagery and the Visual System." Finke's experimental work investigates the "fundamental relations between mental imagery and visual perception" and shows that although there are differences between them, "mental images display a much richer variety of visual properties than had been previously thought" (1986, 88). Indeed, the activity of the brain in seeing an object and in imagining the same object are remarkably similar. Thus, as we read a novel, say, our "mental imagery" may stir up mental activities very similar to those we would have were the object physically present.

2. I would point to Paul Fussell's essay which articulates the visceral horror of war's carnage, the madness and degradations it begets. He speaks to and of the "public innocence about the bizarre damage suffered by the human body in modern war" (1989, 34), and notes that witnessing such damage is another level of damage: "You can't take much of that sort of thing [grisly encounters with shot-up bodies] without going mad" (36).

Chapter 4

1. Robert A. Erikson points out how female many of Crusoe's works are: "When we look specifically at the things Crusoe learns to make on the island, most of these reflect his growing mastery in creating and preserving feminine shapes and maternal spaces. Part of the function of the maternal aspect of his island experience then is that Crusoe learns to behave like a mother and homemaker" (1982, 64). More generally, Erikson discusses many of the maternal features of Crusoe's experiences in the natural world—the sea, the ship, the island itself; he sees a range of emotional responses to the "ambivalent maternal force" Crusoe encounters "from terrrible, destructive, or barren, to productive, erotic, harmonious, or protective" (52). Erikson notes that although women are absent from the island, "there is a profound concern, intimately allied with the 're-making' process, with generation, breeding, new growth and development" (52).

2. In particular, I have in mind the ecology movement that has begun systematically thinking about the consequences of such factors as depletion, exploitation, and dumping. This movement is akin to the civil rights movement and the women's movement in its developed consciousness. Behind the ecology movement is the development of general systems theory, cybernetics, and information theory. See, for example, Ludwig von Bertalanffy (1975). Gregory Bateson's "Roots of Ecological Crisis" points to the ecological crisis as rooted in epistemological errors, especially ones that split individuals or groups from

their environment: "When you narrow down your epistemology and act on the premise 'What interests me is me, or my organization, or my species,' you chop off consideration of other loops of the loop structure. You decide that you want to get rid of the by-products of human life and that Lake Erie will be a good place to put them. You forget that the eco-mental system called Lake Erie is part of your eco-mental system—and that if Lake Erie is driven insane, its insanity is incorporated in the larger system of *your* thought and experience" (1972, 484). Bill McKibben's *End of Nature* (1989) also explores the ramifications of development, the realization of a natureless planet, and the paradigms that human beings have chosen and can choose from. See also Davis (1990).

3. Defoe did not manage to keep what he had; he lost in a repetitious way. Reading his biographies (Sutherland 1938, Moore 1958, or Backscheider 1989), one is impressed with the pattern of losses in the form of money but also in the form of support, to the point of betrayal, from fellow dissenters, business partners, political figures, his own son. As a man who took risks, economic and political, he made himself vulnerable; he then had to scramble very hard to maintain balance. It is impressive, for example, to realize, as Backscheider's biography highlights, just how many words Defoe produced in various periods of his life to survive economically. I suspect his economic and emotional losses repeated the loss of his mother before he was eleven and no doubt earlier losses as well. As a young witness and survivor of the Plague and the Great Fire he must have developed a keen sense of loss. Whatever the psychological bottom line might be, there is something nearly compulsive about the pattern of loss.

4. Had Freud considered these words in his work on the antithetical meanings, he would have noted in English that "womb" and "bowel" share letters in a symmetrically inverted way; the relationship of the words may speak to an early sense of their physiological (functional) relationship; and Freud's "Three Essays on Sexuality" (1905) addresses the matter of "theories of birth" (S.E., 5, 195–96). Children confuse or condense the areas of bowel and womb. In David Bradley's *Chaneysville Incident* we find a similar ambiguity and switching.

5. In the 1960s one could discern aspects of this split in Defoe's work by the split in the focus of critical studies. On the one hand Ian Watt focuses on the rise of individualism within "the rise of modern industrial capitalism and the spread of Protestantism" (1965, 60) and sees "economic man" as central to Defoe's work: "All Defoe's heroes pursue money, which he characteristically called 'the general denominating article in the world' [*Review*, III (1706)]; and they pursue it very methodically according to . . . profit and loss bookkeeping . . . the distinctive feature of modern capitalism" (63). On the other hand, the work of Hunter (1966), Grief (1966), and Starr (1965) stresses the spiritual and religious aspect of Defoe's novel. Starr, for example, explicitly argues against Watt and other economic critics and sees in Crusoe's actions a fundamental, spiritual tale,—for example, his rebellion is not only against father but God: "Implicit in Defoe's treatment [of Crusoe's 'original sin'] . . . is a conventional identification of family, social and divine order, all of which are flouted by Crusoe's deed" (77). In the mid-1970s, John Richetti brought these views to a useful synthesis: "I think we must concede the accuracy of *both* these descrip-

tions [economic and spiritual]; Crusoe is . . . neither exclusively a masterful economic individual nor a heroically spiritual slave. He inhabits both ideologies in such a way that he manages to be both at once and therefore to reside in neither" (1975, 23). In the argument I am advancing, I place the dynamic of the split Richetti articulates on a psychological register, between body/desire and mind/will (a split of the mother), or between mother (money) and father (law) (a split between mother and father).

6. For example, Dinnerstein argues that we have "the responsibility to protect nature" (1976, 10) but that the split engendered in our sexual being generates a ruthlessness toward nature as a displaced mother, and "if she does not provide us with everything we would like to have . . . her treasure . . . can if necessary be taken by force" (109). Elsewhere, she says, "The son has set his foot on the mother's chest, he has harnessed her firmly to his uses, he has opened her body once and for all and may now help himself at will to its riches. What remains is the danger that she will be depleted, spoiled. Men's view of this danger has been fatally short-sighted; it has not kept pace with the actual growth of their destructive power" (104).

Davis points to two current paradigms of environmental economists: "The consensus view assumes a 'business as usual' attitude, with an overall growth in consumption. The sustainable-world view assumes radical improvements in effciency with demand stabilizing" (1990, 60). He explores the difference: "As we learn more about the relation human beings have to their planet, we may find that rather than viewing energy as a commodity to be exploited *from* planet Earth, we will increasingly need to think and act in terms of energy *for* the planet Earth" (62). Davis's argument that we cannot simply take, that we have to give and care, has a remarkable resemblance both to Melanie Klein's discussion of the infant's split attitudes toward the mother and to Dinnerstein's argument, partly based on Klein, that child rearing patterns must change if, among other things, "men" are to stop taking so much without caring enough.

7. R. D. Laing delineates the impoverishment that occurs when the self is divided against itself; many of his descriptions fit very clearly with Crusoe's character and the general argument I am advancing here about Crusoe's conflicts. The "mutual enrichment" that can take place in a "creative relationship" (1970, 86–87) becomes impossible for the "ontologically insecure" individual: "The self then seeks by being unembodied to transcend the world and hence to be safe. But a self is liable to develop which feels it is outside all experience . . . a vacuum. Everything is there, outside; nothing is here, inside. Moreover, the constant dread of all that is there, of being overwhelmed, is potentiated rather than mitigated by the need to keep the world at bay" (84).

8. Searles develops a complex argument on the relationship between symbiosis, murderousness, and identity (1979, 45–70). The desire for a symbiotic relatedness strongly counters a desire for individual identity, and parent or child might feel murderous in the face of challenges to symbiotic ties in the forming of identity. Crusoe's murderousness— his destruction of animals and cannibals—can be read as attempts to assert his identity, his separateness. It is the vehemence of these assertions that gives one a sense of overcompensating for a desire not to be separate.

Chapter 5

1. The phrase, *stade de miroir* is Lacan's (1977, 1–7). I use it here for adolescent discovery and rediscovery of the body (see Kaplan 1984). The adolescent self seeing often returns the person to his or her child self seeing or to primal scenes. I sense at times that one's entire life takes place in relation to one's current *stade de miroir*.

2. I think of Foucault's opening essay in *The Order of Things: An Archaeology of The Human Sciences* (1970, 3–16). In it he analyzes Velazquez's "Las Maninas," particularly in relation to various levels of reflection and gazing.

3. The biography I rely on for my impression of the atmosphere at home is Elizabeth Gaskell's *Life of Charlotte Brontë* (1971), even though Gaskell is not the last word in Brontë biography; see, for example, Tom Winnifrith, *The Brontës and Their Background: Romance and Reality* (1973). Some of the background facts one gets about Brontë's growing up is that the family did have to be very quiet at times, that the children were prodigious writers, and that the father at times invited the children to speak with a mask.

4. Several have written on this matter; see Burns (1952), McCurdy (1947), Smith (1974), Dingle (1972), Solomon (1959), and McGuire (1988).

Chapter 6

1. My use of "symbiosis" follows Margaret Mahler's *On Human Symbiosis and the Viscissitudes of Individuation*. The term is used metaphorically and, as Mahler says, "It was chosen to describe that state of undifferentiation, of fusion with mother, in which the 'I' is not yet differentiated from the 'not-I' " (1968, 9).

2. The notion of a "narcissistic defense" is Hyman Spotnitz's and is described in his *Psychotherapy of Preoedipal Conditions: Schizophrenia and Severe Character Disorders*. Spotnitz explains the defense as an "internalizing of . . . destructive impulses," and thus one "attacks his ego to preserve his external object" (1976, 105). As to the genesis of the defense, Spotnitz says it "seems to originate in a relationship that was gratifying to the infant in some respects, especially in meeting his biological needs . . . but failed to meet the need of his mental apparatus for cooperation in discharging destructive energy. . . . The infant got to understand that his mother might be damaged by his rage; perhaps she discouraged such reactions by withholding her favors" (104). I employ Spotnitz's concept primarily as a way of describing the self-attack in several characters in Woolf's work, as well as in Woolf herself. As we investigate Woolf's biography, the etiology of the defense becomes more significant if still hypothetical.

3. I use the term in the sense described in R. D. Laing's *Divided Self*. Laing describes a "creative relationship" as one "in which there is mutual enrichment of the self and the other" and this is compared to a "sterile relationship" (1976, 80). The latter might evolve, for example, when one fears "he will be engulfed or otherwise lose his identity" in an interaction with the other (80) and closes himself off from the other—and thereby deprives himself of emotional enrichment.

4. A sense of the female's genital vulnerability, which Woolf's work specifically focuses on (however indirectly or unconsciously), has been recognized by several psychoanalytic

writers. See Karen Horney, "The Dread of Women" and "The Denial of the Vagina" in *Feminine Psychology* (1967, 133–46, 147–61). See also Melanie Klein, *The Psychoanalysis of Children*, in which she proposes a female anxiety to parallel male castration fears: "the girl's deepest fear is of having the inside of her body robbed and destroyed" (1975, 194).

5. I refer here to D. W. Winnicott, *Playing and Reality*. Winnicott describes the "good enough" mother in the following way: "A baby is held, and handled satisfactorily, and with this taken for granted is presented with an object [i.e., the mothering figure] in such a way that the baby's legitimate experience of omnipotence is not violated. The result can be that the baby is able to use the object, and *to feel as if this object is a subjective object, and created by the baby*" (1971a, 112, my emphasis).

6. There are several biographical issues here—how old was Woolf when she was first sexually abused, how long did this abuse go on, who was responsible for it, and what was Woolf's overt attitude? In *Moments of Being*, Woolf is not specific about her age when first abused; she tells us only that she "was very small" (1976, 69). She is, however, specific about the perpetrator—it was Gerald Duckworth, not George. Quentin Bell's biography cites a letter of Woolf's to Ethel Smyth which describes the same incident and tells us her age—"about 6 or so"—but refers to the perpetrator only as her "half brother." Because there are later references in other letters to her having been molested by George Duckworth, Bell assumed that the half-brother referred to was George. Bell's work informs us that, according to his sources, Woolf continued to be molested and fondled by George even as late as 1904 (1972, 43). The attitude of Woolf toward these half-brothers and their abuse is important to address, especially in light of Nigel Nicolson's introduction to Woolf's letters (1975). Nicolson takes issue with Bell's contention that the sexual abuse had a profound effect on Woolf. Nicolson argues on the basis of letters, which Bell had not seen, that Woolf was on amiable terms with George and thus not so traumatized as Bell thinks. Nicolson does not seem to know much about family abuse and family networks. I would stand behind Bell's position and would argue further that the social deception for which Nicolson falls is as much at the root of Woolf's later problems as the assaults that initiated it. Woolf internalized the anger she felt, and like all such psychological operations, it would take a long time to surface. That she writes about it indicates that it does surface.

7. One of the first psychoanalysts to make a similar connection is Karl Abraham in his "Experiencing of Sexual Trauma as a Form of Sexual Activity." Abraham discusses a child who is hurt in the course of playing a forbidden game; the child suppresses the pain and tells no one about it. Abraham says, "The child had yielded to the attraction of doing something forbidden, and it now has the feeling that the accident is its own fault" (1972 [1907], 98). See also Alice Miller's works (1983, 1986).

8. Part of what I have in mind is Leonard Woolf's description of Virginia Woolf's recuperation procedures in *Beginning Again: An Autobiography of the Years 1911 to 1918*. He explains that when the first of Virginia's symptoms of illness appeared, "If she went to bed and *lay down doing nothing in a darkened room, drinking large quantities of milk* and eat-

ing well, the symptoms would slowly disappear and in a week or ten days she would be well again" (1964, 76, my emphasis).

Chapter 7

1. The phrase is Jacques Lacan's, and he uses it to describe the crucial locus of Melanie Klein's work. He says of Klein that it is through "her we know the function of the imaginary primordial enclosure formed by the *imago* of the mother's body; through her we have the cartography, drawn by the children's own hands, of the mother's internal empire" (1977, 20–21). Klein's work is influential in my thinking about this novel. The focus on the belly and its symptoms makes Klein's ideas appropriate.

2. See the section of Freud's *Interpretation of Dreams* (1953a [1901]) where he discusses "the means of representation" in dreams. Freud sees a "syntax" in the sequencing of items in a dream (S.E., 4, 310–38).

3. I take the wire to its most primitive roots. D.W. Winnicott has described string, used in children's play, as a concrete metaphor for a desire for communication or union, a denial of separation (1971a, 17–19, 42–43). Ella Freeman Sharpe associates string with "milk, water and semen" (1978, 56–57). One can see these other elements in Bradley's opening passage, especially in light of what follows; Winnicott gives us a higher level of generality than "umbilicus," and Sharpe offers us other concrete possibilities in addition to the prototype of birth and separation.

4. The notion of the transitional object is Winnicott's. He says such objects are found "between oral eroticism and true object-relations . . . between primary unawareness of indebtedness and the acknowledgement of indebtedness" (1971a, 2). He sees the object as "a symbol of the union of the baby and the mother . . . the place in space and time where and when the mother is in transition from being (in the baby's mind) merged in with the infant and alternatively being experienced as an object to be perceived rather than conceived of" (96).

5. The issue of reparation is a primary concern of Klein's; her notion is carried into the realm of aesthetic creation by Hannah Segal, who argues that "all creation is really a recreation of a once loved and once whole, but now lost and ruined object. . . . It is when the world within us is destroyed, when it is dead and loveless, when our loved ones are in fragments, and we ourselves in helpless despair—it is then that we must re-create our world anew, reassemble the pieces, infuse life into dead fragments, re-create life" (1981, 190).

6. I am thinking here of the "wisdom" that Gregory Bateson discusses in contradistinction to "mere purposive rationality," which so often leads to foul-ups in systems. Two essays elaborate on this distinction: "From Versailles to Cybernetics" (1972, 469–77) and "Style, Grace, and Information in Primitive Art" (1972, 128–52).

7. The relationship between metacommunication and interpersonal relationships has been explored by Bateson in his various essays on schizophrenia, e.g., "Double Bind, 1969" (1972, 271–78). Bateson's work is seminal; he opened up a way of thinking about interpersonal communications which many have followed up on. For example, see Laing, Phillipson, and Lee (1972) and, more recently, Slipp (1984). The significance of these

works in relation to the novel rests in their attention to and analysis of interpersonal verbal (and nonverbal) interaction, especially in the messages about the relationship as coded in the surface messages.

8. Harold Searles has recognized the defensive and sometimes damaging impact of "interpretation." See "The Effort to Drive the Other Person Crazy—an Element in the Aetiology and Psychotherapy of Schizophrenia" (1965, 254–83). See also Phyllis Whitcomb Meadow's "A Research Method for Investigating the Effectiveness of Psychoanalytic Techniques" (1974, 79–94). Meadow demonstrates the increased resistance often precipitated by interpretation.

References

The abbreviation for Feher (1989) *Fragments for a History of the Human Body*, is *FHHB*.

Abraham, Karl. 1927 [1907]. "The Experiencing of Sexual Trauma as a Form of Anxiety." In *Selected Papers on Psychoanalysis*, translated by D. Bryan and A. Strachey, 47–63. New York: Bruner/Mazel.

Achebe, Chinua. 1959. *Things Fall Apart*. Greenwich, Conn.: Fawcett.

Anzieu, Didier. 1989. *The Skin Ego: A Psychoanalytic Approach to the Self*. New Haven: Yale University Press.

———. 1990. "Formal Signifiers and the Ego-Skin." In *Psychic Envelopes*, edited by Didier Anzieu. London: Karnac Books.

Atwood, Margaret. 1972. *Surfacing*. New York: Warner Books.

———. 1986. *The Handmaid's Tale*. Boston: Houghton Mifflin.

Austen, Jane. 1957 [1816]. *Emma*. Cambridge, Mass.: Riverside Press.

Backscheider, Paula R. 1989. *Daniel Defoe: His Life*. Baltimore: Johns Hopkins University Press.

Baldwin, James. 1953. *Go Tell It on the Mountain*. New York: Dell.

Bandler, Richard, and John Grinder. 1978. *The Structure of Magic: A Book about Language and Therapy*. Palo Alto, Calif.: Science and Behavior Books.

Banks, Russell. 1990. *Affliction*. New York: Harper Perennial.

Barker, Francis. 1984. *The Tremulous Private Body: Essays on Subjection*. London: Methuen.

Barth, John. 1960. *The End of the Road*. New York: Avon.

Bateson, Gregory. 1972. *Steps to an Ecology of Mind*. New York: Ballantine Books.

———. 1979. *Mind and Nature: A Necessary Unity*. New York: E.P. Dutton.

Beardsley, T. M. 1989. "Different Strokes . . ." *Scientific American* 261, 3 (September):34–36.

Beckwith, Carol. 1989. "Geerewol: The Art of Seduction." *FHHB*, pt. 2, 200–216.

Bell, Quentin. 1972. *Virginia Woolf: A Biography*. New York: Harcourt Brace Jovanovich.

Benjamin, Jessica. 1988. *The Bonds of Love: Psychoanalysis, Feminism, and the Problem of Domination*. New York: Pantheon.

Berne, Eric. 1956. "The Psychological Structure of Space with Some Remarks on *Robinson Crusoe*." *Psychoanalytic Quarterly* 25:549–57.

Bertalanffy, Ludwig von. 1975. *Perspectives on General Systems Theory*. New York: George Braziller.

Bettelheim, Bruno. 1960. *The Informed Heart: Autonomy in a Mass Age*. New York: Avon.

————. 1979. *Surviving and Other Essays.* New York: Knopf.

————. 1983. *Freud and Man's Soul.* New York: Knopf.

Bleich, David. 1979. *Subjective Criticism.* Baltimore: Johns Hopkins University Press.

Bloch, Dorothy. 1978. *"So the Witch Won't Eat Me": Fantasy and the Child's Fear of Infanticide.* Boston: Houghton Mifflin.

Bloom, Harold. 1973. *The Anxiety of Influence: A Theory of Poetry.* New York: Oxford.

Boston Women's Health Course Collective. 1971. *Our Bodies, Our Selves: A Course by and for Women.* Boston: New England Free Press.

Bowie, Theodore, and C. Christenson, eds. 1970. *Studies in Erotic Art.* New York: Basic Books.

Bradley, David. 1981. *The Chaneysville Incident.* New York: Avon.

Brontë, Charlotte. 1966. *Jane Eyre.* Edited by Q. D. Leavis. New York: Penguin, 1966.

Brown, Norman O. 1959. *Life against Death.* New York: Vintage.

Burns, Wayne. 1952. "Freudianism, Criticism and *Jane Eyre.*" *Literature and Psychology* 2, 5 (November):4–13.

Burroughs, William. 1959. *Naked Lunch.* New York: Grove Press.

————. 1981. *Cities of the Red Night.* New York: Holt, Rinehart and Winston.

Carse, James. 1986. *Finite and Infinite Games.* New York: The Free Press.

Castaneda, Carlos. 1974. *The Teachings of Don Juan: A Yaqui Way of Knowledge.* New York: Washington Square Press.

Castle, Terry J. 1979. "'Amy, Who Knew My Disease': A Psychosexual Pattern in Defoe's *Roxana.*" *Journal of English Literary History* 46:81–96.

Chasseguet-Smirgel, Janine. 1984. *Creativity and Perversion.* New York: Norton.

————. 1985. *The Ego Ideal: A Psychoanalytic Essay on the Malady of the Ideal.* Translated by Paul Burrows. New York: Norton.

Chicago, Judy. 1979. *The Dinner Party: A Symbol of Our Heritage.* Garden City, N.Y.: Anchor Books.

Chicago Psychoanalytic Literature Index. 1978. Chicago: Chicago Processing Laboratories.

Chodorow, Nancy. 1978. *The Reproduction of Mothering: Psychoanalysis and the Sociology of Gender.* Berkeley: University of California Press.

Chomsky, Noam. 1957. *Syntactic Structures.* The Hague: Mouton.

————. 1965. *Aspects of the Theory of Syntax.* Cambridge: MIT Press.

————. 1980. *Rules and Representations.* New York: Columbia University Press.

Clark, Kenneth. 1972. *The Nude: A Study in Ideal Form.* Princeton: Princeton University Press.

Cleland, John. 1963 [1749]. *Memoirs of a Woman of Pleasure.* New York: G. P. Putnam.

Coles, Robert. 1967. *Children of Crisis: A Study in Courage and Fear.* Boston: Little, Brown.

Davis, Ged R. 1990. "Energy for Planet Earth." *Scientific American* (September):55–62.

Defoe, Daniel. 1964. *Roxana.* Edited by Jane Jack. New York: Oxford University Press.

————. 1972. *Robinson Crusoe.* Edited by J. Donald Crowley. London: Oxford University Press.

DeSalvo, Louise. 1989. *Virginia Woolf: The Impact of Childhood Sexual Abuse on Her Life and Work.* Boston: Beacon.

Dickens, Charles. 1956 [1853]. *Bleak House.* Cambridge, Mass.: Riverside Press.
Dingle, Herbert. 1972. "The Origin of Heathcliff." *Brontë Society Transactions* 16:131–38.
Dinnerstein, Dorothy. 1976. *The Mermaid and the Minotaur: Sexual Arrangements and Human Malaise.* New York: Harper Colophon.
Duden, Barbara. 1989. "A Repertory of Body History." *FHHB,* pt. 3, 470–575.
Duverger, Christian. 1989. "The Meaning of Sacrifice." *FHHB,* pt. 3, 367–85.
Eco, Umberto. 1976. *A Theory of Semiotics.* Bloomington: Indiana University Press.
Erikson, Erik. 1963. *Childhood and Society.* 2d ed. New York: Norton.
Erikson, Robert A. 1982. "Starting Over with *Robinson Crusoe.*" *Studies in the Literary Imagination* 15, 2 (Fall):51–73.
Feher Michel, ed. 1989. *Fragments for a History of the Human Body.* Parts One–Three. 3 vols. New York: Zone Books.
Finke, Robert. 1986. "Mental Imagery and the Visual System." *Scientific American* 28, 2 (March):88–95.
Fliess, Robert. 1961. *Ego and Body Ego.* New York: International Universities Press.
Foucault, Michel. 1970. *The Order of Things: An Archaeology of the Human Sciences.* New York: Pantheon Books.
———. 1980. *The History of Sexuality.* Vol. 1: *An Introduction.* Translated by Robert Hurley. New York: Vintage.
———. 1986. *The History of Sexuality.* Vol. 2: *The Use of Pleasure.* Translated by Robert Hurley. New York: Vintage.
Fraser, Rebecca. 1988. *The Brontës: Charlotte Brontë and Her Family.* New York: Fawcett Columbine, 1988.
Freire, Paulo. 1972. *Pedagogy of the Oppressed.* New York: Herder and Herder.
Freud, Anna. 1969. *The Writings of Anna Freud.* Vol. 5, 1956–65. New York: International Universities Press.
Freud, Sigmund. 1953a [1901]. *The Interpretation of Dreams.* S.E. 4. London: Hogarth Press.
———. 1953b [1905]. "Fragment of an Analysis of a Case of Hysteria." S.E. 7. London: Hogarth Press.
———. 1957a [1910]. "A Special Type of Choice of Object Made by Men." S.E. 11, 163–75.
———. 1957b [1912]. "On the Universal Tendency to Debasement in the Sphere of Love." S.E. 11, 177–90.
———. 1961 [1923]. *The Ego and the Id.* S.E. 19. London: Hogarth Press.
———. 1966 [1886]. "Observations of a Severe Case of Hemi-Anaesthesia in a Hysterical Male." S.E. 1, 23–31.
Friedan, Betty. 1964. *The Feminine Mystique.* New York: Dell.
Fromm, Erich. 1973. *The Anatomy of Human Destructiveness.* New York: Holt, Rinehart and Winston.
Fussell, Paul. 1989. "The Real War, 1939–1945." *Atlantic* 269 (Summer):32–40.
Gallop, Jane. 1988. *Thinking Through the Body.* New York: Columbia University Press.
Gaskell, Elizabeth Cleghorn. 1971. *The Life of Charlotte Brontë.* New York: Everyman's Library.
Gay, Peter. 1984. *Education of the Senses: The Bourgeois Experience, Victoria to Freud.* New York: Oxford University Press.

Gilbert, Sandra M., and Susan Gubar. 1979. *The Madwoman in the Attic: The Woman Writer and the Nineteenth-Century Literary Imagination.* New Haven: Yale University Press.

Gilligan, Carol. 1982. *In a Different Voice: Psychological Theory and Women's Development.* Cambridge, Mass.: Harvard University Press.

Gissing, George. 1977 [1893]. *The Odd Women.* New York: Norton.

Gliserman, Martin. 1973. "The Intersection of Biography and Fiction: A Psychological Study of Daniel Defoe and His Novels." Ph.D. diss., Indiana University.

Gordon, Mary. 1978. *Final Payments.* New York: Ballantine.

Green, André. 1986. *On Private Madness.* Madison, Conn.: International Universities Press.

Grief, Martin J. 1966. "The Conversion of Robinson Crusoe." *SEL: Studies in English Literature, 1500–1900* 6:551–74.

Harris, Marvin. 1977. *Cannibals and Kings: The Origins of Cultures.* New York: Random House.

Healey, George, ed. 1955. *The Letters of Daniel Defoe.* London: Oxford University Press.

Hemingway, Ernest. 1940. *For Whom the Bell Tolls.* New York: Charles Scribner's Sons.

———. 1954 [1926]. *The Sun Also Rises.* New York: Charles Scribner's Sons.

Hofstadter, Douglas. 1979. *Godel, Escher, Bach: An Eternal Golden Braid.* New York: Norton.

Horney, Karen. 1967. "The Distrust between the Sexes." In *Feminine Psychology,* edited by H. Kelman. New York: Norton.

Hulme, Keri. 1986. *The Bone People.* New York: Penguin.

Hunter, J. Paul. 1966. *The Reluctant Pilgrim: Defoe's Emblematic Method and Quest for Form in "Robinson Crusoe."* Baltimore: Johns Hopkins University Press.

Illich, Ivan. 1977. *Toward a History of Needs.* New York: Pantheon.

Irigaray, Luce. 1993. *Sexes and Genealogies.* Translated by Gillian Gill. New York: Columbia Univeristy Press.

James, Henry. 1960 [1903]. *The Ambassadors.* Boston: Riverside Press.

Johnson, Don. 1989. Review of *The History of Sexuality. The Whole Earth Review* 63 (Summer):58.

Johnson, Mark. 1987. *The Body in the Mind: The Bodily Basis of Meaning, Imagination, and Reason.* Chicago: University of Chicago Press, 1987.

Kaplan, Louise. 1984. *Adolescence: The Farewell to Childhood.* New York: Simon and Schuster.

Katan, Anny. 1973. "Children Who Were Raped." *Psychoanalytic Study of the Child* 28:208–24.

Kidel, Mark, and Susan Rowe-Leete. 1989. "Mapping the Body." *FHHB,* pt. 3, 447–69.

Kingston, Maxine Hong. 1977. *The Woman Warrior: Memoirs of a Girlhood among Ghosts.* New York: Knopf.

Klein, Melanie. 1975 [1932]. *The Psychoanalysis of Children.* Translated by Alix Strachey. New York: Delta.

———. 1980. *Envy and Gratitude and Other Works, 1946–1963.* London: Hogarth Press, 1980.

———. 1981 [1937]. *Love, Guilt and Reparation and Other Works, 1921–1945.* London: Hogarth Press, 1981.

Koestler, Arthur. 1978. *Janus: A Summing Up*. New York: Random House.

Kohut, Heinz. 1985. *Self Psychology and the Humanities: Reflections on a New Psychoanalytic Approach*. New York: Norton.

Kovel, Joel. 1981. *The Age of Desire: Case Histories of a Radical Psychoanalyst*. New York: Pantheon.

Kunzle, David. 1989. "The Art of Pulling Teeth in the Seventeenth and Nineteenth Centuries: From Public Martyrdom to Private Nightmare and Political Struggle?" *FHHB*, pt. 3, 29–89.

Lacan, Jacques. 1977. *Ecrits: A Selection*. Translated by Alan Sheridan. New York: Norton.

Laing, R. D. 1970. *The Divided Self: An Existential Study in Sanity and Madness*. New York: Pantheon.

Laing, R. D., H. Phillipson, and A. Lee. 1972. *Interpersonal Perception: A Theory and a Method of Research*. New York: Perennial.

Langer, Lawrence. 1991. *Holocaust Testimonies: The Ruins of Memory*. New Haven: Yale University Press.

Laqueur, Thomas. 1989. " 'Amor Veneris, vel Dulcedo Appeletur.' " *FHHB*, pt. 3, 91–131.

Lasch, Christopher. 1978. *The Culture of Narcissism: American Life in an Age of Diminishing Expectations*. New York: Norton, 1978.

Laub, Dori. 1991. "Truth and Testimony: The Process and the Struggle." *American Imago* 48, 1 (Spring):75–91.

Lawrence, D. H. 1973 [1913]. *Sons and Lovers*. New York: Viking Press.

Le Goff, Jacques. 1989. "Head or Heart? The Political Use of Body Metaphors in the Middle Ages." *FHHB*, pt. 3, 13–26.

Lévi-Strauss, Claude. 1963. *Structural Anthropology*. New York: Basic Books, 1963.

Levertov, Denise. 1964. *O Taste and See*. New York: New Directions.

Lichtenstein, Heinz. 1977. *The Dilemma of Human Identity*. New York: Jason Aronson.

Lifton, Robert Jay. 1986. *The Nazi Doctors: Medical Killing and the Psychology of Genocide*. New York: Basic Books.

Mahler, Margaret. 1968. *On Human Symbiosis and the Vicissitudes of Individuation*. New York: International Universities Press.

Marcuse, Herbert. 1962. *Eros and Civilization: A Philosophical Inquiry into Freud*. New York: Vintage.

McCurdy, Harold. 1947. "A Study of the Novels of Charlotte and Emily Brontë as an Expression of Their Personalities." *Journal of Personality*. 16:109–52.

McDonald, Robert. 1976. "The Creation of an Ordered World in *Robinson Crusoe*." *Dalhousie Review* 56:23–34.

McGuire, Kathryn. 1988. "The Incest Taboo in *Wuthering Heights*: A Modern Appraisal." *American Imago* 45, 2 (Summer):93–100.

McKibben, Bill. 1989. *The End of Nature*. New York: Random House.

McNeill, David. 1970. *The Acquisition of Language: The Study of Developmental Linguistics*. New York: Harper & Row.

Meadow, Phyllis Whitcomb. 1974. "A Research Method for Investigating the Effectiveness of Psychoanalytic Techniques." *Psychoanalytic Review* 6, 1:79–94.

Miller, Alice. 1983. *For Your Own Good: Hidden Cruelty in Child-Rearing and the Roots of Violence*. Translated by H. and H. Hunater Hannum. New York: Farrar, Strauss & Giroux.

————. 1986. *Thou Shalt Not Be Aware: Society's Betrayal of the Child*. New York: New American Library.

Miller, Jonathan. 1978. *The Body in Question*. New York: Random House.

Millett, Kate. 1969. *Sexual Politics*. New York: Avon Books.

Mitchell, Juliet. 1974. *Psychoanalysis and Feminism: Freud, Reich, Laing, and Women*. New York: Pantheon.

Moore, John Robert. 1958. *Daniel Defoe: Citizen of the Modern World*. Chicago: University of Chicago Press.

Mopsik, Charles. 1989. "The Body of Engenderment in the Hebrew Bible, the Rabbinic Tradition and the Kabbalah." *FHHB*, pt. 1, 49–73.

Morrison, Philip, Phylis Morrison, and the Office of Charles and Ray Eames. 1982. *Powers of Ten: About the Relative Size of Things in the Universe*. New York: Scientific American Books.

Morrison, Toni. 1991. *Beloved*. New York: Signet Classics.

Nelli, René. 1989. "Love's Rewards." *FHHB*, pt. 2, 219–335.

Nin, Anaïs. 1969. *Delta of Venus: Erotica by Anaïs Nin*. New York: Harcourt Brace Jovanovich.

Novak, Maximillian. 1976. *Economics and the Fiction of Daniel Defoe*. New York: Russell and Russell.

Ohmann, Richard. 1969a [1964]. "Generative Grammars and the Concept of Literary Style." In *Contemporary Essays on Style: Rhetoric, Linguistics, and Criticism*, edited by G. A. Love, 133–48. Glenville, Ill.: Scott, Foresman.

————. 1969b [1966]. "Literature as Sentences." In *Contemporary Essays on Style: Rhetoric, Linguistics, and Criticism*, edited by G. A. Love, 149–90. Glenville, Ill.: Scott, Foresman.

Orwell, George. 1983 [1949]. *Nineteen Eighty Four*. New York: Signet Classics.

Parry, Jonathan. 1989. "The End of the Body." *FHHB*, pt. 2, 491–517.

Pearlman, E. 1975. "Robinson Crusoe and the Cannibals." *Mosaic* 10:39–55.

Peckham, Morse. 1967. *Man's Rage for Chaos: Biology, Behavior and the Arts*. New York: Schocken Books.

Poe, Edgar Allen. 1972. *The Portable Edgar Allen Poe*. New York: Viking Press.

Pointon, Marcia. 1990. *Naked Authority: The Body in Western Painting*. Cambridge: Cambridge University Press.

Reich, Annie. 1973. "Pathological Self-Esteem Regulation." (1960) In *Annie Reich: Psychoanalytical Contributions*. New York: International Universities Press.

Reich, Wilhelm. 1949. *Character Analysis*. 3d ed., enlarged. New York: Noonday Press.

Richetti, John J. 1975. *Defoe's Narratives: Situations and Structures*, 21–62. Oxford: Oxford University Press.

Ritvo, Peter. 1974. "Current Status of the Concept of Infantile Neurosis." *Psychoanalytic Study of the Child* 28:159–81.

Roheim, Geza. 1952. *The Gates of the Dream*. New York: International Universities Press.

Scarry, Elaine. 1985. *The Body in Pain: The Making and Unmaking of the World*. New York: Oxford University Press.

Searles, Harold. 1960. *The Nonhuman Environment: In Normal Development and in Schizophrenia*. New York: International Universities Press.

————. 1965. *Collected Papers on Schizophrenia and Related Subjects.* New York: International Universities Press.

————. 1979. *Countertransference and Related Subjects.* New York: International Universities Press.

Segal, Hanna. 1981. *The Work of Hanna Segal: A Kleinian Approach to Clinical Practice.* New York: Jason Aronson.

Segal, Julia. 1985. *Phantasy in Everyday Life.* Harmondsworth, England: Penguin Books.

Sharpe, Ella Freeman. 1978. *Dream Analysis.* New York: Brunner/Mazel.

Showalter, Elaine, ed. 1985. *The New Feminist Criticism: Essays on Women, Literature, and Theory.* New York: Pantheon.

Siegel, Bernie, S. 1986. *Love, Medicine and Miracles.* New York: Harper & Row.

Sissa, Guila. 1989. "Subtle Bodies: The Body of Semen." *FHHB*, pt. 3, 133–56.

Slipp, Samuel. 1984. *Object Relations: A Dynamic Bridge Between Individual and Family Treatment.* New York: Jason Aronson.

Smith, David. 1974. "Incest Patterns in Two Victorian Novels." In *Literature and Psychology*, 135–52.

Solomon, Eric. 1959. "The Incest Theme in *Wuthering Heights.*" *Nineteenth Century Fiction* 4:80–83

Spackman, I. J., et al. 1987. *A KWIC Concordance to Daniel Defoe's "Robinson Crusoe."* New York: Garland.

Spitz, René A. 1965. *The First Year of Life: A Psychoanalytic Study of Normal and Deviant Development of Object Relations.* New York: International Universities Press.

Spotnitz, Hyman. 1976. *Psychotherapy of Preoedipal Conditions: Schizophrenia and Severe Character Disorders.* New York: Jason Aronson.

Starobinski, Jean. 1989 [1964]. "A Short History of Bodily Sensation." *FHHB*, pt. 2, 353–405.

Starr, G. A. 1965. *Defoe and Spiritual Autobiography.* Princeton: Princeton University Press.

Stolorow, Robert, and George Atwood. 1979. *Faces in a Cloud: Subjectivity in Personality Theory.* New York: Jason Aronson.

Stone, Robert. 1973. *Dog Soldiers.* Boston: Houghton Mifflin.

————. 1981. *A Flag for Sunrise.* New York: Knopf.

Suleiman, Susan Rubin, ed. 1986. *The Female Body in Western Culture: Contemporary Perspectives.* Cambridge: Harvard University Press.

Sutherland, James. 1938. *Defoe.* New York: J. B. Lippincott.

Thompson, Hunter S. 1971. *Fear and Loathing in Las Vegas: A Savage Journey to the Heart of the American Dream.* New York: Random House.

Valenstein, Arthur. 1973. "On Attachment to Painful Feelings and the Negative Therapeutic Reaction." *Psychoanalytic Study of the Child* 28:365–92.

Vigarello, Georges. 1989. "The Upward Training of the Body from the Age of Chivalry to Courtly Civility." *FHHB*, pt. 2, 149–99.

Wasson, Richard. 1981. "Class and the Vicissitudes of the Male Body in Works by D.H. Lawrence." *D.H. Lawrence Review* 14, 3 (Fall): 289–305.

Watt, Ian. 1965. *The Rise of the Novel: Studies in Defoe, Richardson and Fielding.* Berkeley: University of California Press.

Whorf, Benjamin Lee. 1956. *Language, Thought and Reality: Selected Writings of Benjamin Lee Whorf.* Cambridge: MIT Press.

Winnicott, D. W. 1958. *Collected Papers: Through Paediatrics to Psychoanalysis.* London: Tavistock.

————. 1965. "String: A Technique of Communication." In *The Maturational Processes and the Facilitating Environment,* 153–57. New York: International Universities Press.

————. 1971a. *Playing and Reality.* London: Tavistock.

————. 1971b. *Therapeutic Consultations in Child Psychiatry.* New York: Basic Books.

Winnifrith, Tom. 1973. *The Brontës and Their Background: Romance and Reality.* New York: Harper & Row.

Woolf, Leonard. 1964. *Beginning Again: An Autobiography of the Years 1911 to 1918.* New York: Harcourt Brace Jovanovich.

Woolf, Virginia. 1925. "Defoe." In *The Common Reader.* New York: Harcourt, Brace.

————. 1955 [1927]. *To the Lighthouse.* New York: Harcourt, Brace and World.

————. 1975. *The Letters of Virginia Woolf.* Vol. 1, 1888–1912, edited by Nigel Nicolson and J. Trautmann. New York: Harcourt Brace Jovanovich.

————. 1976. *Virginia Woolf: Moments of Being: Unpublished Autobiographical Writings,* edited by Jeanne Schulkind. New York: Harcourt Brace Jovanovich.

Wurlitzer, Rudolph. 1970. *Nog.* New York: Pocket Books.

Index